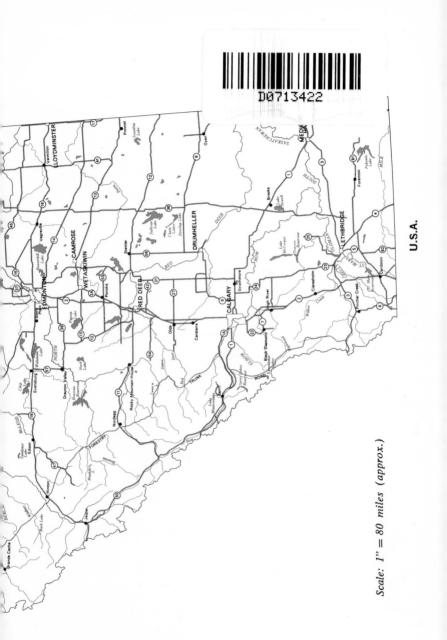

Scale: 1" = 80 miles (approx.)

U.S.A.

...OURSES IN THE PROVINCE OF ALBERTA

THE

FISHES

of

ALBERTA

by

MARTIN J. PAETZ

and

JOSEPH S. NELSON

Photographs by the Authors and Acknowledged Contributors

Available by mail order
from
THE BOOKSERVICE
QUEEN'S PRINTER
GOVERNMENT OF ALBERTA
EDMONTON
T5G 2Y5

1970

Lithographed by Commercial Printers

a division of Bulletin-Commercial Printers Limited, Edmonton

Distributed by

THE QUEEN'S PRINTER, EDMONTON

Price $6.00

This book is dedicated to the late PROFESSOR R. B. MILLER, Ph. D. Dr. Miller contributed a great deal to the knowledge of the fisheries of this province, and to the broader field of Zoology from 1939 until the time of his passing some 20 years later. It was his enthusiasm, encouragement, and collecting that laid the ground work for eventual production of this volume.

Martin J. Paetz was born in the prairie ranching country at Youngstown, Alberta, and received his early education in rural schools. After leaving the prairies he attended Edmonton and Calgary normal schools and taught school in several locations in the province prior to entering the University of Alberta to undertake studies in the field of Zoology with a major interest in fisheries management. He received his B.Sc. in 1952, his M.Sc. in 1957, and is currently carrying on work towards a Ph.D. in Zoology. Mr. Paetz joined the Fish and Wildlife Division of the Department of Lands and Forests as a fishery biologist in 1952, was named Assistant Superintendent of Fisheries in 1959, and Chief Fishery Biologist in 1961, the position he holds at the present time.

During the period of his employment with the Provincial Government he has travelled the length and breadth of the province and it was during this work that he had the opportunity to make numerous collections of fish and record observations on their distributions. His interest in using this information as a nucleus of this book was stimulated by the late Dr. R. B. Miller with whom he was associated in biological survey work for a number of years.

Dr. Joseph S. Nelson is a faculty member in the Zoology Department of The University of Alberta and resides in the Patricia Heights area of Edmonton. He was born in San Francisco but, from before the age of 1, was brought up in British Columbia. His early schooling was obtained at a copper mine in the Princeton area; high school was attended in Vancouver. During this time he developed an interest in astronomy and biology. The four summers of his undergraduate university years were spent on salmon investigations along much of coastal British Columbia and in the Yukon Territory, with the Federal Department of Fisheries. In 1962 he received his Master of Science degree from The University of Alberta after studying fishes in the Kananaskis River system. Following this, he returned to British Columbia and studied suckers in the Prince George region for a thesis for his Doctor of Philosophy degree and then spent 3 years as Research Associate and Assistant Director of Indiana University Biological Stations with the Indiana Aquatic Research Unit. In 1968, Dr. Nelson joined the University of Alberta as Assistant Professor where he teaches the courses on fish biology and on animal distribution. His students work on a variety of problems concerning Alberta fish while most of his own current research is on those delightful small fish called sticklebacks.

CONTENTS

ACKNOWLEDGMENTS

We have become indebted to many individuals during the preparation of this book. To our many benefactors we express our deep appreciation for their help and generosity.

Mr. H. E. Hamly of Commercial Printers has given us help and encouragement far beyond his regular duties. His interest and the interest of the Honourable A. R. Patrick, Minister of Mines and Minerals, and Mr. L. S. Wall of the Queen's Printer, made this book possible.

Drs. R. M. Bailey, E. J. Crossman, D. E. McAllister, W. B. Scott and Messrs. C. Gruchy and T. A. Willock constructively criticized our preliminary keys. The University of Alberta students in the Zoology Department's course on Ichthyology in 1968 used the keys and made suggestions for their improvement.

Drs. G. E. Ball, H. F. Clifford, C. C. Lindsey, and J. R. Nursall constructively criticized various parts of the text. Dr. J. C. Holmes provided much unpublished information of fish parasites and made other useful suggestions.

Some specimens of Alberta fish housed outside the Province were loaned for examination by Mr. T. A. Willock and Dr. N. J. Wilimovsky. The co-operation of Dr. V. Lewin and Mr. N. Panter in the University of Alberta Museum of Zoology is appreciated. Mr. T. A. Willock generously supplied several of the fish and habitat photographs. Messrs. A. N. Paulson, E. B. Cunningham, R. J. Paterson, C. A. Gordon, and W. Schenk also supplied photographs. Mr. N. Kiss took many of the fish photographs.

The encouragement and information provided by Dr. S. B. Smith, Messrs. R. J. Paterson, A. C. Sinclair, K. A. Zelt and several regional biologists (notably F. G. Bishop, C. B. Lane, and M. R. Robertson) of the Alberta Fish and Wildlife Division, and Messrs. H. B. Watkins and W. A. West, formerly of that Division, is gratefully acknowledged. Messrs. C. G. Paterson, W. Roberts, B. D. Smiley, and T. A. Willock provided much useful information. Messrs. J. I. Nichols, E. Kuyt, and J. C. Ward of the Department of Indian Affairs and Northern Development provided information not otherwise available to us. Mr. J. R. Card provided many of the data on lakes and rivers.

Technical help was obtained from Messrs. L. D. Gudmundson, L. E. Dunn, Miss C. L. Paley, and Mrs. E. Hunt, and the technical assistance of Mr. T. A. Drinkwater and his staff of the Department of Lands and Forests in the preparation of maps was particularly valuable.

INTRODUCTION

The Province of Alberta is generously endowed with a diversity of lakes and streams. Numerous bodies of water which offer excellent fishing opportunities exist on the plains and in the mountains. Alberta is situated on the easterly sloping height of land in western Canada between the 49th and 60th parallels of north latitude. The 756 mile long eastern boundary is located at 110° west longitude and the western boundary is marked by 120° west longitude in the northern portion and the continental divide in the southern portion. The province covers an area of 255,285 square miles of which some 6,485 square miles are fresh water.

Factors such as topography, climate, vegetative cover, and geological history profoundly influence the distribution of fish species in an area. It is thus useful to consider some of the features which characterize the province and some of the events of the past which have influenced our present day fish fauna. Included within the province are three main physiographic regions; the rugged Cordillera in the southwest, the great plains which occupy the majority of the area in the north-west to south-east direction, and the Canadian Shield in the extreme north-east corner. Alberta is the only Canadian province which contains these three regions. From altitudes of up to 12,294 feet in the Rocky Mountains (Mt. Columbia) the land surface slopes, abruptly at first then more gently, in easterly and north-easterly directions. The lowest elevation of about 600 feet above sea level is found in the north-east near Fort Smith where the Slave and Salt rivers cross the Alberta-Northwest Territories border.

A combination of climate and topography have produced several well marked vegetative zones. Forested land dominated by spruce, fir, pine, larch, poplar, and birch, which occupies most of the northern half of the province as well as a relatively narrow band along the east slopes of the mountains, comprises about 158,000 square miles. To the south and east of the forest lies a transition zone or parkland characterized by moderate to gently rolling topography and aspen poplar groves alternating with prairie. This zone gives way to the prairie or grasslands in the vicinity of a line between Olds and Grassy Island Lake. From here the semi-arid prairies extend south to the International border.

The province is drained by eight river systems. Most of our water is carried by the Hay, Peace, and Athabasca rivers in northerly and north-easterly directions and eventually reaches the Arctic Ocean by way of the Mackenzie River. The small Petitot system with Bistcho Lake drains westerly into the Liard basin, thence into the Mackenzie. The majority of the region traversed by these drainage systems is forested land. The Beaver, North Saskatchewan, and South Saskatchewan River systems drain the central and most of the southern parts of the province and flow eastward to form part of the Hudson Bay drainage via the Churchill and Nelson rivers. The extreme southern part of the province is drained by the Milk River whose water is eventually delivered to the Gulf of Mexico via the Missouri and Mississippi rivers. The total linear mileage of flowing water in the province, excluding intermittent streams, has been estimated to be between 12,000 and 13,000 miles. While the total area of over 6,000 square miles miles covered by water in the province may seem at a glance to be considerable, it is actually quite small compared to the 80,000 square miles of water contained in the province of Ontario.

In order to have an understanding of how the present day fish fauna came to occupy the various streams and lakes throughout the province it is necessary to retrace briefly some of the events of the past 15,000 years. Prior to that time Alberta was all but covered by a mass of ice which is recorded as the Wisconsin glaciation. Actually, geological evidence tells us that the ice cover was the result of two huge ice sheets. The Cordilleran advanced from a center in British Columbia to as far as the eastern edge of the Rocky Mountains and the much larger Keewatin ice sheet ground across the province from the north east and joined with the Cordilleran sheet. Only a portion of the Cypress Hills and a tongue of land extending north from Montana into the Porcupine Hills area escaped being covered by these ice masses. Since it is generally accepted that no fishes could have survived the Wisconsin glaciation in the area we now know as Alberta, the story of our present fish fauna really begins with the retreat of this ice sheet from southern Alberta about 15,000 years ago and its gradual recession from the province to its disappearance from the northeastern corner about 10,000 years ago. It is important at this point to note that the southern edge of the ice extended only a short distance into Montana thus permitting fish to survive in the upper part of the Missouri River system as well as in the richer Mississippi region; most of our species came from the latter area. Much of the Columbia drainage in Washington and Oregon was ice-free during glaciation and served as the second-most important refugium for our fish. A good deal of the Yukon and most of Alaska were also left unglaciated, so that these areas also provided a refuge for fish which had occupied the area prior to the Wisconsin glaciation. Relatively few of Alberta's fish came in from this northern area.

As the vast ice sheet receded, large meltwater lakes were formed behind the ice front. Notable among these post-glacial lakes were Miette Lake which extended from below present Brule Lake, westward across the Yellowhead Pass, to a point near Mount Edith Cavell; Lake Edmonton which reached from west of the present Pembina River to just east of Edmonton and south to Lacombe; Lake Peace which roughly occupied most of the area from Lesser Slave Lake to the Hay River; and Lake Tyrell which covered a large area west and south of, and including present Lake Athabasca. At various times these lakes drained through different outlets, the details of which cannot be presented here. However, it is important to note that Lake Miette at one time drained both toward the west into the Fraser system and to the north-east towards the Arctic Ocean. Lake Peace also drained toward the Arctic while Lake Edmonton drained towards the east to Lake Agassiz which had an outlet to the Mississippi. In the southern part of the province the early course of post glacial drainage systems was also complex. There were times for example when the St. Mary, Waterton, and Belly rivers flowed into the Milk drainage instead of the South Saskatchewan as they do now. As the ice retreated northward, however, the modern drainage patterns emerged so that the flow of these western rivers shifted from the Milk to the South Saskatchewan system. Meltwater lakes were of course also formed in this area along the receding ice front. Lake St. Mary, Lake Waterton, Lake Caldwell, Lake Cardston, Lake McLeod, and Lake Lethbridge are some examples of water bodies that once existed south and north of the 49th parallel.

With this brief description of the great glaciers and probable events as they retreated as background, it is possible to visualize some of the routes by which fish have naturally been able to re-inhabit our province. Four major dispersal routes have been suggested but it is not completely known which of these routes were used by the various species or how many of them arrived by more than one route.

In the south and south-west, it is believed that fish used three avenues for invasion. From the refugia which existed in the Mississippi-Missouri system, fish are almost certain to have dispersed in two directions. The most important route was probably by way of Lake Agassiz (which lay over a large area in Manitoba and Saskatchewan), and thence up the Saskatchewan River. A drainage shift between the Milk and South Saskatchewan rivers and the lakes mentioned above, which covered a considerable area of southern Alberta, was a second and important route. Some of our species did not make this transfer and are confined to the Milk drainage. The third route was eastward from a refuge in the Columbia basin over the continental divide through headwater lakes which may have drained both towards the Pacific and towards the Hudson Bay. Dolly Varden, cutthroat trout, and mountain whitefish probably utilized several headwater areas such as the 5,339 foot Kickinghorse Pass between Field and Lake Louise. Here, at the Great Divide, drainage still splits in two directions, east into the Bow via Bath Creek and west into the Kickinghorse River (underground part of the way at present). Willock (1969 a,b) suggests that 19 species may have reached the Milk River system by these three routes.

The fish which came to occupy the central and northern parts of the province (prior to introductions by man) are also thought to have used three routes; from the south-east through Lake Agassiz, southward from a refuge in the unglaciated portion of the Yukon, and thirdly, eastward from the interior of British Columbia via the Peace drainage and the Fraser-Athabasca drainage. Again it is difficult to say whether some fish used more than one of these routes but it is generally accepted that at least some of them did. The distribution patterns of certain species, however, indicate that they probably came from only one direction. Rainbow trout, for example, which are abundant in waters on the south and east slopes of the Swan Hills and throughout most of the upper parts of the Athabasca system and which are reported by early fishermen to have been present in these areas many years before introductions were possible (R. Krause and C. Picarello, personal communication), probably came from the headwaters of the Fraser River. Squawfish, redside shiner, and largescale sucker invaded Alberta through the Peace River from the Columbia drainage (via several possible early transfer routes from Columbia to Fraser and thence Fraser to Peace drainage). The absence of Arctic

5

grayling from the Saskatchewan River system and its presence in the Peace and Athabasca drainages suggest that this species came from the north. In total, however, the Lake Agassiz route is likely to have contributed more to our fish fauna than any other route. These fishes are generally our most abundant and widespread species. On the other hand, the seven Columbia River fishes mentioned above are generally limited to western Alberta.

The dispersal of fish since glaciation has been a continuing process for many species and is one which has been accentuated by man. The construction of canals between drainage systems, i.e., the United States St. Mary canal between the St. Mary and Milk Rivers and St. Mary-Milk River Irrigation development have provided artificial avenues for dispersal. Deliberate and accidental introductions have also played an important role in adding species which were not native to the province and in extending the ranges of some of those which are native. Brook trout, brown trout, golden trout, and kokanee are examples of the introductions of non-native species and the widespread stocking of rainbow trout is just one example of a species whose distribution has been extended into areas which it originally did not occupy.

The number of native forms known at present in Alberta is 45 and with the inclusion of four introduced species the total is only 49 (this excludes several introductions listed in Appendix I which are known only from one or two localities). This is less than the number found in both the neighboring provinces of British Columbia and Saskatchewan and less than one third of the number found in Ontario. By way of further contrast, many states in the Ohio-Mississippi drainage can boast of having over 160 native species. The reasons for the relatively impoverished Alberta fish fauna are probably both geographical and ecological. The continental divide has constituted a barrier to dispersal of a number of species from the west and the cold waters of the east slopes of the Rocky Mountains have proven to be unsuitable habitat for some of the warm water fishes which are found to the east and south-east. As might be expected, those species which have invaded Alberta following glaciation are generally adapted to a wide variety of environments. Most of our fish are wide-ranging. None of our species has all or even most of its range within Alberta.

In producing this edition of The Fishes of Alberta the authors wish to point out that some of the distribution patterns and much of the biology of the species are poorly known. Therefore, such an undertaking will always be subject to revision as new information becomes available. In addition it should be noted that it has not been possible to include every locality record on distribution maps where many collections have been made in close proximity to one another. This book brings together as much of the present knowledge of our fish fauna as is considered practical. The published information of other workers is included along with more than twenty years of effort in collection and observation on the part of the authors and many others. In so doing we hope to provide a source of information for laymen, fishermen, and scientists as well as for students of biology. To attempt to strike such a balance is not an easy task but it is hoped that this objective has been at least partially achieved.

FISH ECOLOGY

As fish naturalists know, most species tend to predominate in particular areas within a body of water. Different individuals may venture into all available areas within a lake or stream but, in general, each species has its own particular preferred habitat. One species may spend the summer in deep cold areas of lakes while another may prefer the shallow weedy areas. It is the dynamic interplay of many factors — environmental preferences and tolerances to such things as temperature and oxygen concentration, relationships with other species, availability of spawning area, and the location of their preferred food — that determines where a particular species will predominate. Variation in the relative abundance of various species between lakes is also related to these same factors. Most details of the individual factors and their interrelations await investigation.

Most species of fish in Alberta have considerable ecological tolerance as revealed by field observations. Many species are at home both in lakes and rivers and are not restricted to any particular habitat. This is undoubtedly related to the fact that all of Alberta's native fish have quite wide distributions. A relatively large number of our species extend across North America and have obviously had good powers of dispersal.

In the summertime, fish in most deep Alberta lakes have a wide temperature range in their environment. The surface water may be 65°F while the bottom water may be close to 45°F. Although the uninsulated body of a fish is always at about the same temperature as its immediate environment, each species tends to prefer a particular range of temperature. Providing that other conditions are suitable they will occupy the depth where that temperature range occurs. For example, northern pike and yellow perch have a relatively high temperature preference and tend to occupy shallow waters while lake whitefish and lake trout have a relatively low temperature preference and tend to be found in deep waters in the summer. Fish can usually swim their fastest and are healthiest at their preferred temperature.

Temperature is probably "measured" by the fish with sensory organs along the lateral line. The particular temperature which a fish prefers depends, in part, on the temperature of water it has been exposed to in the preceding days and on the fish's age. Individuals accustomed to cold winter temperatures generally have a strong preference for warm water. If a lake warms up unusually fast in the spring, fish may move into water which is warmer than they can withstand and as a result they may perish. The lethal temperature, or temperature at which fish will be killed, varies between fish species and on the past temperature experience of the fish. A fish accustomed to 40°F, for example, may die if it moves into a preferred temperature of 70°F in shallow bay areas or in thermally polluted water but it may be able to tolerate that temperature quite well, although possibly preferring a lower temperature, in the summer. As would be expected, it appears that natural selection results in individuals of a species having a temperature preference which favors their ultimate ability to successfully reproduce.

Fish also vary in their requirements for dissolved oxygen. Whitefish and trout require relatively high oxygen concentrations while carp and sticklebacks can tolerate very low oxygen conditions. In some Alberta lakes of moderate to shallow depth which are protected from strong wind action, the bottom becomes very low in oxygen during late winter and late summer. During these times, fish are forced to move up into shallower water. During summer months this often means that cold water species must move into water warmer than they prefer, which may prove to be lethal. Thus, cold water species such as lake whitefish and lake trout cannot live in lakes that lack the cool well-oxygenated zone so typical of northern Alberta lakes.

Oxygen diminishes in the winter when the lake is sealed off from the atmosphere. This oxygen depletion is due to the respiration of living organisms and to the decomposition of dead organisms which consume oxygen and release carbon dioxide and sometimes hydrogen sulphide. This process begins at the bottom and proceeds upwards. The loss is hastened by snow cover and cloudy ice which eliminates sunlight penetration and thereby prevents algae from adding oxygen to the water during photosynthesis. Massive fish die-offs may occur during late winter due to lack of oxygen and also during circulation of the lake following ice break-up if oxygen concentration is very low or if enough toxic materials accumulate during the winter. Similar die-offs may also occur in the summer and in the fall but this is rare in Alberta. Fish mortalities are usually not complete. Much to the fishermen's and fishery biologist's distress, game species, which require more oxygen than do most non-game species, are usually killed off first or may be the only species to die. Oxygen depletion is relatively rapid in warm highly productive lakes of moderate to shallow depth in central and eastern Alberta and slow or non-existent in the cold low productive lakes of the Rocky Mountains.

The series of seasonal events in a deep lake are shown in the following diagram. Lakes are frozen over for about 4-6 months in

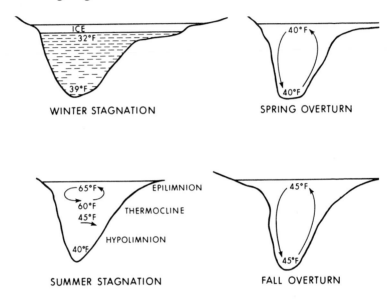

Example of seasonal temperature changes in a deep lake.

central Alberta and 4-7 months in the Rocky Mountains. During this time the water temperature ranges from 32°F under the ice to as much as 39°F lower down, the temperature at which fresh water is highest in density. Ice thickness is seldom greater than 3 feet. After ice break-up the surface water is quickly warmed until the entire lake is of uniform density. Deeper water is warmed only by currents produced by wave action forcing down surface water through eddy currents. During this time of circulation there is little or no stratification in temperature and oxygen. If periods of little or no wind action occur, the surface waters may warm up and become sufficiently lighter than the deeper cooler water that even strong winds cannot thoroughly mix the surface with the bottom waters. The upper layer of warm water, which circulates under wind action and tends to be well-oxygenated, is termed the epilimnion (meaning upper lake). It is this area where algae and rooted aquatic plants occur, their depth in the epilimnion being determined largely by the depth of sunlight penetration which is, in turn, governed by the turbidity of water. Immediately below this warm surface layer there is a zone in which the water temperature drops rapidly and this zone is termed the thermocline or metalimnion. This layer, several feet thick, usually is pushed deeper into the lake as the summer season progresses which in turn causes some fish species to move into deeper water, provided that other conditions are suitable. The depth of a thermocline in a lake depends on the amount of wind action and may start anywhere from about 6 to 60 feet. Most shallow lakes and many moderately deep Alberta lakes with strong wind action never develop a thermocline. Depending upon annual climatic differences, a lake may develop a thermocline one year but not during another. In thermally stratified lakes the area of cool water below the thermocline is termed the hypolimnion (meaning under lake). This area, due to the lack of circulation from the surface, cannot gain oxygen during the summer as can the epilimnion. In lakes of moderate depth the hypolimnion may be much smaller in volume than the epilimnion and may become very oxygen deficient while in deep lakes the hypolimnion may exceed the epilimnion in volume and may not become seriously deficient in oxygen. When temperatures drop in the late summer and early fall the epilimnion cools to a temperature near that of the hypolimnion. Then, when the density difference is small, winds cause the circulation of the lake once more and the thermocline is lost and the lake is uniform in temperature from top to bottom. Despite the isothermal state of the lake, many species of fish are still found at different depths because of other factors. During fall turn-over, bottom water comes into contact with the surface and if the winds are sufficiently strong, the lake will become saturated in oxygen before freeze-over in November or December. After ice cover forms the entire lake is cut off from contact with the atmosphere.

Horizontal zonation of fish around a lake's margin, in contrast with vertical zonation, is also commonly observed. Shoreline areas may consist of barren rock, sand, gravel, marl, and rooted aquatic plants. Each such zone may differ in the relative abundance of species due to different preferences.

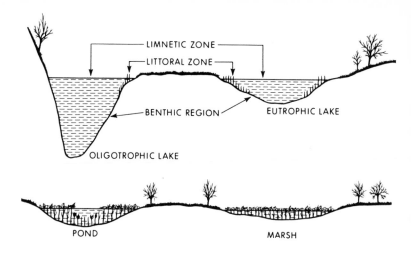

The ecological regions of two extreme types of lakes and their succession into the pond and marsh stage. The littoral region is the shallow water area characterized by rooted emergent or floating vegetation; the limnetic region consists of open water; the benthic region is the entire bottom. Organisms which are at the mercy of currents in the limnetic and littoral region are termed planktonic (animals — zooplankton; plants — phytoplankton). The benthos consists of organisms that move on the bottom, are attached to it, or burrow into it. Oligotrophic lakes typically have a small littoral region, are very deep, and are low in dissolved nutrients and organic matter. Eutrophic lakes typically have an extensive littoral region, are relatively shallow, and are rich in dissolved nutrients and organic matter. Sedimentation tends to change an oligotrophic lake into a eutrophic lake. Ponds result from further shallowing which enables submerged vegetation to cover the bottom. Additional build up on the bottom results in a marsh with emergent vegetation, cattails and sedges, and no limnetic region. Finally, the acidic spagnum moss or alkali sedge peat bog so common in Alberta, which may have had its start at any one of the above stages, may result. It is essentially a swamp which is wet and spongy and dominated by trees and shrubs.

Information on some of the diversity of our lakes is presented in Appendix II.

Stream fish also live in a variable environment and their differences in preference are also reflected in differences in distribution. Streams usually have sufficient oxygen and are uniform in temperature from top to bottom. However, species may be segregated on the basis of differences in bottom materials, strength of current, and depth of water. In streams, as in lakes, the presence of aquatic vegetation is necessary for some species. For example, brook sticklebacks require vegetation in order to build their nest. The absence of suitable aquatic plants eliminates the possibility of the species completing its life cycle in the North Saskatchewan River. Plants are rare or absent due to the large fluctuation in water level in this silty stream and due to the low light penetration and the scouring action of ice and flood waters. A marked differences in species can be observed in proceeding from the lower elevations of rivers in eastern Alberta upstream to the headwaters in the Rocky Mountains. Although certain temperature conditions and stream gradients are associated with these differences, the explanation for the differences is largely unknown. Species confined to the upper portions of Alberta rivers are often found in the lower portions of rivers elsewhere.

Information on the size of our large rivers is presented in Appendix III.

In all environments, the interaction of individuals of different species is also highly important in determining where a species will live and its relative abundance. Individuals may be absent from an area due to their inability to compete with individuals of another species rather than to a lack of tolerance to the physical environment. Young brown trout, for example, often force native cutthroat trout and Dolly Varden out of their preferred areas and into less favorable ones.

The abundance and annual rate of increase in numbers of fish are governed by the productivity of the water, that is, by its ability to produce organisms which in turn may be utilized as food. Waters rich in inorganic nutrients and having a long gentle sloping shoreline are more productive than waters with low nutrient salts and steep rocky shorelines. Water transparency is important in determining at what depth phytoplankton (algae) and rooted plants can live and is consequently related to a lake's production. Increased production in phytoplankton, however, decreases water transparency and further production is checked. Waters which are turbid due to high silt content tend to be unproductive and very clear water is a sign of low productivity. Some lakes, such as Astotin in Elk Island National Park, are highly productive. Algae blooms in the summer can leave the water a bright blue-green or green and allow little light penetration. Wind may concentrate these waterblooms into a paint-like mess which can be highly toxic. Oxygen depletion is often so severe that only brook sticklebacks presently live in the lake (despite the introduction of other species). Salts are so high in some lakes in southeastern Alberta, even higher than in the ocean, that none of our native species can live in them.

Some species are primarily bottom feeders, others are open-water plankton feeders, still others may be surface feeders, and finally some species are fish feeders. Their mouth shape and position and their gillrakers often show obvious adaptations for the type of food upon which they feed. Most trout-like fish are quite adaptable and are not highly specialized in their feeding requirements.

Every body of water has a certain limited carrying capacity. There is a maximum poundage of fish that can be supported over a period of time. This capacity, which may vary from year to year, depends primarily upon climatic factors and is only realized if species of all different feeding habits are present. A lake with only bottom feeding whitefish or suckers will not reach its maximum carrying capacity. On the other hand, the carrying capacity for an individual species is usually highest when competitive species are absent. A given lake capable of supporting 30 pounds of trout per acre may have many stunted adults or a few large ones. Limited spawning area and high predation rates may be conducive for the latter. Over-stocking, of course, will only result in lean fish when the abundance of food is limiting.

Spawning time in fish is governed by daylength and water temperature. Every month has one or more Alberta species spawning, each species responding to a slightly different daylength and water temperature as a triggering device for spawning. Fish vary in their methods of reproduction. Sticklebacks build nests of aquatic vegetation, have an elaborate courtship behavior, and care for the relatively few eggs and for the young after hatching. Salmon dig cavities, called redds, in gravel and cover the deposited eggs but do not care for them afterwards. Suckers, at the other extreme, release many thousands of eggs after a very short and simple courtship, without providing any care for them. Some species go on rather lengthy migrations for spawning, as appears to be the case for goldeye in the North Saskatchewan River, or may spawn near areas they frequent for food.

Natural selection tends to favor species mating with their own kind but interbreeding, resulting in hybrids, does occur between some species. Two species may be prevented from hybridizing by spawning at different times, such as rainbow and brown trout. If two species spawn at the same time, they may prefer to spawn in different areas. Failing this, they may have developed a strong tendency to mate with individuals of their own kind. If the above three mechanisms fail, resulting in hybridization between two closely related species of fish, the hybrids usually survive but fail to successfully reproduce. Hybridization is usually commonest in areas of environmental disturbance, species introduction, and rarity of one parental species. Whitefish-cisco hybridization in Alberta, which occurs under quite natural conditions, is one notable exception. It is the ultimate failure of the hybrids to interbreed with their own kind and with their parental species that maintains a species integrity and adaptiveness to the environment.

Stauffer Creek, near Caroline, a typical brown trout stream.

A fisherman's creel of Arctic grayling (top) from Little Smoky River and Yellowstone cutthroat trout (bottom) from Dutch Creek, Oldman River drainage.

Milk River 10 miles east of Milk River town, June 5, 1967. Mr. T. A. Willock found flathead chub and longnose dace to be the most abundant fish while longnose suckers, stonecats, sauger, and burbot were common.

Lower Milk River looking north-west about 10 miles from the Montana border, September 4, 1966. Mr. T. A. Willock found flathead chub, stonecats, sauger, and silvery minnows to be typical of this area.

17

North Fork of the Milk River, about 15 miles west of Milk River town, August 22, 1967. Mr. T. A. Willock has found mountain whitefish, mottled sculpins, cutthroat trout, and mountain sucker at this site.

A prairie stream, Etzikom Coulee, in southern Alberta between Warner and Wrentham, August 23, 1967. Mr. T. A. Willock found white suckers, fathead minnows, and lake chub to be abundant while brassy minnows were rare.

Peace River at Dunvegan, between Grande Prairie and Fairview, at unusually low water level. Downstream view toward east near a provincial campsite, July 23, 1968, showing gravel and sand bottom. The following species, in order of abundance, were seined in bay and current at right: lake chub, flathead chub, longnose sucker, longnose dace, trout-perch, redside shiner, squawfish, yellow perch, walleye, largescale sucker, and slimy sculpin.

Smoky River at highway 34 between Grande Prairie and Valleyview. Downstream view toward north near a provincial campsite, July 24, 1968, showing gravel bottom. The following species, in order of abundance, were seined in current at left: flathead chub, redside shiner, lake chub, longnose dace, longnose sucker, trout-perch, mountain whitefish, largescale sucker, and white sucker.

19

Simonette River 5 miles south of highway 34 between Grande Prairie and Valleyview. Upstream view immediately east of Forestry Trunk Road at a provincial campsite, July 24, 1968, showing gravel and sand bottom. The following species, in order of abundance, were seined in this area and downstream: flathead chub, redside shiner, lake chub, longnose sucker, trout-perch, white sucker, longnose dace, mountain whitefish, and finescale dace.

Little Smoky River downstream of highway 43 at Little Smoky between Valleyview and Whitecourt. Downstream view toward north, July 25, 1968. The following species, in order of abundance, were seined in current at left: lake chub, white sucker, longnose sucker, trout-perch, redside shiner, and yellow perch.

Preble Creek, Northwest Territories, near Mile 117 on Highway 5, west of Fort Smith. Downstream view, about 2 miles north of the Alberta border, June 28, 1970. The following species, in order of abundance, were collected along this gravel and sand stretch (with much filamentous algae): brook stickleback, pearl dace, lake chub, fathead minnow, white sucker, northern redbelly dace, finescale dace, and longnose sucker. The five minnows were also in the adjacent Sass River, although in different proportions; brook sticklebacks and longnose suckers were also present.

Slave River, at upper end of Portage Mountain Rapids, Alberta. Upstream view, about 2 miles south of the Northwest Territories border, June 25, 1970. Four miles downstream, at the water intake system for Fort Smith, Arctic lamprey have been obtained. A short distance upstream, at Fitzgerald, burbot and northern pike are common. Tributary streams between Fitzgerald and Hay Camp in Wood Buffalo National Park, near their confluence with the Slave, yielded: burbot, longnose sucker, northern pike, spottail shiner, emerald shiner, and walleye. The dominant species varies in proceeding upstream from this area. For example, at Peace Point, in the Peace River, Wood Buffalo National Park, spoonhead sculpins, trout-perch, and longnose dace are common inshore.

21

Hornaday Creek, 6 miles south of Hay Camp, Wood Buffalo National Park, Alberta, a short distance from the Slave River, June 25, 1970. Downstream from this site, near the Slave River, burbot, northern pike, and longnose sucker were abundant while longnose dace and white sucker were very rare.

Salt River, 14 miles southwest of Fort Smith, near a sink-hole area on the road to Pine Lake and Peace Point. Downstream view, June 26, 1970. Ninespine stickleback, northern pike, and longnose sucker were common. Further downstream at the confluence of Brine Creek, Alberta, and at Highway 5, Northwest Territories, ninespine stickleback, brook stickleback, spoonhead sculpin, longnose sucker, northern pike, walleye, and white sucker were obtained. Minnows are apparently rare in this Slave River tributary (C. G. Paterson collected emerald and spottail shiners in 1966). They are common in nearby sink-holes and in the adjacent Little Buffalo system (5 minnow species known).

Scalp Creek, west of the Red Deer Ranger Station. This section is an example of an unproductive trout stream with swift water and barren bottom.

Harold Creek, west of Water Valley. This foothill stream is productive with protective cover and moderate current.

An example of an aquatic habitat formed by beaver activity.

Pyramid Lake, Jasper National Park. An example of a cold oligotrophic lake where lake trout are found.

FISH CULTURE IN ALBERTA

The term 'fish culture,' generally applied to the artificial propagation and rearing of fish, may include one or more of a number of steps beginning with the extraction of eggs and milt from ripe adult fish, followed by fertilization, incubation, hatching, and finally rearing the offspring to a size suitable for specific purposes. The artificial propagation of fish is not just a technique developed in recent times, for simple methods of fish culture were practiced by the Chinese as early as 2100 B.C. Other references to it are made during the time of the Roman Empire, and again in the 14th and 18th centuries. It was not, however, widely used until after its introduction to the British Isles in 1834 and to the United States in 1857. From then on it grew and improved rapidly to the present day. There are now fish cultural stations on this continent which boast such sophisticated equipment as automatic fish feeders controlled by computers.

Prior to 1932, when the natural resources were transferred from federal to provincial jurisdiction, the responsibility for fish cultural activities in Alberta was assumed by the Canadian government. For several years after that date the federal government continued to supply fish for the province since no provincial fish hatcheries existed. From 1940 to the present, the provincial government has carried on its own fish propagation programs for waters outside the National Parks, while federal activities in this field have been restricted to waters within the parks. Fish culture in Alberta has been used primarily to provide various species of trout, and to some extent Arctic grayling and salmon, for stocking natural waters to improve their sport fishing potential. However, a whitefish hatchery was also operated for approximately sixteen years in an attempt to replenish stocks of lake whitefish in commercially fished waters.

The first trout hatchery was established at Banff in 1913. This was followed by construction of a second in Waterton National Park in 1928. A third hatchery in Jasper National Park also had its beginnings in the 1920's, but this facility was not really a significant producer of trout until its reconstruction and expansion in 1941. In recent years the fish cultural activities of the western National Parks have been consolidated at the Jasper site, and the Waterton and Banff trout hatcheries have been closed.

During the early years of fish hatchery operations in the National Parks in Alberta, the primary objective was to introduce game fish into the many mountain lakes which lacked native species of trout. This was done with a view to enhancing the recreational potential of these waters. By 1952, approximately 120 lakes, which were previously devoid of fish, had been stocked in these parks and in the adjacent parks in British Columbia. The number of such stocked lakes has undoubtedly increased further since that time. The principal species used in this stocking program were rainbow, cutthroat, brook, and to a lesser extent, lake trout, splake, and brown trout. Many fine angling fisheries such as the brook trout fisheries in Maligne, Crandell, Trefoil, and Cameron lakes have been created. It may also be said, however, that due to lack of knowledge in the early years, some unwarranted introductions of other species of trout were made in waters which contained populations of native trout such as the cutthroat. The use of hatchery-reared trout in the western National Parks is now chiefly confined to lakes where natural reproduction is limited or absent, or where fish populations have been reduced or completely lost through winter-kill (Solman 1952).

The first trout hatchery in the province outside the National Parks was established in 1936 in Calgary by Mr. J. B. Cross of the Calgary Brewing and Malting Company. It was not, however, until 1940 that this hatchery began to produce several species of trout in sufficient quantities for distribution to the province's lakes and streams. Shortly thereafter the provincial government entered into an agreement with the company whereby the latter would supply and maintain the hatchery facilities and personnel of the Department of Lands and Forests would carry out the fish cultural operations. Although the hatchery has been expanded substantially since 1940, this cooperative arrangement has remained in effect to the present day.

In conjunction with the Calgary Hatchery, a number of fish rearing stations have been operated at various times and places, and with varying degrees of success. These rearing stations were designed to raise trout from fingerling size to the yearling stage or older. The most important of these stations is the one currently in use, known as the Raven station near Caroline, Alberta. It was established in 1937 and was supplied for a time with trout from the Banff Hatchery. Other rearing ponds were located at Pincher Creek, Big Hill Springs near Cochrane, Westmount in Calgary, and on the banks of Sundance Creek near Edson. These small stations were operated for a limited time in the 1940's with the exception of Westmount ponds which continued operation until 1956. Abandonment of these stations took place because of water quality problems, and also due to the fact that improvement of fish transporting equipment rendered them more or less obsolete. All subsequent trout rearing has been carried out at the Raven station which was reconstructed and enlarged to meet requirements in 1962.

Raven fish rearing station near Caroline, 1963. The ponds in the foreground are where the fingerlings are reared prior to planting.

In addition to these fish cultural facilities, a station to maintain 'brood stock' which supplied eggs to the Calgary hatchery, was operated on the well-known Hunter Ranch west of Fort McLeod from 1941 to 1953. The establishment of large commercial trout hatcheries in the United States from which large quantities of fertilized trout eggs could be purchased at reasonable cost, led to the closing of the brood stock station at the Hunter Ranch.

For some time prior to, and after the establishment of the Calgary fish hatchery, trout were stocked in provincial waters for the purpose of creating angling fisheries in lakes which contained no fish; to introduce species which by popular opinion were superior to existing native game fish; and to supplement naturally reproducing populations of trout in our east slope streams. As in

27

the National Parks, this policy resulted in the introduction of exotics such as the brown trout and brook trout and in the introduction of rainbow and cutthroat trout into waters outside their native range. It was not until the late 1940's that the value of attempting to supplement naturally reproducing stocks of stream trout with hatchery fish was seriously questioned by the late Dr. R. B. Miller. His investigations and research indicated that hatchery reared trout suffered high mortalities when stocked in streams in which wild trout were present and that there was little chance of the hatchery product contributing to the fisheries unless larger trout were used on a put-and-take basis. As a result of these investigations, the practice of routine stocking of fingerling and yearling hatchery trout in Alberta streams was all but discontinued in 1952. Since that time, although hatchery trout production has continued to increase, the emphasis on the use of these fish has shifted to providing stocks for angling in the many lakes and reservoirs in the province where natural reproduction of the species does not occur. In some streams and in beaver ponds where spawning is also limited, the stocking of hatchery trout is still being carried on.

The whitefish hatchery located at Canyon Creek on the south shore of Lesser Slave Lake was established in 1928. Its main purpose was to incubate large numbers of fertilized whitefish eggs to within several weeks of hatching. In late March and early April these 'eyed-eggs' were transferred to various lakes throughout the province with the intention of supplementing the natural supply of lake whitefish, and thus increase the yield to commercial fishermen. In some cases the eggs were distributed to lakes which contained no whitefish. The present populations of Muriel Lake, Lake McGregor and Lake Newell, to mention a few, are the result of the introduction of eggs from the Canyon Creek hatchery. The practice of planting whitefish eggs to supplement natural reproduction was continued until the early 1940's when research, again by Miller, showed that this program was having little or no effect on the numbers of whitefish available to the commercial fishery. It was on the basis of this evidence that the whitefish hatchery was closed in 1944 and no further whitefish culture has been carried on in the province.

In conclusion it may be said that although the role of the fish hatchery has changed significantly over the years, it continues to play an important part in fish management in Alberta. The main-

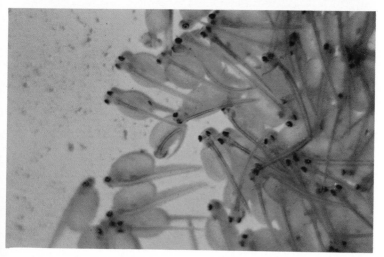

Lake trout before hatching (the eyes are visible) and just after hatching (note the relatively large yolk sac).

The removal of hatchery trout from rearing pond in preparation for planting.

Steps involved in loading hatchery fish into special tank truck.

Releasing trout from hatchery truck into an Alberta lake (Upper Kananaskis Reservoir).

tenance of many excellent trout fisheries where natural reproduction is not possible, the replenishment of fish populations which have been depleted or eradicated by natural disasters such as winter-kill, have already been mentioned. In addition, there are intensive fish farming operations which, at present, are just beginning in Alberta but which will depend on hatcheries for their supply of fish. There is also growing evidence that natural trout populations in our streams soon may not be able to supply the demands made upon them by an increasing number of anglers. Experience in the United States and elsewhere has shown this to be so, and the only avenues available to maintain stream fishing in heavily populated areas appear to be the catch-and-release programs or the stocking of catchable-sized hatchery trout. Where fishermen are willing to bear the substantial cost of the latter method of providing fish for the creel, the trout hatchery has become the important tool in providing the fish required. In support of fish cultural operations in this province it should be noted also that many useful introductions of trout species have been made to waters which previously were not providing high quality sport fishing. We have learned, however, that prior research and considerable caution must be exercised before introductions of new species are undertaken.

HOW TO IDENTIFY A FISH

Keys are generally the best means of finding out what a certain organism is. Identification through the use of these keys may be facilitated by comparing the unknown specimen with the outline drawings on page 49 and the species pictures. Reliance on only comparing a specimen with a picture, however, is poor practice and often results in error. Consistent use of the keys will result in their mastery and give much satisfaction to the user and confidence in identifications.

The following keys are designed to separate characters so that an identification can be made by means of a series of alternative choices. To identify a fish, the user should examine the first alternative, determine which member of the couplet best describes the specimen (a or b) and proceed to the next alternative indicated by the number at the end of the correct member couplet and continue to successive alternatives until a name is reached. The number in parentheses after the couplet number enables the user to retrace the path of alternatives quickly.

In identification one must keep in mind the wide variability of some characters due to the environment and due to actual genetic differences both between populations and between individuals of the same population. The amount of variation in a few species precludes a simple and unfailing key.

An attempt has been made to include enough diagnostic characters so that mistakes at one alternative will not lead to incorrect identifications and so that the key will be of use with specimens having obviously deformed key characters. This also reduces the chance of failing to recognize a species new to the province. The comparative descriptions for each species in the text should insure accurate identifications. The danger of misidentifying a species new to Alberta and thus not in the key can be further avoided by checking the characteristics of those specimens in Appendix I, by checking all questionable identifications in Bailey and Allum (1962), Carl, Clemens, and Lindsey (1967), Cross (1967), Hubbs and Lagler (1964), McPhail and Lindsey (1970), Moore (1968), Scott and Crossman (1969), and Trautman (1957), and by comparison with specimens previously identified by competent workers. The key is not intended for hybrids or teratological individuals.

34

The keys include only those families and species that are considered to be part of the established Alberta fish fauna (golden trout and kokanee are exceptions). They exclude some exotic fish successfully introduced, unsuccessfully introduced species, and species adjacent to the province and very likely in our waters but as yet not recorded. These 27 odd species, with means of recognizing most, are listed in Appendix I.

Within the borders of Alberta, fossils are found of marine fish which lived as long ago as about 400,000,000 years. The fossil fish exhibit more diversity then do the living forms. Information on Alberta fish fossils may be found in Gardiner (1966) and O'Brian (1969) and their references.

Many technical terms are used in the keys for the sake of brevity. Most of these terms are explained in the following section.

COUNTS, MEASUREMENTS, AND ATTRIBUTES
(WITH DEFINITIONS)

Counts of meristic characters given in the species key and general species description are usually from regional works outside Alberta and from recent systematic studies. Some meristic data are from Alberta material but, in general, very little is known on the meristic peculiarities of the province's fishes. It would be expected that different populations of the same species would each be slightly different in some characters. Measurements and attributes have generally been taken from Alberta material.

Maximum lengths noted for Alberta fish are presented primarily to form a basis for obtaining verifiable records from the province in the future. At present, the maximum length often represents the largest individual from a small collection.

Many characters may be measured or counted in different ways. The methods recommended by Hubbs and Lagler (1964) are generally followed. Some of the technical terms used in the keys and methods of counting and measuring are mentioned below. Several features are shown on the drawings on pages 40 to 42.

adipose fin — the small fleshy rayless fin on the back between the dorsal and caudal fins in members of the salmon, catfish, and trout-perch families.

anterior — that which is in the front part or in front of another part.

barbel — an elongate fleshy process provided with the sense of touch or smell found in sturgeon, catfish, burbot, and some minnows.

basal end of a fin — point where last ray joins body.

base of a fin (or basal length) — the length of the fin where it is attached to the body.

basibranchial — a series of median bones behind the tongue and between the gills.

branchiostegal rays — long curved bones supporting the branchiostegal membrane which encloses the gill chamber ventrally.

caudal peduncle — portion of the body between end of anal fin and base of the caudal fin; see scale counts and the following figure.

cheek — area between the eye and preopercle bone.

compressed — flattened from side to side.

concave — curved inward, like the inside of a circle.

convex — curved outward, like the outside of a circle.

ctenoid scale — a scale bearing tiny spines on its posterior portion and feeling rough to the fingers, typical of the perch family.

cycloid scale — a scale roughly circular in outline, lacking spines and relatively smooth to the fingers, typical of most Alberta fish.

decurved — curved downward.

depressed — flattened from top to bottom.

dorsal — pertaining to the back or upper side.

fork length — the straight line distance from the most anterior point of the snout to the central part of the margin of the caudal fin (whether forked or not).

frenum — a vertical bridge of tissue across which the premaxillary groove does not cross, connects the upper lip to the snout and thus makes the premaxillaries nonprotractile. Present in all salmonids, pike, goldeye, longnose dace, trout-perch, and Iowa darter.

gill cover — or opercle, the large thin bones on each side of the head which cover the gills.

gillrakers — slender rodlike structures under the opercular flap attached to the gill arches. Counts are customarily made on the first arch (always in this book), which must usually be dissected out.

gonad — the ovary or testis.

head length — distance from the most anterior part of the head to the most posterior part of the opercular membrane.

heterocercal caudal fin — a tail fin in which the upper lobe has a distinct fleshy base and is longer than the lower lobe, as in the sturgeon.

homocercal caudal fin — a tail fin in which the upper and lower lobes are about equal or the fin is rounded, in all Alberta fish except the sturgeon.

hypural bones or plate — the modified haemal spines of the last few vertebrae on which the caudal fin-rays articulate, determined without dissection by moving the tail fin from side to side.

inferior mouth — a mouth which is ventral to the terminal position, the snout usually overhangs the upper lip.

insertion (of the pelvic fin) — the line along which the fin is attached to the body, front end of paired fins.

isthmus — the ventral portion of the head behind the lower jaw and between the opercular flaps.

lateral — toward the side or on the side.

lateral line — a series of pores along the side, variously developed or absent.

maxilla — the bone of the upper jaw lying behind (as in salmonids) or above (as in percids) the premaxilla.

median — situated on the middle or axial plane.

meristic — any body part occurring in serial repetition; for example scales and fin rays.

opercle or operculum — the large, flat, and thin bones on each side of the head covering the gills, also called gill-cover.

origin (of the dorsal, adipose, and anal fins) — the most anterior point of attachment to the body.

palatine — a paired bone in the roof of the mouth lying on either side of the vomer and behind the premaxilla.

papilla — a small fleshy projection.

papillose — covered with papillae.

parr marks — vertical dark bars on the sides of some young fish such as grayling, trout, charr, and mountain whitefish.

peritoneum — the membrane lining the inside (external surface) of the body cavity, seen by slitting open the fish ventrally.

pharyngeal teeth — see introductory section of the minnow family.

physoclistous — having lost the embryonic duct connecting the air bladder and the esophagus, generally the condition in spiny-rayed fishes.

physostomous — having a functional duct connecting the air bladder and the esophagus, generally the condition in soft-rayed fishes.

plicate — a series of wrinkle-like folds of skin.

posterior — that which is in the hind part or behind another part.

premaxilla — the bone at the tip of the upper jaw.

protractile — capable of being extended out as in the case of the upper jaw in fish lacking a frenum.

pseudobranch — accessory gill on the inner surface of the opercle.

pyloric caeca — finger-like processes attached to where the intestine leaves the stomach.

38

ray of a fin — supporting structures to the fin membranes, includes both soft-rays and spines.

scale counts

(a) *along lateral line* — the number of scales along the lateral line or along its normal position and terminating at the base of the caudal fin (end of hypural plate). Several variations of this count exist. In the salmonids often only the sensory pores along the lateral are counted (which gives a lower count) or the scales one or two rows above the lateral line are counted (giving a higher count).

(b) *above the lateral line* — the number of scales from the origin of the dorsal fin, including the small scales, to, but not including, the lateral-line scale.

(c) *around the caudal peduncle* — the circumference scale count around the narrowest part of the trunk between the anal fin and the tail fin.

snout length — distance from the anterior-most point of the snout to the front margin of the eye.

soft-ray — rays which are branched, segmented, and usually flexible. Unless otherwise stated, a dorsal and anal fin ray number includes only the principal rays (the number of branched rays plus one unbranched ray, with the last ray in dorsal and anal fin counts consisting of two ray elements in which one is branched and the other is usually unbranched). The first principal dorsal or anal fin ray is usually unbranched and is followed by a branched ray. In salmonids, many workers include all the anterior rudimentary rays and the principal rays includes all rays whose length is at least ½ the length of the longest ray.

spine — rays which are not branched or segmented and usually stiff and sharp.

standard length — the straight line distance from the anterior-most point of the snout to the end of the hypural plate.

terminal mouth — when both the upper and lower jaws form the extreme anterior tip of the head.

total length — the straight line distance from the anterior-most point of the snout to the extreme end of the caudal fin.

upper jaw length — distance from tip of snout to end of maxilla.

ventral — pertaining to the bottom or lower side.

vomer — median bone in the roof of the mouth.

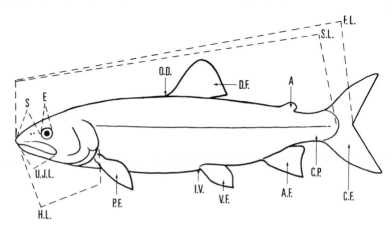

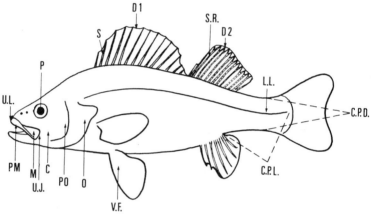

Lateral view of two fish showing some of the structures and methods of measuring used in identification.

Upper — trout. A — adipose fin; AF — anal fin; CF — caudal or tail fin; CP — caudal peduncle; DF — dorsal fin; E — eye diameter; FL — fork length; HL — head length; IV — pelvic fin insertion; OD — dorsal fin origin; PF — pectoral fin; S — snout length; SL — standard length; UJL — upper jaw length; VF — pelvic fin (in abdominal position).

Lower — perch. C — cheek; CPD — caudal peduncle depth; CPL — caudal peduncle length; D1 — first dorsal fin (spiny); D2 — second dorsal fin (soft rayed); LL — lateral line; M — maxilla; O — opercle; P — pupil; PM — premaxilla; PO — preopercle; S — spine; SR — soft ray; UJ — end of upper jaw; UL — upper lip; VF — pelvic fin (in thoracic position).

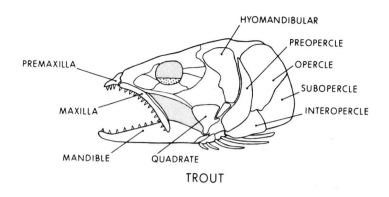

TROUT

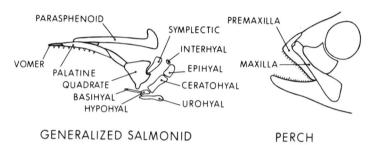

GENERALIZED SALMONID

PERCH

Relationship of some of the skull bones.

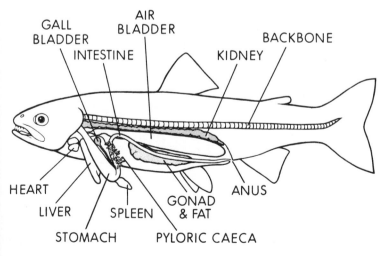

Internal anatomy of a fish

41

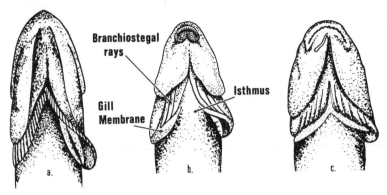

Ventral view of the heads of three Alberta fishes showing the various means of gill membrane attachment.

  (a) Gill membranes (or branchiostegal membrane) free from isthmus, not attached to each other and gill slits extended far forward, northern pike.
  (b) Gill membranes united to isthmus and gill slits not extended far forward, white sucker.
  (c) Gill membranes broadly connected to each other with an underneath cavity, burbot.

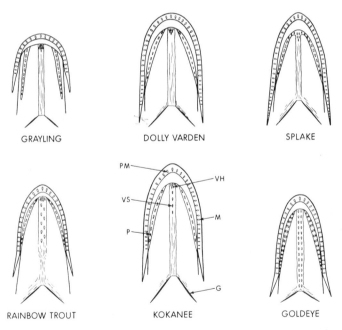

View of roof of mouth in six Alberta fish showing various tooth patterns. G — gill slit; M — teeth on maxillae; P — teeth on palatine; PM — teeth on premaxillae; VH — teeth at head of vomer or prevomerine teeth; VS — teeth on shaft of vomer.

SPECIES AND CLASSIFICATION

Species represent different kinds of organisms; they comprise individuals which share common features. The existence of different species and our ability to recognize them results from their adaptation to different environments and their failure to grade into one another through free interbreeding. A species consists of groups of interbreeding individuals which are capable of successfully interbreeding with other such groups in the species but which cannot successfully interbreed with individuals of other species. Thus, all individuals of the yellow perch can successfully interbreed with one another but they are reproductively isolated from walleye.

Species which are considered to be relatively closely related, usually because of their similar shape and anatomy, are placed in the same genus. Thus the genus *Salmo* includes the true trout, all of which share certain common characteristics. The generic name shows relationships by classifying the species (in contrast, common names often tell us nothing of relationships or may actually suggest false relationships). There are no rules on how much of a morphological difference is necessary to designate genera. It is entirely a matter of opinion and it is common for research workers to have differences of opinion on this subjective matter. As a consequence, fish biologists may assign species to different genera. For example, all workers agree that Dolly Varden and brook trout share more characters in common with one another than either do with lake trout. This evidence is used by some to support placing the lake trout in a separate genus, namely *Cristivomer*. The majority of workers, however, feel it more important to indicate relationships through generic names as much as practical, and place the above three species of charr in the same genus, namely *Salvelinus*.

The latinized scientific name of a species is a two-part name; it is a binominal consisting of a generic name and a specific name and it is employed throughout the world. The generic name is given first and its first letter is always capitalized. If a species is not considered to have any close evolutionary relationship with any other known species it may be the only species placed in a genus. Such a genus, to which only one species has been assigned, is said to be monotypic in contrast to a polytypic genus such as

Salmo which has many species. The second or specific name always begins with a letter in lower case. If the specific name is an adjective in the nominative singular, it must agree in gender with the generic name. The spelling of the specific name can thus vary if the species is placed in different genera. For example, the lake chub may be *Couesius plumbeus* or *Hybopsis plumbea.* Together, the generic and specific names comprise the species name. This name is always written in italics. A third or subspecific name is sometimes employed for species with particular types of variation in their morphology in different areas. The first species to be described in a particular genus is termed the type species for the genus. It has special significance under the rules of nomenclature.

Each species has an author, the person who first adequately described the species and named it under the rules of binominal nomenclature. An author's name is indicated, as is done in the text at the start of each species account, by placing his surname after the species name. If the author originally described the species in another genus than it is now recognized, the author's name is placed in parentheses. Thus *Salvelinus malma* (Walbaum) means that the specific or trivial name *malma* was placed in a different genus by Walbaum than it is now recognized.

Changes in the scientific name of a species is a source of frustration to all but it is sometimes necessary under the rules of zoological nomenclature. Species may be placed in different genera as our ideas concerning evolutionary relationships change. A generic name is changed when it is discovered that it has been used earlier for another taxon. For example, a few years ago all workers placed the brook stickleback in the genus, *Eucalia.* However, this name had been used for a butterfly before it had been used for the fish. Since a generic name cannot be used for two different animals, the fish name had to be changed. In this case, *Culaea* was adopted as a generic name.

Different genera which are considered to be relatively closely related are combined into the same family. Thus, the genera comprising grayling, whitefish, and trout are placed in the same family, Salmonidae. A large number of species may be placed in the same family if a great deal of speciation has resulted amongst similar appearing forms. The family of minnows thus contains about 2000 species. On the other hand, the family of trout-perch contains only two species.

Related families are placed in the same order, and related orders into the same class. All Alberta fish, representing 12 families and 7 orders, belong to the same class, Osteichthyes or Teleostomi. Other classes are represented in the province by fossils.

Different common names often exist in different areas for the same species. This presents no problem when there is no communication between people employing the different "language" but uniformity in names is obviously desirable. In hopes of bringing about stability and uniformity in names, The American Fisheries Society has a list (Bailey, 1970) of common and scientific names for fish. This list, in turn, has been guided by the suggestions of The International Commission on Zoological Nomenclature. We favor retention of the original spelling of patronyms (a name based on that of a person) as advised by the International Commission. However, for uniformity within fish names, we follow the list of Bailey (1970) in employing the one added "i" for all patronyms.

DISTRIBUTION MAPS

Locality records for the 49 distribution maps were derived from numerous sources. Records for northern Alberta are almost entirely based on museum collections and Theses in the Department of Zoology of The University of Alberta and collections and reports made by the staff of the Provincial Fish and Wildlife Division. Records from southern Alberta are primarily from collections of the Fish and Wildlife Division, Henderson and Peter (1969), and Willock (1969b). Older literature was also employed when desirable. In some cases, one dot serves for several nearby collections. Introduced populations which are not known to be self-sustaining are generally not shown on the maps.

The section on distribution of each species in the text contains a statement of the general range of the fish in the world and in the province.

KEY TO THE 12 FAMILIES OF FISHES OF ALBERTA

Note — Four families with representatives not considered to be truly part of the Alberta fauna are diagnosed in Appendix I and are not in this key. See outline drawings on p. 49 and 250.

1 a   Pelvic fins abdominal (placed back, generally on middle third of body), their base overlapped only slightly or not at all by the pectoral fins; one dorsal fin (with or without an adipose fin) _____ 2

1 b   Pelvic fins, if present, thoracic or jugular (placed forward, generally on front third of body), their base beneath or in front of the anterior half of the pectoral fins; two dorsal fins with rays or one fin preceded by isolated spines _____ 9

2 a (1)   Caudal fin heterocercal; entire mouth posterior to front of eye; bony shields present in 5 separated rows on body; flattened snout projecting beyond mouth by a distance exceeding width of mouth.
> Sturgeon family — ACIPENSERIDAE, p. 50.

2 b   Caudal fin homocercal; front part of mouth anterior to eye; no bony shields; snout not projecting beyond mouth by a distance exceeding opening of mouth _____ 3

3 a (2)   Adipose fin present _____ 4

3 b   Adipose fin absent _____ 6

4 a (3)   Body without scales; 4 pairs of barbels on front part of head; each pectoral fin with a hard spinous ray.
> Catfish family — ICTALURIDAE, p. 201.

4 b   Body with scales; barbels absent; pectorals without spinous ray _____ 5

5 a (4)   Adipose fin origin distinctly behind the basal end of anal fin; pectoral fin slightly overlaps pelvic fin base; some ctenoid scales; weak spines in dorsal and anal fins.
> Trout-perch family — PERCOPSIDAE, p.209.

46

5 b   Adipose fin origin in front of basal end of anal fin; pectoral fin not overlapping pelvic fin base; cycloid scales; no spines in fins.

         Salmon family — SALMONIDAE (grayling, cisco, whitefish, charr, trout, and salmon), p. 55.

6 a (3)   Gill membranes not attached to isthmus and gill slits extended far forward ventrally; jaw teeth present; branchiostegal rays 7 or more _____   7

6 b   Gill membranes attached to isthmus and gill slits not extended far forward; jaw teeth absent; branchiostegal rays 3 _____   8

7 a (6)   Body elongate, standard length more than 4 times body depth; snout length about equal to length of anal-fin base; scales above lateral line more than 12; portions of head scaly; ventral surface of body rounded.

         Pike family — ESOCIDAE, p. 112.

7 b   Body comressed, standard length less than 4 times body depth; snout several times shorter than anal-fin base; scales above lateral line fewer than 9; head without scales; ventral surface of body forming a sharpish edge.

         Mooneye family — HIODONTIDAE, p. 118.

8 a (6)   Lips usually thick and covered with papillae or plicae; distance from anal-fin origin to tip of snout more than 2½ times distance from anal-fin origin to base of caudal fin; pharyngeal teeth in a single row with more than 15 teeth.

         Sucker family — CATOSTOMIDAE, p. 174.

8 b   Lips usually not thick, not covered with papillae or plicae; distance from anal-fin origin to tip of snout less than 2½ times distance from anal-fin origin to base of caudal fin (except in some cyprinids not native to Alberta); pharyngeal teeth in 1 or 2 rows with fewer than 6 teeth in any row.

         Minnow family — CYPRINIDAE, p. 123.

9 a (1) Dorsal fin preceded by a row of isolated spines, not interconnected with a membrane; each pelvic fin, when present, reduced to a single spine and a small soft-ray; branchiostegal rays 3.

> Stickleback family — GASTEROSTEIDAE, p. 213.

9 b Dorsal fin not preceded by a row of isolated spines; each pelvic fin with more than 2 distinct soft-rays; branchiostegal rays 5 or more _____ 10

10 a (9) Single long barbel on tip of lower jaw; pelvic fins inserted in front of pectoral fins; first dorsal fin without spines; second dorsal fin with more than 65 rays.

> Cod family — GADIDAE, p. 205.

10 b No barbels on lower jaw; pelvic fins inserted beneath pectoral fins; first dorsal fin with spines; second dorsal fin with fewer than 24 rays _____ 11

11 a (10) Body covered with ctenoid scales; first dorsal fin about equal in length to second dorsal fin (the first fin with more than ½ the number of rays as the second fin); anal spines one or two.

> Perch family — PERCIDAE, p. 220.

11 b Body without scales (small prickles may be present); first dorsal fin usually about ½ as long as second dorsal fin (the first dorsal fin with about ½ the number of rays as the second fin); no anal spines.

> Sculpin family — COTTIDAE, p. 239.

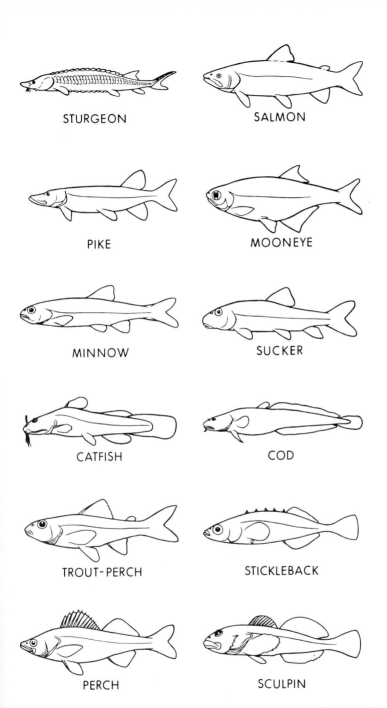

STURGEON

SALMON

PIKE

MOONEYE

MINNOW

SUCKER

CATFISH

COD

TROUT-PERCH

STICKLEBACK

PERCH

SCULPIN

OUTLINE DRAWINGS OF MEMBERS OF ALBERTA'S FISH FAMILIES

STURGEON FAMILY — ACIPENSERIDAE

Representatives of the sturgeon family occur in fresh waters and along coastlines in the Northern Hemisphere. All species, however, must spawn in fresh water. The family contains about 22 species, placed in 4 genera. Five species occur in Canada with 1 in Alberta.

The sturgeon family contains the largest fresh-water fish in the Northern Hemisphere, sometimes reaching lengths of over 20 feet. Sturgeon flesh is very flavorsome and the eggs are much valued for caviar. In some areas, the fish are important commercially and for sport.

All sturgeons have a ventral sucking mouth with 4 barbels located in a row anterior to the mouth, used for detecting food. Five rows of hard scutes line the body and upper lobe of the caudal fin is elongate (heterocercal). The skeleton is primarily cartilaginous.

The closest living representatives of the sturgeons are the paddlefishes (Polyodontidae), confined to fresh water in China and the United States. These two families are placed in the order Acipenseriformes. This primitive order is placed in the ancient group of fishes, the superorder Chondrostei or Palaeoniscoidei, in contrast to all other Alberta fish which belong in the superorder Teleostei.

Acipenser fulvescens Rafinesque

Acipenser — sturgeon

fulvescens — in reference to its
    fulvous (brownish-yellow) color.

Lake sturgeon

DESCRIPTION

Color olive-grey to dark grey, whitish underneath. Peritoneum silvery with blackish viscera.

Body subtriangular (somewhat rounded) in section, rounded
at caudal peduncle. Head slightly rounded between the eyes
with a median shallow groove; distance between the eyes 3 (in
young) — 6 (in adults) times eye diameter; eyes small; nostril
openings large; snout long, flattened and pointed in young, somewhat conical in adults; mouth ventral with front margin behind
front margin of eye, lower lip with 2 slightly papillose lobes;
teeth absent in adults, inconspicuous in very young; premaxillaries fused with maxillaries but mouth is protrusible; 4 long
barbels in transverse row in front of mouth; small opening
(spiracle) between eye and upper corner of opercle (the only
fish in Alberta with this remnant of the hyoid gill slit). Gill
membranes attached to a broad isthmus; isthmus about ⅓ width of

head. Pectoral fin on lower half of body and nearly horizontal. Body with 5 rows of shield-like plates (pointed in young, smooth in adults). Upper lobe of caudal fin elongated (with a patch of ganoid scales on the upper lobe). Median dorsal plates in front of dorsal fin about 14, usually 2 behind; dorso-lateral plates in each row about 35; ventro-lateral plates in each row about 9 in front of pelvic fin insertion, with usually 2 median ones before the anal fin. About 35 closely set dorsal fin rays and about 25 closely set anal fin rays. One branchiostegal ray (on the interhyal) and 25-40 short gillrakers on a curved arch.

Length up to about 7 feet. Maximum length noted from Alberta is 67 inches fork length from the South Saskatchewan River.

DISTRIBUTION

Alberta to Quebec and Nebraska to Alabama.

Known in Alberta from the North and South Saskatchewan and Brazeau rivers (see map on page 54).

BIOLOGY

Lake sturgeon occur in the shallow bottom areas of lakes and large rivers with generally clean bottoms. Their food consists of bottom organisms such as clams, snails, insect larvae, some fish, and plant material. Spawning probably occurs in the late spring with maturity reached when an individual is about 15 years old and about 35 inches in fork length. Spawning then occurs every 5 or so years. As many as 500,000 eggs may be produced by a large female. Individuals may live for longer than 50 years and with the possible exception of lake trout, are Alberta's longest-lived fish. Sturgeon were once much more abundant in the North Saskatchewan River and their decrease may have been due to pollution and ecological changes in the river due to settlement. Because of their rarity in Alberta they provide no commercial fishery.

ANGLING

Owing to the scarcity of this species angling for sturgeon on a special licence has only recently been legalized in Alberta following a long closure. Sturgeon are taken exclusively with bait using casting or spinning gear and hand lines. The bait is allowed to sink to the bottom of a pool in the river and a long wait is often in store for the angler before he is rewarded with a strike. Although some sturgeon are found in the North Saskatchewan River, the majority of annual catch is taken from the South Saskatchewan between the junction of the Bow and Oldman Rivers and the eastern boundary of the province.

HISTORICAL NOTE

First described by C. S. Rafinesque in 1817 from the Great Lakes as *Accipenser fulvescens*. First recorded from Alberta by Whitehouse (1919) from the Bow River at Bassano as *Acipenser transmontanus* (a Pacific drainage species which gets no closer to Alberta than Kootenay Lake and the Columbia River above Revelstoke).

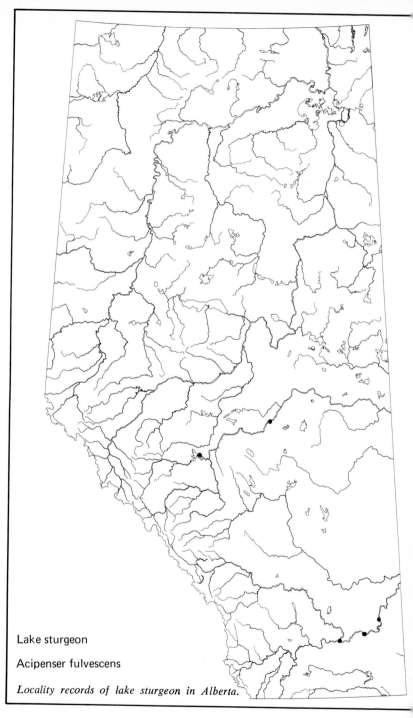

Lake sturgeon

Acipenser fulvescens

Locality records of lake sturgeon in Alberta.

SALMON FAMILY — SALMONIDAE

Representatives of the salmon family are native to cold-waters throughout the Northern Hemisphere. Most species are fresh water but many are anadromous or have anadromous members. Salmonids have been successfully introduced throughout the world onto all continents except Antarctica. In addition, many species have been planted in areas within their native range.

Three subfamilies are recognized, each of which has representatives native to Eurasia and North America. There is little agreement on the number of species in most of the groups but the number in parentheses after each genus may be considered a conservative estimate.

The subfamily Thymallinae (grayling) contains a single genus, *Thymallus* (4).

The Coregoninae (cisco, whitefish, and inconnu) contains three recognized genera, *Coregonus* (21), *Prosopium* (6), and *Stenodus* (1).

The Salmoninae (lenok, taimen, charr, trout, and salmon) contains five recognized genera, *Brachymystax* (1), *Hucho* (4), *Salvelinus* (10), *Salmo* (7), and *Oncorhynchus* (6).

In the family, about 32 species are native to Canada while 9 are native to Alberta.

Salmonids have 7-20 branchiostegal rays on the epihyal and ceratohyal (Thymallinae 8-12; Coregoninae 7-12; *Salvelinus* and *Salmo* 8-14; *Oncorhynchus* 10-20), 57-75 vertebrae, cycloid scales, and an adipose fin. In addition, Alberta species share the following characteristics: body moderately compressed (except in cisco and lake whitefish where it is usually strongly compressed); head region between eyes slightly to moderately rounded; space between the eyes roughly about 1 (in young) — 1½ (in adults) times eye diameter; eyes moderate to large; mouth terminal, upper jaw occasionally projecting slightly forward, and slightly oblique (except as noted for the cisco and whitefishes); wide frenum (no continuous groove separating upper jaw from snout, premaxillaries not protrusible); gill membranes extending far forward, not attached to each other or to isthmus; pectoral fin on lower half of body and base slightly to moderately oblique; pelvic appendage present; dorsal fin origin in front of pelvic fin insertion; adipose fin origin usually over middle of anal fin base; lateral line straight and complete (in Dolly Varden it is usually very slightly decurved anteriorly); peritoneum silvery with small black spots often present.

This family contains the majority of species important in the commercial and sport fishery in Canada. Within the salmonids, there is considerable adaptive radiation as is true for many other families of fish. Various species such as cisco show adaptations toward feeding on plankton (and have a large terminal mouth with small teeth and numerous long gillrakers), on bottom fauna such as most whitefish (and have a small subterminal mouth with small teeth and relatively few short gillrakers), or on other fish such as lake trout (and have a large terminal mouth with well developed teeth and relatively few short gillrakers). Many salmonids, such as Dolly Varden and brown trout, show remarkable adaptiveness in changing their diet to suit the environment.

Salmonids are placed by most workers in the large order Isospondyli or Clupeiformes, together with the mooneye and pike families, while others place them in the order Salmoniformes, along with the pike and numerous other families not represented in Alberta. Salmonids are close relatives of the smelts (Osmeridae).

KEY TO THE 13 SPECIES

Note—Eight species adjacent to Alberta or introduced and of questioned status in Alberta in Appendix I, not in key.

1 a   Scales above lateral line fewer than 12; scales along lateral line fewer than 100; teeth on jaws small or absent _____ 2

1 b   Scales above lateral line more than 17; scales along lateral line more than 110; teeth on jaws well developed (subfamily SALMONINAE) ___ 6

2 a (1)   Dorsal fin with 16 or more rays; dorsal fin base equal to (in young) or greater than (in adults) head length; maxilla with small teeth; adults with scattered distinct black spots usually restricted to anterior half of body, young with about 12 to 16 vertical parr marks (dark blotches) along lateral line (subfamily THYMALLINAE).

Thymallus arcticus — Arctic grayling

| 2 b | Dorsal fin with 15 or fewer rays; dorsal fin base shorter than head length (about ½ head length in young); maxilla toothless; body without distinct black spots, young with or without parr marks (subfamily COREGONINAE) _____ | 3 |

| 3 a (2) | Each nostril with a single flap between openings; young, up to about 4 inches, with about 8 to 11 roundish parr marks (dark blotches) along the lateral line. |

Prosopium williamsoni — mountain whitefish

| 3 b | Each nostril with two flaps between openings; young without parr marks _____ | 4 |

| 4 a (3) | Upper jaw blunt and projecting well forward beyond lower jaw; profile of upper jaw extending downwards and backwards; gillrakers usually 33 or fewer. |

Coregonus clupeaformis — lake whitefish

| 4 b | Upper jaw sharp and not projecting forward beyond lower jaw; profile of upper jaw extending forward and downward (in line with forehead); gillrakers 34 or more _____ | 5 |

| 5 a (4) | Gillrakers usually 43 or more; ratio of head length divided by snout to eye distance about 3.7-4.2. |

Coregonus artedii — cisco

| 5 b | Gillrakers usually 42 or less; ratio of head length divided by snout to eye distance about 3.2-3.8. |

Coregonus zenithicus — shortjaw cisco

| 6 a (1) | Body, especially above the lateral line, with pale spots or markings (grey, red, orange, or white), never black spots in adults; teeth on head of vomer only (occasionally a few teeth on the anterior vomerine shaft in lake trout), not on more posterior shaft; lateral-line scales more than 175 ___ | 7 |

6 b   Body, especially above the lateral line, with dark spots; teeth on head and along almost full length of shaft of vomer; lateral-line scales fewer than 165 (except in some cutthroat trout) _____ 9

7 a (6)   Irregular whitish or greyish spots on back (seldom circular or wavy); spots on side usually without color; caudal fin deeply forked; pyloric caeca more than 90.

Salvelinus namaycush — lake trout

7 b   Circular or wavy markings on back; spots on side often with red, orange, and blue; caudal fin only slightly forked; pyloric caeca fewer than 45 ____ 8

8 a (7)   Circular red, orange, or white spots on side, no halo-like marks, no wavy markings on back; dorsal fin without markings.

Salvelinus malma — Dolly Varden

8 b   Some red spots with blue halos on side, elongate or wavy pale or green markings on back; dorsal fin with dark markings.

Salvelinus fontinalis — brook trout

9 a (6)   Anal fin rays 13 or more; gillrakers 30 or more; wide gap separating palatine and vomerine teeth on anterior roof of mouth.

Oncorhynchus nerka — kokanee

9 b   Anal fin rays 12 or fewer; gillrakers 22 or fewer; narrow gap separating palatine and vomerine teeth 10

10 a (9)   Dark spots, if present, on caudal fin confined to upper lobe; many of the large dark spots on body surrounded by pale halos; young with orange adipose fin and usually with a row of red spots (white when preserved) along lateral line between parr marks.

Salmo trutta — brown trout

10 b   Dark spots on both lobes of caudal fin; no halos around dark body spots; young without orange on adipose fin and without row of red spots along

58

lateral line (the next three species are often impossible to separate adequately, hybrids frequently occur) _____ 11

11 a (10) Reddish dash on inside of lower jaw in crease (visible externally); usually no marked whitish leading edge on anal and pelvic fins; dark spots below lateral line often closer and more numerous on posterior than anterior half of body; usually no broad red band on sides of adults; basibranchial teeth usually present.

Salmo clarki — cutthroat trout

11 b Reddish dash pale or absent on inside of lower jaw; whitish border usually present on anal and pelvic fins; dark spots below lateral line about equally common on anterior and posterior halves of body; broad red bands on sides often present; basibranchial teeth usually absent _____ 12

12 a (11) Relatively numerous small roundish dark spots above and below the lateral line and on a darkish background; sides and belly silvery to yellowish-green; parr marks usually present only in young; usually only an indistinct white tip on the dorsal fin in adults; occur in a variety of environments.

Salmo gairdneri — rainbow trout

12 b Relatively few large round dark spots confined to above the lateral line and on a pale background; sides and belly yellow to rosy-red; parr marks usually present in adults; distinct white tip on the dorsal fin; confined in Alberta to high altitude lakes.

Salmo aguabonita — golden trout

Thymallus arcticus (Pallas)
Thymallus — an ancient name of the
    grayling, pertaining to the
    fish's odor of thyme
arcticus — of the arctic

Arctic grayling.

DESCRIPTION

Color dark bluish dorsally, iridescent greenish-grey or bronzy laterally. Black spots on adults, commonest on anterior half above the lateral line. Dorsal and pelvic fins colored, especially brilliant in spawning males which also have a dark body. Young with 12-16 elongated dark brown parr marks crossing the lateral line, above which are several irregular rows of dark marks.

Upper jaw extended behind anterior margin of eye, almost to middle of eye. Teeth small, present on jaws, head of vomer, palatines, and usually on tongue; wide gap between vomerine and palatine teeth at anterior end. Two nostril openings on each side separated by a distinct gap with only the anterior nostril having a distinct flap. Caudal fin deeply forked. Scales one row above lateral line 75-95; above lateral line about 9 or 10; around caudal peduncle about 24-26. Dorsal fin rays 16-24; anal fin rays 10-12. First arch gillrakers 14-22. Pyloric caeca 13-18.

Dorsal fin, and less noticeably the pelvic fin, longer in mature males than in females.

Maximum length 24 inches and weight 3 pounds. Maximum known length from Alberta is 14 inches fork length from Marten Creek (Ward, 1951) and maximum weight is 2 pounds 13 ounces from the Embarrass River.

DISTRIBUTION

Ob River in western Soviet Union, St. Lawrence Island and Alaska to northeastern Northwest Territories and northwestern British Columbia (south to Stikine River) through much of the Peace River headwaters to Owl River in Manitoba. Native stocks in the Michigan area and Missouri drainage are probably extinct. Introduced within and outside native range.

Known in Alberta from Hay, Peace, and Athabasca drainages (see map page 63). Specimens have occasionally been taken from the Belly River, Oldman River drainage.

BIOLOGY

Grayling are confined to cold streams and lakes and are extremely susceptible to various forms of pollution. They feed primarily on terrestrial and aquatic insects, secondarily on bottom organisms and plants, and rarely on fish. Spawning occurs in streams in May and early June at about 40-45°F. At this time, the males defend their spawning territories. During mating, the male arches his large dorsal fin over the back of the female and the pair undergo intense quivering. During this time the eggs are buried into gravel. An average female produces about 7000 eggs. Grayling live for as long as 12 years. Ward (1951) and Bishop (1967) present details about the life history of this species.

ANGLING

Angling for this species in Alberta is for the most part confined to stream fishing since very few lakes in the province contain year round resident populations. They are an easily caught sport fish, and the larger fish are often rapidly depleted even under moderate angling pressure. Grayling are excellent fish for the fly fisherman and generally may be taken on a wide variety of patterns, both wet and dry. They may, however, also be taken with spinning tackle using natural baits or small lures. The summer period from mid-June to mid-September is the best time for general grayling fishing, with the period from mid-July to the end of August being the best time for dry fly fishing. Grayling are an excellent table fish.

HISTORICAL NOTE

First described by P. S. Pallas in 1776 from a tributary of the Ob River as *Salmo arcticus*. Preble (1908) reported it present from Peace River and from Lake Athabasca downstream as *Thymallus signifer*. Kendall (1924) gives a description of specimens from Lake Athabasca. Bajkov (1926) noted it from the Athabasca and Snake rivers and Pyramid Lake in Jasper Park.

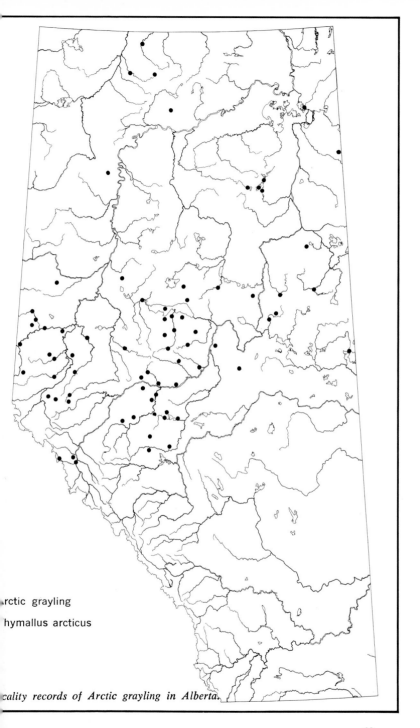

Arctic grayling

Thymallus arcticus

Locality records of Arctic grayling in Alberta.

63

Coregonus artedii Lesueur

Core gonus — a name used by Artedi
 for European whitefish, meaning
 the pupil of the eye, angle.

artedii — named for P. Artedi, ichthyologist
 associate of Linnaeus.

Cisco, two color phases.

DESCRIPTION

Color steel blue with emerald-green overcast dorsally, silvery ventrally. Young without parr marks.

Mouth terminal. Anterior edge of upper jaw directed forward and slightly downward (antrorse); snout sharp. Upper jaw extended behind front margin eye, often to midline. Minute teeth sometimes present on premaxilla and tongue; none on maxilla and lower jaw. Two conspicuous nasal flaps on each side as in the lake whitefish. Adipose eyelids present. Caudal fin deeply forked. Scales along lateral line 75-90 (fewer pored scales); above lateral line about 7-10; around caudal peduncle about 19-25. Dorsal fin rays 8-11 and anal fin rays 10-13. Gillrakers on first arch 40-54. Pyloric caeca about 100.

Maximum length 20 inches and weight 3 pounds. Maximum length noted in Alberta is 12 inches fork length from Myer's Lake.

DISTRIBUTION

Alberta and Northwest Territories to Quebec and Great Lakes region south to Wabash drainage in northern Indiana.

Known in Alberta from Slave, Peace, Athabasca, and Beaver drainage; introduced into southern Alberta in Bow drainage (see map on page 67).

BIOLOGY

Cisco tend to be pelagic and prefer cooler depths of lakes with plentiful oxygen. Young and adults feed on open water plankton. They generally spawn from November to December at about 40°F in lakes over a wide variety of bottoms and depths. Maturity is reached by about age 3 and an average female produces about 10,000 to 25,000 eggs. Hatching occurs about April or May. Miller (1950a) found individuals living up to 9 years in age and presented evidence that in unfished lakes natural mortality may be about 70% a year, at least for fish of age 6. Within limits, he found that fishing mortality decreases natural mortality. Cisco hybridize with lake whitefish throughout much of their area of overlap including in several Alberta lakes. Cisco form a valuable source of mink food on ranches in the Lesser Slave Lake-Lac La Biche area.

Cisco are the most frequently infected hosts of the last larval stage of the tapeworm *Triaenophorus crassus* (see lake whitefish for greater discussion). They are also susceptible to small copepod parasites of the genus *Ergasilus* which attach to the gills. Heavy infections with *Ergasilus,* plus reduced oxygen levels due to algal blooms, were instrumental in producing mass mortality of cisco in Lac La Biche in 1962. Roundworms of the genus *Cystidicola* are sometimes found on the cut surfaces of the fish after cleaning. These parasites live in the air bladder of cisco and other coregonines, from which they are accidentally dragged onto the meat during cleaning. The roundworm *Philonema,* occurring in the body cavity, can cause degeneration of the gonads.

HISTORICAL NOTE

First described by C. A. Lesueur in 1818 from Lake Erie and Niagara River as *Coregonus artedii.* This species bears a close relationship with *Coregonus albula* and *C. sardinella.* In Alberta, Kendall (1924) noted the cisco in Lake Athabasca as *Leucichthys athabascae* and in Lac La Biche as *L. tullibee.* Dymond and Pritchard (1930) noted it from Lesser Slave Lake and nearby Fawcett Lake as *L. tullibee.*

Ciscoes in Alberta are poorly known and more species may be present than are currently recognized.

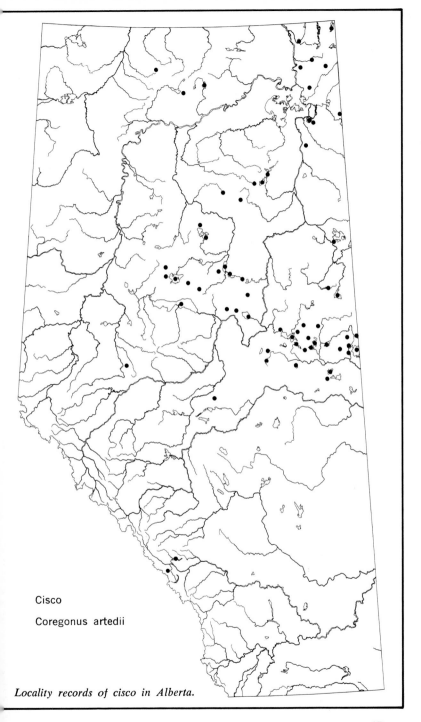

Cisco

Coregonus artedii

Locality records of cisco in Alberta.

67

Coregonus zenithicus (Jordan and Evermann)

zenithicus — in reference to Duluth, "the
  Zenith City", where specimens were seen.

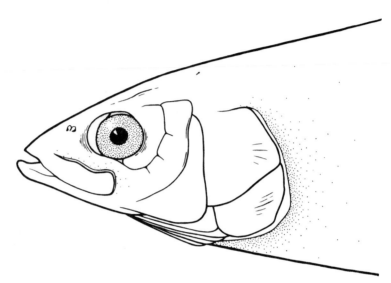

Head of shortjaw cisco from Barrow Lake, 12 inches standard length.

DESCRIPTION

Generally similar to *Coregonus artedii*. Distinguished from other cisco by the following combination of characters: gillrakers usually 38-42 (37-41 reported from Alberta); lower jaw usually very slightly projecting beyond upper jaw (the opposite relationtionship for that in Alberta is shown in some books); body deepest at center not deepest in front part as in *C. nigripinnis*.

DISTRIBUTION

Northeastern Alberta and Northwest Territories to Ontario.

Known in Alberta only from Barrow Lake (Slave drainage), however, further work will probably show it to be present in other lakes of the McKenzie lowlands.

BIOLOGY

Probably similar to that of *C. artedii*. In Barrow Lake, Paterson (1969) reported specimens from 11 to 18 inches fork length being captured in 6-15 feet of water (in contrast, the individuals of *C. artedii* were all much smaller and younger and at depths greater than 45 feet). It is of interest to note that *C. zenithicus* in other areas is reported to be smaller than *C. artedii* and that its size in Barrow Lake exceeds the maximum size reported elsewhere.

HISTORICAL NOTE

First described by D. S. Jordan and W. B. Evermann in 1909 from Lake Superior as *Argyrosomus zenithicus,* the long-jaw. Reported in the Alberta portion of Lake Athabasca by Dymond and Pritchard (1930) but the first verifiable record was made by Paterson (1969) in Barrow Lake.

The Alberta population seems to superficially resemble the longjaw cisco, *Coregonus alpenae,* and more taxonomic work needs to be done on it.

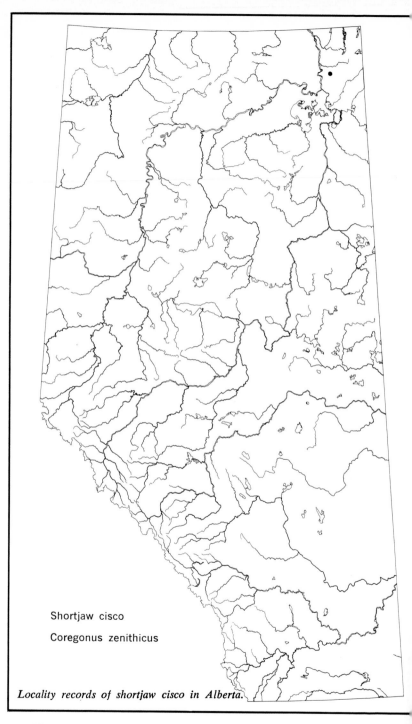

Shortjaw cisco

Coregonus zenithicus

Locality records of shortjaw cisco in Alberta.

Coregonus clupeaformis (Mitchill)
clupea formis — herring shape

Lake whitefish from Utikama Lake

DESCRIPTION

Color olive green to olive blue dorsally, silvery laterally. Young without parr marks.

Mouth subterminal. Anterior edge of upper jaw directed downward and backward (retrorse); snout rounded. Upper jaw extended behind to anterior margin of eye but not to midline. Teeth inconspicuous. Two conspicuous nasal flaps on each side as in ciscoes. Adipose eyelid present. Caudal fin deeply forked. Scales along lateral line 77-90; above lateral line about 10 or 11; around caudal peduncle about 22 or 23. Dorsal and anal fin rays 10-12. Gillrakers on first arch usually 23-33. In Frog Lake, south of Cold Lake, they range from 28-37 (average 32.6). Pyloric caeca about 150-190.

Nuptial tubercles (small horny whitish bumps) present on head and scales at spawning time (more conspicuous on males).

Maximum length 36 inches and weight 15 pounds (a specimen 25 inches fork length and weighing 19¼ pounds was taken from Lesser Slave Lake in 1936).

71

DISTRIBUTION

Alaska to Labrador and northern half of British Columbia to New Brunswick with southern limits in Lakes Michigan and Erie. Introduced within and outside native range, including southern British Columbia.

Known in Alberta from Petitot, Hay, Slave, Peace, Athabasca, Beaver, North Saskatchewan, upper Battle, lower Bow, and Oldman drainages; most populations in the latter two drainages may not be native — probably native to Waterton Lake (see map on page 74).

BIOLOGY

Lake whitefish are generally restricted to the cool well-oxygenated regions of lakes, usually near the bottom but they are occasionally pelagic. In Alberta, they seldom enter rivers. They feed primarily on bottom organisms, notably chironomids and snails and secondarily on amphipods and insects. Spawning occurs from October to December with an average egg production of about 8,000 per pound of fish. As is perhaps true for most Alberta fish, only about 10% of fertilized eggs survive to become fry. Most mature by age 7 with males maturing at a younger average age than females. Miller (1947, 1949b, 1956a) noted that in Pigeon Lake the maximum age was 8 and that during a period of intense fishing the average age of caught fish decreased from 5 to 2 years while the age at which maturity was reached also decreased from 5 to 2 years; growth rates increased.

Lake whitefish comprise an extremely valuable commercial fishery in Alberta. For example, in Lake Wabamun, west of Edmonton, up to 600,000 pounds of whitefish have been taken in one year. This species has recently had a limited sport fishery during the winter months. In the past, many lakes fished commercially had their whitefish populations supplemented with hatchery eggs. Natural reproduction, however, provides more fish than can survive and the hatchery operations did little or nothing to increase a population. Lake whitefish hybridize with cisco in parts of their area of overlap including in several Alberta lakes.

Lake whitefish, along with cisco and occasionally other salmonids, carry the last larval stage of the tapeworm *Triaenophorus crassus*. The parasite is picked up by ingestion of the copepod *Cyclops bicuspidatus,* its first larval host, in July or

August. A tapeworm makes its way out of the stomach and tends to concentrate in the muscle of the dorsal half of the fish between the head and dorsal fin. Slightly higher concentrations appear on the right side than on the left side. In the muscle the tapeworm forms cysts which are harmless to man but are not appetizing. When their numbers reach a certain concentration, the fish cannot be marketed in the United States. Also, Miller (1945a), in Lesser Slave Lake, found that this tapeworm can cause a slight decrease in the growth rate and a marked decrease in the length of infected whitefish. Larvae in whitefish produce most of the economic loss, but those in cisco are more important in carrying on the life cycle. *Triaenophorus crassus* is rarely found in lakes devoid of cisco. Attempts to control the infections in whitefish by reducing cisco populations have been partly successful. The life cycle of *T. crassus* (reviewed by Miller, 1952) is completed with the ingestion of an infected fish by a northern pike. Whitefish are also susceptible to *Cystidicola,* a roundworm in the air bladder and to the larvae of a species of *Diphyllobothrium* (not *D. latum,* and probably not infectious to humans), which occurs on the stomach wall.

ANGLING

Lake whitefish angling has really only achieved significance in Alberta within the last decade or so, in a limited number of lakes. Wabamun and Pigeon Lakes near Edmonton yield the best returns with the majority of the fish being taken in late fall and throughout the winter. Flies with chenille bodies and weighted heads are commonly used in open water fishing while jigging a variety of very small lures with a short stiff casting rod is the favorite technique of the ice fisherman. Because of its general abundance throughout the province this fish will probably become the mainstay of the winter sport fishery.

HISTORICAL NOTE

First described by S. L. Mitchill in 1818 from Sault Ste. Marie as *Salmo clupeiformis.* Noted in Lake Wabamun and "many lakes of northern Alberta" by Whitehouse (1919) as *Coregonus labradoricus.* Kendall (1924) noted them in Lake Athabasca and the Athabasca River 8 miles above the Embarras River. They may have been described from Beauvert Lake, near Jasper, by Bajkov (1926) as *Coregonus nasus* (see Dymond, 1943:192, for a discussion on this designation), but it is more likely that his report is completely erroneous.

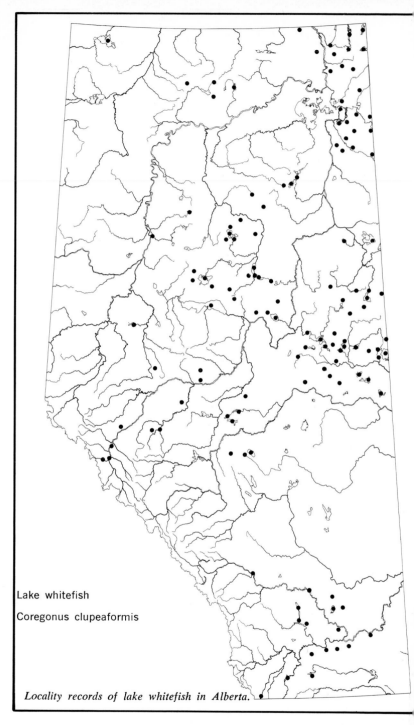

Lake whitefish

Coregonus clupeaformis

Locality records of lake whitefish in Alberta.

MOUNTAIN WHITEFISH

Prosopium williamsoni (Girard)

Prosopium — a mask, from the large
bones in front of the eyes.

williamsoni — named for Lt. R. S. Williamson,
of the U.S. Pacific Railroad exploration.

Mountain whitefish

DESCRIPTION

Color greyish-blue to light brown dorsally, silvery laterally. Young with 8-11 roundish parr marks along the lateral line and a few spots above.

Mouth subterminal and snout somewhat pointed. Upper jaw usually extended to anterior margin of eye but never reaching to midline. Teeth inconspicuous. One flap separating the two closely spaced nostril openings on each side of head as in all other Alberta salmonids except grayling, cisco, and lake whitefish. Caudal peduncle relatively narrow compared to other salmonids (about equal to base length of the long adipose fin). Caudal fin deeply forked. Scales along lateral line 74-92; above lateral line 8-11; around caudal peduncle 19-24. Dorsal fin with 9 or 10 branched rays (all rays 11 or 12) and anal fin with 8 or 9 branched rays (all rays 10 or 11). Gillrakers on first arch 19-26. Pyloric caeca usually 70-130.

Maximum length 22 inches and weight 5 pounds. Maximum known length from Alberta is 19 inches fork length (5 pounds) from the Athabasca River.

DISTRIBUTION

Taku River in northwestern British Columbia to Peace River drainage in Alberta and south throughout most of British Columbia to Nevada, including the Missouri headwaters in Montana and Wyoming.

Known from the western half of Alberta in Peace, Athabasca (as far east as the La Biche River, known in Lac La Biche from 1 specimen), North Saskatchewan, Red Deer, Bow, Oldman, and North Fork Milk drainages (see map on page 78).

BIOLOGY

Mountain whitefish are generally abundant in streams and the relatively shallow portions of lakes. They feed mostly on bottom fauna but terrestrial insects occasionally make up a large part of their diet. McHugh (1940) examined the diet of these fish throughout much of the Bow drainage and found it to consist primarily of bottom aquatic insect larvae (mainly chironomids and ephemerids). Spawning occurs in October and early November; no redd or nest is built as in other Alberta stream salmonids. Females lay an average of about 2,000-8,000 eggs (more in exceptionally large fish). The eggs hatch about March. The young school and do not hide under rocks as do most other stream salmonids; they thus do not seem to compete for space with young brown trout. Maturity is generally reached at age 3. McHugh (1941) noted their growth from several Bow River drainages and reported ages up to 18 years (age 9 is perhaps more typical as a maximum). In southwestern Alberta mountain whitefish are often called grayling, a practice which causes some confusion with the Arctic grayling. Mountain whitefish have been found with the tapeworm *Triaenophorus crassus* in Lesser Slave Lake (Miller, 1945a). They are commonly infected with the air bladder nematode, *Cystidicola,* and occasionally with a large copepod *(Coregonicola)* on the gills. No commercial fishery exists for mountain whitefish.

ANGLING

Mountain whitefish contribute substantially to the angler harvest from our east slope streams but they are usually not as popular as trout or charr. They are common in medium and larger sized clear, cold rivers and are readily available to the angler throughout the year but mountain whitefish are particularly abundant in early fall when they appear to form large schools. Since most of the fish creeled are less than one pound in weight they provide the best sport on a fly rod using flies in sizes varying from No. 10 to No. 16. Wet flies are usually most successful since these fish forage chiefly along the bottom of the stream. Small spinning lures will also take mountain whitefish but the most widely used method of angling is drifting natural baits such as stoneflies or maggots along the stream bottom. The species supports an attractive winter fishery in the Bow River in the vicinity of Cochrane to Banff.

HISTORICAL NOTE

First described by C. F. Girard in 1856 from Des Chutes River, Oregon, as *Coregonus williamsoni*. First noted in Alberta by Eigenmann (1895) from the Bow River at Calgary and Banff. Vick (1913) noted it to be widespread in the Banff area (e.g., Boom, Moraine, and Spray lakes) and Lower Kananaskis Lake (which may be erroneous since it was not present in surveys conducted from 1938 onward). Whitehouse (1919) noted reports of the species from west of Red Deer in the Raven and Clearwater rivers. Dymond (1943) described 6 specimens and Miller (1945a) noted the species from Lesser Slave Lake as *Prosopium oregonium*.

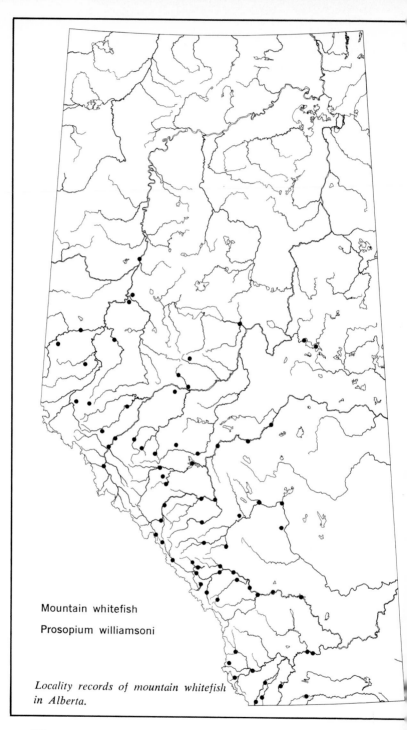

Mountain whitefish

Prosopium williamsoni

Locality records of mountain whitefish in Alberta.

Salvelinus namaycush (Walbaum)
Salvelinus — an old name of the charr
namaycush — an Indian name

Lake trout

DESCRIPTION

Color olive to brownish-grey dorsally, sides light silvery. Faint greyish vermiculations on back and irregular greyish spots on sides. Dorsal and caudal fins with light spots but without white edging or sharply different colors. Tips of jaws and roof of mouth whitish in spawning males. Newly hatched fry very lightly pigmented, much less so than that of brook trout. Young with 8-11 elongate parr marks crossing the lateral line, fins transparent, and few or no greyish blotches or vermiculations.

Upper jaw extended well past the hind margin of eye, except in young where it is still extended past the midline. Teeth well developed, absent from the posterior shaft of the vomer but single row usually present on anterior shaft; little or no space between the vomer and palatine anteriorly. Tongue teeth usually in a parallel row. Basibranchial ("hyoid") teeth well developed. Origin of adipose fin sometimes even with basal end of anal fin. Caudal peduncle relatively narrow compared with other salmonids.

Caudal fin deeply forked. Lateral line sensory pores about 120-130; scales one row above lateral line 175-228; above lateral line about 30-35; around caudal peduncle about 60. Branched dorsal and anal fin rays 8-10 (all rays 10-12). Gillrakers 17-24. Pyloric caeca 81-170.

Spawning individuals usually develop small pearl organs on the scales.

Maximum length about 4 feet and weight about 100 pounds. Maximum lengths noted from Alberta are 30 inches fork length from Swan Lake (Paterson, 1968), and 36 inches from Pyramid Lake (Rawson and Elsey, 1950); however, the world's largest lake trout was taken in Lake Athabasca in 1961 and weighed 102 pounds.

DISTRIBUTION

Alaska to Labrador, including some Arctic Islands, and northern British Columbia as far south as the Shuswap Lake area, through the Great Lakes to Nova Scotia. Apart from the Arctic charr, this species extends farther north than any other North American member of this family.

Known in Alberta and believed native from Slave, Peace, and Beaver drainages and headwater lakes of the Athabasca (e.g., Moab, Pyramid, Rock, Graham, and Legend), North Saskatchewan (e.g., Glacia and Swan), and South Saskatchewan (e.g., Waterton and Minnewanka) drainages (see map on page 82).

BIOLOGY

Lake trout tend to be restricted to relatively deep cool lakes. In early spring when the water temperature throughout the lake is uniformly cold, individuals may be found at all depths but as the season progresses they seek deep areas where the temperature is less than 50°F. In Alberta the diet of lake trout is quite variable. Where they have the choice, their diet as adults is primarily on other fish, such as in Lake Athabasca, Waterton lakes, and Minnewanka Resevoir. Where other fish are not readily available, as in Swan Lake, good growth can occur on crustaceans and insects. Lake trout under about 10 inches feed predominately on chironomid larvae. Spawning in Alberta occurs on rocky or gravel shoals from mid-September to October. The average female produces from 4,000-11,000 eggs of somewhat larger size than in brook trout. Maturity is usually reached at about age 6-10.

Lake trout and brook trout were first artificially crossed in Canada in 1946 at Banff and successfully reared hybrids were produced in 1947, from Lake Minnewanka and Third Vermilion Lake parents (Stenton, 1950). Generally the only successful cross involves female lake trout and male brook trout. The hybrids, called splake, are generally somewhat intermediate in most characters with their parents (Stenton, 1952). Agnes Lake, near Lake Louise, has a splake population which has reproduced for several generations. Splake have been extensively introduced as a sport fish in parts of Canada but the first introduction outside Jasper, Banff, and Wood Buffalo (Pine Lake) National Parks in Alberta was made in 1968 in the Edson area. Natural hybridization between lake trout and brook trout or between these or other charr does not occur. Although not investigated in Alberta, lake trout are susceptible to parasites known in our other salmonids.

ANGLING

Lake trout are taken mainly by casting or trolling on large metal lures. In the spring they may be readily caught in shallow water but during the summer, trolling in deep water with metal lines and weighted lures is the most common method of fishing for them. Their popularity with sportsmen is due largely to the fact that they are considered as trophy fish and to their excellent table qualities.

HISTORICAL NOTE

First described by J. J. Walbaum (based on Pennant's description) in 1792 from Hudson Bay as *Salmo namaycush*. First reported from Alberta by Eigenmann (1895) who obtained large *Salvelinus* from Devils Lake, Banff National Park, up to 17 inches (reported to him to reach 40 inches). Vick (1913) noted them in Lake Minnewanka, near Banff, and Whitehouse (1919) noted them from "northern lakes of Alberta". Recorded from Lake Athabasca by Preble (1908) and Kendall (1924). Bajkov (1926) noted them to be uncommon in Jasper National Park lakes. Lake trout are placed in the monotypic genus *Cristivomer* by a few workers.

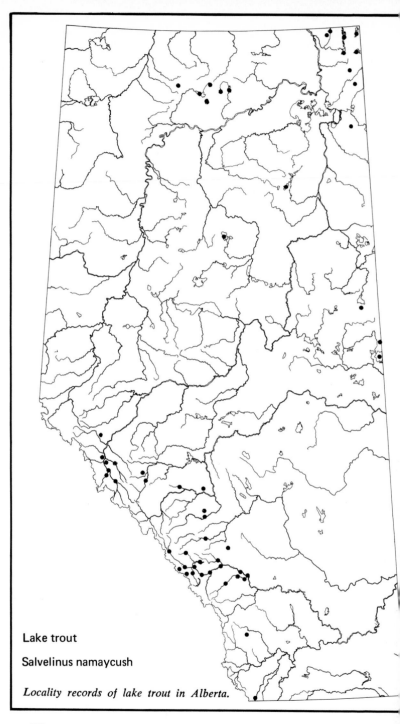

Lake trout

Salvelinus namaycush

Locality records of lake trout in Alberta.

DOLLY VARDEN
bull trout

Salvelinus malma (Walbaum)
malma — vernacular name in Kamchatka.

Dolly Varden from McLeod River drainage

DESCRIPTION

Color olive-green to blue-grey dorsally with silvery tones laterally. Yellow, orange, or red spots (white in preserved specimens) on dorsal surface and sides. Pelvic and anal fins often with whitish leading edge, not followed with black. Roof of mouth whitish and belly and lower sides sometimes orange to red in spawning males. Young with 7-10 wide oval parr marks along the lateral line; fins transparent.

Upper jaw extended past hind margin of eye in fish over about 3 inches. Teeth well developed but absent from shaft of vomer; very small gap between vomer and palatine teeth anteriorly. Basibranchial ("hyoid") teeth present or absent. Caudal fin moderately forked; only a slight notch in fingerlings. Pores along lateral line 105-142; scales one row above lateral line 186-254; above lateral line about 40; around caudal peduncle about 60. Branched dorsal fin rays 9-11 (all rays 13-16) and branched anal fin rays 8-10 (all rays 11-15). Gillrakers 12-24. Pyloric caeca 15-45.

Maximum length 50½ inches and weight 32 pounds. Maximum known length from Alberta is 34 inches fork length from the Clearwater River and maximum weight 14 pounds 13 ounces from Brazeau Reservoir.

DISTRIBUTION

Japan, Korea, and Kamchatka, through the Aleutians and south along coastal streams to northern Oregon; McLeod River in California; throughout British Columbia and east to westernmost Alberta.

Known in Alberta from head-waters of the Peace, Athabasca, Red Deer, Bow, and Oldman drainages and in the North Saskatchewan River (see map on page 86) as far downstream as Edmonton.

BIOLOGY

Dolly Varden frequent lakes and streams from sea level to high mountains; in addition, an anadromous (sea-run) form exists. Their primary food source is bottom fauna and other fish. Spawning occurs in the fall with the average female depositing about 5000 eggs. Maturity is usually reached in their fifth year. Although not investigated in Alberta, Dolly Varden are susceptible to parasites known in our other salmonids. Hybrids between Dolly Varden and brook trout are suspected to occur in the Clearwater River.

ANGLING

Although Dolly Varden are occasionally taken by fly fishermen, the most common angling technique is spinning or casting with medium sized lures or bait. They usually frequent the deeper pools of streams or the junctions of tributary streams and larger rivers. In lakes they are caught at various depths by casting or trolling.

HISTORICAL NOTE

First described by J. J. Walbaum (based on descriptions by earlier workers) in 1792 from Kamchatka as *Salmo malma*. The common name, Dolly Varden, was first applied in California in reference to the fish's resemblance in color pattern to dress oods with spots called Dolly Varden. This species is very closely related to the Arctic charr, *Salvelinus alpinus*. First reported from Alberta by Eigenmann (1895) from the Bow River at Banff and Calgary and in the Elbow River. Eigenmann listed these specimens as *Salvelinus namaycush* but noted differences between these river forms and the larger ones from Devils Lake (which are probably properly referred to as *S. namaycush*). Vick (1913) noted them from "nearly all the mountain lakes and streams" in Banff National Park area (e.g., Boom, Hector, Bow, Mystic, Harrison, Moraine, Sawback, Spray, and Lower Kananaskis lakes) up to 20 pounds as *Salvilinus parkei*. Whitehouse (1919) recorded them from the Red Deer up to 6 or 7 pounds as *Salvelinus parkii*. This taxon was proposed by G. Suckley in 1861 as *Salmo parkei* from Kootenay River specimens and it shows certain differences from the northern coastal form. Bajkov (1926) noted them from Jaques Lake and Rocky River in Jasper National Park as *Salvelinus alpinus malma*.

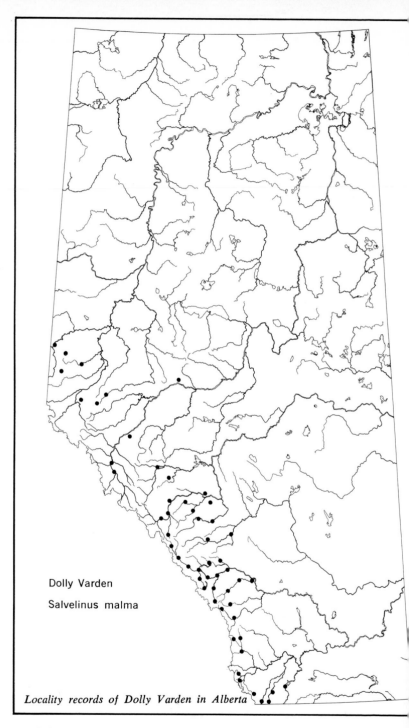

Dolly Varden

Salvelinus malma

Locality records of Dolly Varden in Alberta

alvelinus fontinalis (Mitchill)
ontinalis — living in springs

Brook trout

DESCRIPTION

Color olive-green dorsally; sides lighter. Distinct light-colored worm-like vermiculations on top of head, back, and dorsal fin. Sides with red or pink spots which often have blue halos; no black spots. Pectoral, pelvic, and anal fins with a white leading edge lined with black. Few spots on edges of caudal fin. Tips of jaws and roof of mouth blackish and sides and belly reddish in spawning males. Young with 7-11 broad oval parr marks along the lateral line. Small young with transparent dorsal fin, young over 2 inches long with a spotted dorsal fin, and young over 3 inches with conspicuous vermiculations and spots. The newly hatched fry are much more pigmented than newly hatched lake trout.

Upper jaw exceptionally long, extended well past hind margin of eyes even in 2 inch young. Teeth well developed, not

87

on vomerine shaft; no space between vomerine and palatine teeth anteriorly. Tongue teeth convergent anteriorly. Basibranchial ("hyoid") teeth usually absent. Caudal fin only slightly forked. Pores along lateral line about 109-127; scales one row above lateral line 197-243; above lateral line about 38-40; around caudal peduncle about 70-80. Branched rays in dorsal fin 8 or 9 (all rays 10-13) and branched rays in anal fin 7-9 (all rays 8-12). Gillrakers 14-22. Pyloric caeca 23-46.

Maximum length about 35 inches and weight about 15 pounds. Maximum noted size in Alberta is 29¾ inches fork length (weight 12 pounds 14 ounces) angled from Pine Lake, Wood Buffalo National Park, in 1967. Individuals of similar length are known from near Caroline.

DISTRIBUTION
Native in northeastern Manitoba, around Hudson Bay drainage to the Ungava Bay area and Newfoundland to the Carolinas and Lake Superior drainage; some Mississippi headwaters. Anadromous (sea-run) populations occur in coastal areas. Introduced throughout much of the world in temperate regions, including South America and New Zealand.

Successfully introduced in the western half of Alberta in Athabasca, North Saskatchewan, Red Deer, Bow, and Oldman drainages and in Pine Lake, Wood Buffalo National Park (see map on page 90).

BIOLOGY
Brook trout frequent cool streams, beaver ponds, and the clear shallow areas of lakes. In most waters their diet consists mainly of caddis fly larvae, chironomids, mayflies, ampipods, and *Daphnia*. Reproduction occurs in September and October with maturity usually reached at ages 2-4. An average female produces about 300-1000 eggs. The normal maximum life span is 8 years, but in Alberta streams few have been found beyond the age of 5 years. Brook trout and brown trout hybridize in nature in Montana and elsewhere in the United States. Hybrids between Dolly Varden and brook trout are suspected to occur in the Clearwater River. Artificially produced brook trout and lake trout hybrids called splake are common in the sport fishery of the Rocky Mountain parks (see discussion of lake trout). Hybrids between brook trout and Quebec red trout (see Appendix I) have been

stocked into Lake Louise (1962) and Bow Lake (1962) in Banff National Park and into Third Trefoil (1962) in Jasper National Park. No survival is known.

ANGLING

Brook trout are generally considered easy to catch and are a popular sport fish. They may be taken on wet or dry flies, various types of spinning lures, and on baits. The most popular stream fisheries for this species are tributaries of the Red Deer and Clearwater rivers where the trout are abundant and pan size. A number of mountain lakes in Jasper and Waterton parks also provide excellent angling.

HISTORICAL NOTE

First described by S. L. Mitchill in 1815 from near New York City as *Salmo fontinalis*. Vick (1913) and Whitehouse (1919) note their introduction into the Banff area from Lake Nipigon stock about 1910. Introduced into Maligne Lake, south-east of Jasper, in 1928.

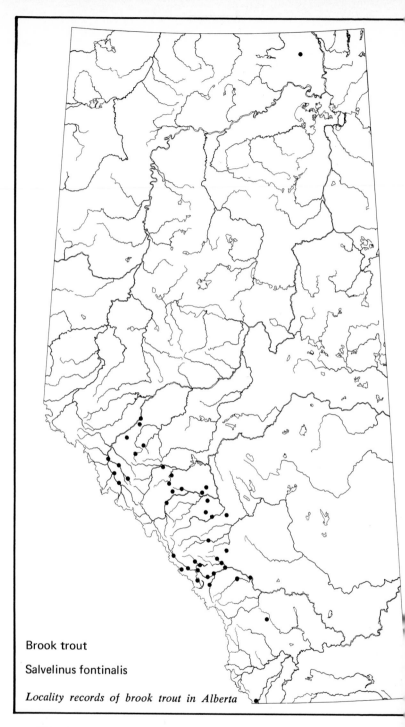

Brook trout

Salvelinus fontinalis

Locality records of brook trout in Alberta

Salmo trutta Linnaeus
Salmo — the Latin name for the
    Atlantic Salmon, meaning to leap
rutta — trout

Brown trout from Stauffer Creek

DESCRIPTION

    Color golden-brown or olive dorsally and laterally. Body
with large black or dark brown spots with pale halos and pink
or red spots (the only salmonid with light and black spots on
body). No vermiculations. Red spots (white in preserved specimens) along the lateral line and alternating with the parr marks
in young longer than about 3 inches. Few or no spots on the
caudal fin. Young with 9-14 wide parr marks (elongate in very
young) along the sides. Young about 1 inch long have a black
leading edge to the dorsal fin and no spots, those over about
2½ inches develop black spots and a whitish tip lined with
black on the dorsal fin. Adipose fin orange with lightish margin
in young, never lined with black. The young are difficult to
distinguish from young Atlantic salmon, which have been introduced into western Alberta (see Appendix I).

Upper jaw usually extended past hind margin of eye in fish over 2 inches long. Teeth well developed, including on shaft of vomer; little or no space between vomerine and palatine teeth anteriorly. Caudal peduncle relatively deep. Caudal fin only slightly forked to squarish. Lateral line pores 105-116; one row above lateral line 116-136; above lateral line about 25-28; around caudal peduncle about 44-46. Principal dorsal fin rays 9-11 (all rays 12-14) and anal fin rays 9-12 (complete count). Gillrakers 16-19. Pyloric caeca 40-65. Generally, males have a rounded anal fin margin while females have a slightly falcate anal fin margin.

Maximum length 32 inches and weight 40 pounds (a weight of about 4 pounds is average for an adult). Maximum length noted in Alberta is 24 inches fork length from the North Raven system and maximum weight is about 12 pounds from Lake Edith.

DISTRIBUTION

Native from Iceland to the White Sea area and from Morocco through Algeria to Turkey; Caspian and Aral seas. Anadromous (sea-run) populations occur in coastal areas. This species has been successfully introduced into more areas than any other salmonid. Populations occur on all continents, except Antarctica, including areas on and near the Equator. Various stocks have also been exchanged within Europe.

Successfully introduced throughout much of western Alberta in Athabasca, North Saskatchewan, Red Deer, Bow, and North Fork Milk drainages (see map on page 94).

BIOLOGY

Brown trout occur in streams, beaver ponds, and lakes. In Alberta, as elsewhere, brown trout appear to be partly responsible for the decline of some native trout and charr populations. Their food consists of terrestrial and aquatic insects, fish, and occasionally other invertebrates and vertebrates. Individuals generally lie in deep pools or under protective covering, often under banks or snags. The young are highly territorial, tending to hide under rocks and aggressively defending their areas from other fish. Spawning is in the fall (primarily November), as in the charrs and unlike in other trout. Hatching probably occurs in late April. Females produce an average of about 1200 relatively small eggs and, like other trout, dig the nest. Brown trout and brook trout hybridize in nature, producing "tiger" trout, in Montana and elsewhere in the United States.

ANGLING

Brown trout are probably the most difficult to catch of all Alberta's sport fish and most able to withstand environmental changes. The bulk of angling for brown trout is in the streams of lower elevations in the area south and east of Rocky Mountain House. Here, stream currents are moderate and abundant cover in the form of rooted aquatic plants and sunken logs is available. Fly fishing, both wet and dry, is a popular form of angling but spinning lures and bait are also used. Angling for brown trout is generally most successful in late afternoon and evening.

HISTORICAL NOTE

Described by C. Linnaeus in 1758 from rivers of Sweden as *Salmo trutta*. First introduced into North America (Michigan) in 1883 from Germany and into Canada in 1884 (Newfoundland) from Scotland (the Loch Leven variety) and 1890 (Quebec) from Germany via New York. First introduced into Alberta in 1924 (Raven River and Jasper National Park) and 1925 (Bow System — this stock, probably the Loch Leven variety, was introduced into Carrot Creek near Canmore when the hatchery truck, destined for eastern Alberta from Banff, broke down). Bajkov (1926) described the species from Jasper Park.

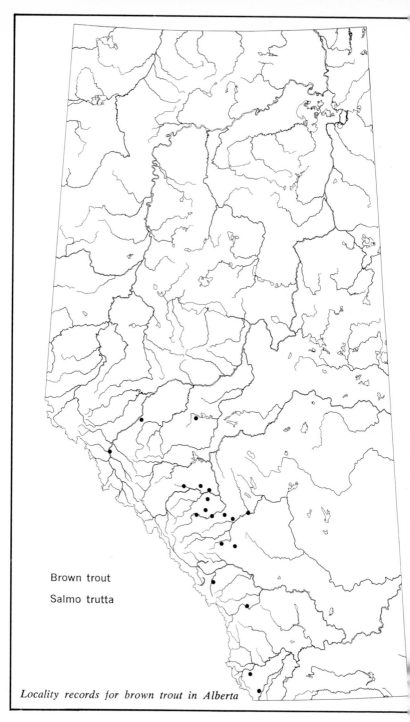

Brown trout
Salmo trutta

Locality records for brown trout in Alberta

94

Salmo clarki Richardson

clarki — after Capt. W. Clark,
    of the Lewis and Clark expedition.

Cutthroat trout, two color phases (upper—upper Castle drainage; lower—Wilson Lake, introduced from Marvel Lake).

95

DESCRIPTION

The following color description applies to the inland *lewisi* form in Alberta. Yellowish-green body with lower sides and belly somewhat reddish, bright red in some spawners. A rosy band along each side of the body from cheek to tail, which is characteristic of rainbow, is common in many Alberta cutthroats. Red streak along inner edge of lower jaw in crease (fades rapidly with death). Large dark body spots most numerous above the lateral line and below the lateral line posteriorly. Spots on dorsal, adipose, and caudal fins. Roof of mouth whitish in spawning males. Young with about 10 oval parr marks along the lateral line and a dark leading edge on dorsal fin. Young are difficult to distinguish from rainbow trout young.

Upper jaw generally extended to hind margin of eye in adults. Teeth well developed, including on shaft of vomer; very narrow space between vomerine and palatine teeth anteriorly. Basibranchial ("hyoid") teeth present but sometimes faint (requires very careful examination under magnification). Caudal fin moderately forked. Scales along lateral line 116-230 (usual for Alberta form 160-200); above lateral line 32-40; around caudal peduncle about 50. Principal dorsal fin rays 8-11 (all rays 10-13) and anal fin rays 8-12 (all rays 11-13). Gillrakers 15-22. Pyloric caeca 27-57.

Maximum size for the species is about 40 inches long and weight about 41 pounds (from Nevada). Maximum weight in Alberta is about 9 pounds.

DISTRIBUTION

Two widespread forms of cutthroat trout are usually recognized in Canada. The coastal form *(clarki)* occurs from southeastern Alaska to northern California in the Pacific drainage. Anadromous (sea-run) populations occur along much of the coast. The interior form, the Yellowstone cutthroat *(lewisi)* occurs in southeastern British Columbia, southwestern Alberta, south to Colorado and Utah.

Native in Alberta to the Bow and South Saskatchewan drainages and introduced into the Red Deer and North Saskatchewan drainages (see map on page 99). One specimen has been collected from the Milk River (Willock, 1969b). Due to fish cultural activities and hybridization with rainbow trout there are few native populations left in Alberta. Upper Picklejar Lake and a few lakes in Banff National Park (e.g., Sawback and Marvel) contain native stocks. The Ram drainage has an introduced pure stock which was obtained from southeastern British Columbia.

BIOLOGY

Cutthroat trout occur in lakes and streams to 7,650 feet elevation in Redoubt Lake, east of Lake Louise (this population may not be native). Their chief food consists of insects, crustaceans, and fish. Spawning occurs in the late spring and early summer at about 50°F with the eggs buried in a gravel nest or "redd" dug by the female. In the inland form, the average egg number is 1100. Young-of-the-year hatch by at least August. Maturity is probably reached by age 2 to 4, when the fish is about 10 inches long. They have a relatively short life span.

As is probably true for other trout, Miller (1954, 1957) found in experiments at Gorge Creek, southwest of Calgary, that cutthroats tend to occupy discreet home territories and are generally able to home back if displaced from them. Mangan (1951), Thomas (1953), and Miller (1955, 1958) also at Gorge Creek, found that hatchery reared cutthroat and other trout when introduced into areas with wild trout were forced out of resting areas and suffered very high mortalities. In some Alberta areas, cutthroats have decreased in numbers following the introduction of rainbow and brown trout. Cutthroat and rainbow trout frequently hybridize in Alberta (Andrekson, 1949; Gilmour, 1950; Miller, 1950). Hybrids were occasionally deliberately produced for stocking in the past, such as in the Kananaskis system.

ANGLING

Cutthroat trout may be taken on wet or dry flies and with spinning lures or bait. Late July and August are favored for dry fly fishing on streams. At this time large well hackled dry flies such as grey or brown bivisibles are popular patterns. Stream fishing for cutthroat is now restricted to upper reaches of mountain streams such as the tributaries to the Castle, Oldman, and Highwood rivers. Some excellent cutthroat fishing is also available in lakes of Banff National Park. The flesh of cutthroat trout is excellent and the fish is of great recreational value to the sportsman.

HISTORICAL NOTE

First described by Sir John Richardson in 1836 from Cathlapootl River, Washington, as *Salmo clarkii*. First reported in Alberta by Eigenmann (1895) from Calgary and Banff as *Salmo mykiss*. Vick (1913) noted it to be widespread in the Banff National Park area (e.g., Boom, Harrison, Consolation, Moraine, Mystic, Sawback, Hector, Bow, Margaret, and Spray lakes and Redearth Creek) and at Twin Falls between Upper and Lower Kananaskis lakes (this falls is now dry and the lakes are hydroelectric reservoirs), Lower Kananaskis Lake, and the Kananaskis River (it is now almost absent from the Kananaskis system — Nelson, 1965). Vick also noted that Lower Kananaskis Lake contained "the finest cutthroat trout in the mountains" and that they were the fish supply depot for the Morley Stoney Indians.

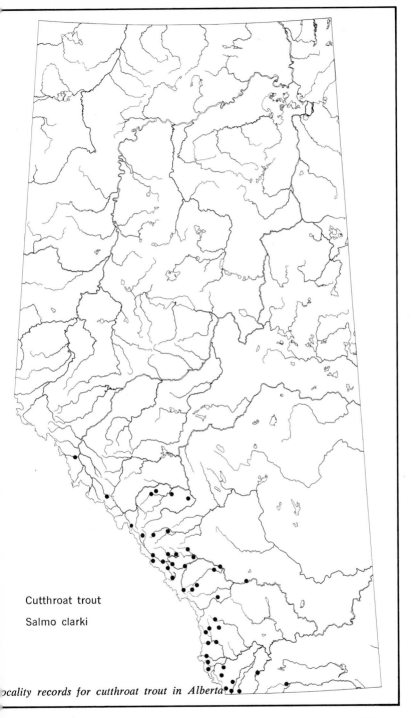

Cutthroat trout

Salmo clarki

Locality records for cutthroat trout in Alberta

99

Salmo gairdneri Richardson
gairdneri — after its discoverer,
    Dr. M. Gairdner, an employee
    of the Hudson's Bay Company

Rainbow trout

DESCRIPTION

Color bluish to greenish dorsally, sides silvery to yellowish-green. Black spots on back, sides, dorsal fin, and caudal fin. Adipose fin with spots or a black margin. Front tip of pelvic, dorsal, and anal fins often orange to yellowish (white in preserved specimens). Spawning fish with broad reddish lateral band which is most pronounced in males. Roof of mouth whitish in spawning males. Young with 8-12 elongate to oval parr marks along side and a distinct black front margin to the dorsal fin. Individuals living at high altitudes tend to retain the parr marks for a longer time and have a brighter colored fin tip than individuals from lower elevations.

Upper jaw extended past hind margin of eye in fish over 4 inches. Teeth well-developed, including those on shaft of vomer; little or no space between vomerine and palatine teeth anteriorly. Caudal fin moderately forked. Scales along lateral line 100-138; oblique scales 2 rows above lateral line 115-162; above lateral line 18-32; around caudal peduncle about 40. Principal dorsal fin rays 10-12 (all rays 12-15) and anal fin rays 8-12 (all rays 12-15). Gillrakers 16-21. Pyloric caeca 27-80.

Maximum length 45 inches and weight 52 pounds. Average weight for the species is one to three pounds. Maximum length noted in Alberta pothole lakes is about 18 inches from Star Lake (Hauptman, 1958); the largest rainbow known from Alberta was taken in 1966 from Reesor Lake in the Cypress Hills and weighed 17 lbs. 10 oz. A 34½ inch individual is known from Mami Lake.

DISTRIBUTION

Southeastern coastal areas of Alaska to northern Mexico and Peace River drainage in British Columbia and Athabasca River drainage of Alberta. Its natural distribution extends farther south in North America than that of any other members of the family. Anadromous (sea-run) populations called steelhead occur along coastal areas. Successfully introduced onto all continents except Antarctica.

Several populations in Athabasca drainage from the south slope of the Swan Hills to the headwaters of the Athabasca River in Alberta are believed to be native. Employees of the Grand Trunk Pacific railway report them being abundant in areas near Hinton and Jasper in 1910 and 1911. Successfully introduced into western Alberta in Athabasca, North Saskatchewan, Red Deer, Bow, Oldman, and Milk drainages and in the Cypress Hills area (see map on page 104). Generally, however, many of Alberta's streams, pothole lakes, and reservoirs seem unsuitable for rainbows and individuals do not reproduce.

Rainbow trout were introduced into northeasternmost Alberta starting in 1958 and 1959. Fry, from a temporary hatchery operation in Fort Smith in 1958 and at Pine Lake, south of Fort Smith in Wood Buffalo National Park, in 1959, were introduced into the five Rainbow lakes, Seven Mile Lake, Little Buffalo River above Campbell Falls, Salt River, and Pine Lake (unpublished report of N. S. Novakowski). No reproduction is known from the above plants.

BIOLOGY

Rainbow trout, like other members of the salmon family, thrive in cool waters, but are able to tolerate temperatures up to 70°F. They occur both in streams and lakes. The term steelhead is often applied to trout caught in the Calgary area, however, since no sea-run populations occur in the province the term is inappropriate. Rainbow trout feed primarily on insects, leeches, molluscs, crustaceans, and occasionally on small fish. Spawning occurs in late spring and early summer. Maturity is usually reached by age 3 or 4. Individuals stocked in high altitude lakes such as Amethyst and Pyramid show relatively poor growth rates. High altitude individuals also spawn later than low altitude ones; in the 6,450 foot Amethyst Lake most spawning is not completed until mid-July. Rainbow and cutthroat trout frequently hybridize in Alberta (Miller, 1950; Gilmour, 1950).

Fishing is generally good for the first few years in many pothole lakes and reservoirs which are stocked with rainbows. Success usually decreases as the large trout, which are less frequently caught by fishermen, become abundant. Modern lake rehabilitation programs are often necessary to maintain a high degree of fishing success. The trout live through very low oxygen conditions in the winter although exceptionally low oxygen results in winter-kill.

A species of *Diphyllobothrium* (not *D. latum*) was found in a high proportion of the rainbow trout taken by M. Denny in the Kananaskis Lakes in 1962. These may be one or more of the seven species found in rainbow trout of the Kootenay Lake area, British Columbia, by Anthony (1967).

ANGLING

This highly rated sport fish may be taken by a wide variety of fishing methods. Rainbows are taken on practically all kinds of lures and baits from willow leaf trolls to salmon eggs. Fly casting and spinning are generally the most popular techniques with local exceptions. In waters where forage fish are the dominant foods items, trolling and spinning generally yield the best results with fly fishing being favored in ponds, lakes, and streams in which insects are the staple food. Many local fly patterns have been designed especially for taking rainbows in the numerous stocked lakes throughout the province. The immense popularity of this trout among anglers is due largely to its spectacular aerial acrobatics when hooked. Rainbows are also excellent tasting and easy to rear in fish hatcheries. Several millions of rainbow trout fingerlings are stocked in the province each year.

HISTORICAL NOTE

First described by Sir John Richardson in 1836 from the Columbia River at Fort Vancouver as *Salmo gairdnerii.* Bajkov (1926), referring to it as *S. irideus,* described the morphology of specimens collected in Jasper National Park.

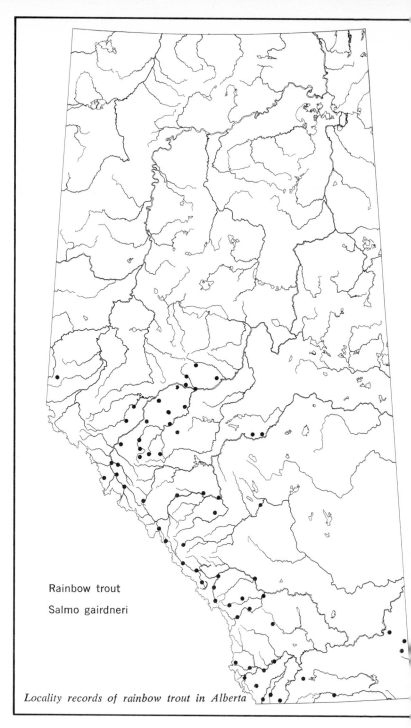

Rainbow trout

Salmo gairdneri

Locality records of rainbow trout in Alberta

Salmo aguabonita Jordan
agua bonita — beautiful water,
     a Spanish name

Golden trout from South Fork lakes.

DESCRIPTION

The golden trout is somewhat similar to the rainbow trout but usually is much more colorful. It tends to have more and smaller scales, a paler yellowish-green body, fewer but larger body spots, brighter orange tips to the fins, and more pronounced parr marks in the adult.

DISTRIBUTION

The native distribution of this trout is probably only the Kern River drainage in the Sierra Nevada Mountains of California at elevations over 10,000 feet. It has been introduced into many high altitude lakes and streams in western North America.

In Alberta it has been introduced into several high-altitude lakes in the southern Rocky Mountains (South Fork, Three Isle, Gap, and Galatea lakes — see map on page 107).

105

BIOLOGY

Much of the general biology of the golden trout is similar to that of the rainbow. It spawns somewhat later than the rainbow and is generally better adapted than other salmonids to high elevations. In South Fork lakes in Alberta, spawning occurs in early July. Since the golden trout is only in a few remote mountainous lakes it is not available to the majority of fishermen. A 4 lb. 7 oz. individual has been taken from the South Fork lakes (also known as the Barnaby Ridge lakes).

ANGLING

Golden trout were introduced in a few selected lakes with a view to provide additional variety to the province's sport fishing. Angling techniques are similar to those used for cutthroat and rainbow trout. Small lures and flies cast from the lake shore are the generally accepted methods of taking this fish.

HISTORICAL NOTE

Described by D. S. Jordan in 1892 from California as *Salmo mykiss agua-bonita*. First introduced into Alberta in 1959 in South Fork lakes.

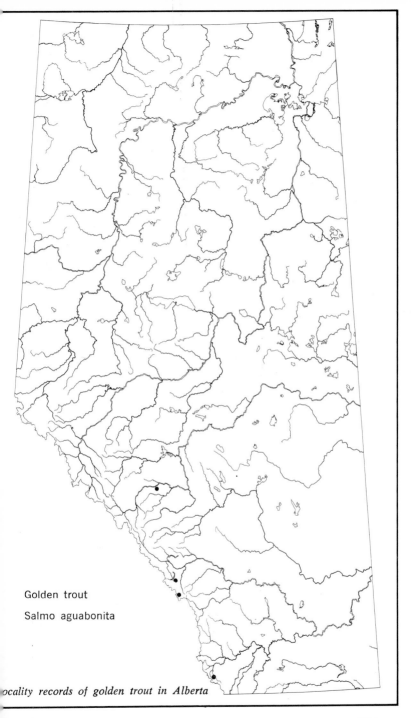

Golden trout

Salmo aguabonita

Locality records of golden trout in Alberta

Oncorhynchus nerka (Walbaum)
Onco rhynchus — hooked snout
nerka — a Russian vernacular name

Kokanee juveniles, 5½ inches standard length

DESCRIPTION

Color green to dark blue dorsally, usually with black spots; sides silvery. Fins, including the adipose, without black spots. Breeding males with a deep red body and greenish head (the females are less brilliantly colored) and with roof of mouth blackish. Young with 8-12 oval parr marks which extend down to the lateral line but little, if any, below it.

Tip of jaw extended past hind margin of eye. Teeth relatively short, present on shaft of vomer; vomerine and palatine teeth separated by a wide gap anteriorly. Caudal peduncle relatively narrow. Caudal fin moderately forked. Scales along lateral line or on one row above lateral line 121-146 (in salmon these two scale counts are similar); above lateral line 18-27. Principal dorsal fin rays 10-13 (all rays 13-17) and principal anal fin rays 13-17 (all rays 15-20). Gillrakers 30-43 (the longest is greater than ½ eye diameter). Pyloric caeca 50-115.

Maximum length is about 27 inches and weight about 9 pounds. The average length of adults is usually about 12 inches.

DISTRIBUTION

Pacific coast drainages from Japan to northern Oregon. Widely introduced outside this area.

In Alberta, kokanee have been stocked in West Twin, Phyllis, Twin, Narrow, Chickako, and Summit lakes and Glenmore Reservoir (see map on page 111).

BIOLOGY

Kokanee travel in schools and are almost always restricted to the cooler waters of lakes. Individuals enter creeks only at spawning time in the fall. Maturity is reached between ages 3 and 5 with spawning males developing a hooked lower jaw. Spawning occurs only in lakes or streams with suitable gravel where the eggs are aerated; reproduction cannot occur in most or all Alberta lakes stocked with kokanee. Unlike other Alberta salmonids, all kokanee (indeed all members of the Pacific salmon genus *Oncorhynchus*) die after their first spawning. Kokanee produce an average of 500 eggs per female.

Kokanee (which are freshwater) and sockeye (which are anadromous) are forms of the same species which have different life histories. There is evidence that each form can produce offspring which take up the life history of the other. Probably most native kokanee populations have been independently derived from sockeye populations.

Kokanee are generally non-competitive with other sport fish and are a forage fish for trout and charr.

ANGLING

Although kokanee are a popular sport fish in British Columbia and western United States, it has not yet achieved this prominence in Alberta. Kokanee are most frequently taken by trolling a combination of metal flashing lures and a small hook baited with a piece of worm; or simply by still fishing using salmon eggs or worms. They may also be taken on flies, particularly when they are seen breaking the surface of lakes. Ice fishing with bait is very popular and effective on some waters.

HISTORICAL NOTE

The species was first described by J. J. Walbaum (after description of earlier workers) in 1792 from sockeye in Kamchatka, USSR, as *Salmo nerka*. Kokanee were first described by G. Suckley in 1861 from Chilliwack Lake, British Columbia, as *Salmo kennerlyi*. The first attempted introduction of kokanee into Alberta was the unsuccessful planting of eyed eggs into St. Mary's Reservoir in 1952. Fingerlings were first introduced in 1961 into Glenmore Reservoir in Calgary.

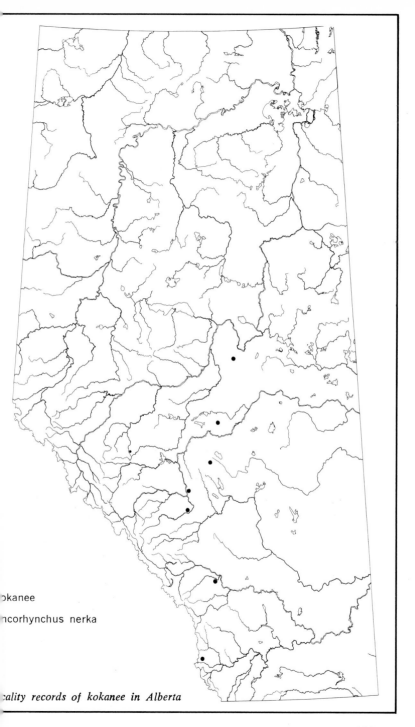

kanee

ncorhynchus nerka

cality records of kokanee in Alberta

PIKE FAMILY — ESOCIDAE

Representatives of the pike family occur in northern parts of the Northern Hemisphere, in Europe, Asia, and North America. Their greatest diversity occurs in eastern North America. This freshwater family contains 5 species, 4 of which range into Canada. Although two species of pike have often been suspected to occur in Alberta (Whitehouse, 1919; and others) only one species is definitely known from the province.

Various members of this family are considered important sport fishes, particularly the northern pike and muskellunge (or maskinonge). The name pickerel, usually applied to walleye in Alberta, is properly applied to a relatively small member of the pike family confined to eastern North America.

The closest relatives to this family are small fresh-water fish, the mudminnows and Alaska blackfish. The pike family is usually placed in the order Clupeiformes, along with the salmon and mooneye families.

NORTHERN PIKE
jackfish

Esox lucius Linnaeus
Esox — a kind of pike
lucius — the latin name for the pike

Northern pike young, 5½ inches standard length, from Ridge Reservoir.

DESCRIPTION

Color in adults olive or brownish-green dorsally, large irregular white or greenish spots laterally in the form of oblique rows. Young with darkish green oblique bars on silvery background. Horizontal black bar in front of and behind the eye and a vertical bar beneath the eye; the latter bar remains longest. Young less than 1½ inches long have a horizontal stripe beneath the eye instead of the vertical bar. Juveniles and adults have dusky spots on the median fins. Peritoneum silvery. A mutant, with a silvery lateral sheen and accounting for up to 10% of the pike population has been noted from Primrose and Cold lakes.

Body elongate and slightly to moderately compressed. Head elongate, broad, flattened anteriorly, and depressed dorsally; distance between eyes about 1½ - 2 times eye diameter; eyes moderate; mouth exceptionally large (tip of maxilla extended to or past front margin of eye and, except in young, more than 3 times eye diameter), terminal (lower jaw extended forward slightly beyond upper jaw, however), and slightly oblique. No groove separating tip of upper jaw from snout. Teeth well developed on jaws, (absent in maxilla), palatines, and head of vomer; weak on tongue and shaft of vomer (pike in Alberta occasionally lose their long teeth). Gill membranes extended far forward, not attached to each other or to isthmus. Cheeks fully scaled, opercles scaleless on their lower halves. Origin of dorsal fin far behind pelvic fins but slightly in front of origin of anal fin. Lateral line complete and straight. Pelvic axillary process absent. Caudal fin moderately forked. Lateral-line scales more than 100, very small; dorsal and anal fin rays less than 20 (including rudimentary rays); branchiostegal rays 13-16; gillrakers short and poorly developed.

Maximum length 50 inches and weight 50 pounds.

Alta: Meristic counts have been obtained as follows from North Saskatchewan drainage.

Scales

Along lateral line: 119-123
Above lateral line: 14-16
Around caudal peduncle: 27-30

Pike between 36 and 42 pounds have been taken from the Athabasca River delta while a 43 pounder (48 inches long) was taken from Lake Newell in 1953 in a commercial fishery.

Three color phases in adult northern pike.

DISTRIBUTION

Northern portions of the Northern Hemisphere. In North America from Alaska and northeastern British Columbia to Missouri and Labrador.

Common throughout most of Alberta in Petitot, Hay, Slave, Peace, Athabasca, Beaver, North Saskatchewan, Battle, Red Deer, Bow, Oldman, South Saskatchewan, and Milk drainages (see map on page 117).

BIOLOGY

Northern pike prefer relatively shallow, weedy, clear waters and although they occur primarily in lakes and marshes they are also common in slow warm streams. In Alberta about 1 million pounds are caught and sold annually for mink food within the province and for human consumption as far away as France. Large individuals are usually taken from Winefred, Seibert, May, Newell, Cold, Ridge, Touchwood, and Athabasca lakes. Their diet is largely made up of fish, crustaceans, insects, and other animal items. In Alberta very young individuals have been found feeding on amphipods while young-of-the-year have been found feeding on minnows, suckers, trout-perch, brook sticklebacks, and amphipods. Adult pike have been found with young muskrats and ducklings in their stomachs. Northern pike spawn in the early spring, often before the ice has completely left the lakes. Spawning areas typically are shallow marshes connected to lakes or over flooded vegetation in the shallow bays. Young less than 1 inch long have been taken on May 30 in Hastings Lake and may reach a length of 11 inches in their first year.

Pike are the final hosts of several tapeworms including four of the genus *Triaenophorus;* one species, *T. crassus,* is harmless to man but its larval stage causes unsightly cysts in the flesh of whitefish and ciscoes. Larvae of another, *T. nodulosus,* occur in the liver of burbot, perch, or other fish. In pike, the adult tapeworms are found in the intestine and may reach lengths of up to 15 inches in late fall to early spring. Miller (1952) gives an excellent review of the tapeworms' life history. Pike in Alberta are also host to the larvae of the broad tapeworm, *Diphyllobothrium latum,* the only fish parasite in Alberta known to infect humans (Anthony, 1967).

ANGLING

Northern pike are an extremely popular game fish and Alberta is generously supplied with them. Pike will readily take a wide variety of plugs and spoons which may be cast or trolled in the shallows of lakes near weed beds or lily pads. Angling success is usually best after the spawning season in May and June although fishing is generally good throughout the entire open water season. Considerable attention is now being given to the trophy aspect of northern pike fishing in Alberta with specimens up to thirty pounds being available in lakes such as Seibert, Winefred, and Athabasca.

HISTORICAL NOTE

First described by C. Linnaeus in 1758 (well known before that time, however) from Europe as *Esox lucius*. First reported in Alberta by Eigenmann (1895) at Medicine Hat as *Lucius lucius*. Whitehouse (1919) reported it in the Red Deer, Saskatchewan, Peace, and Athabasca rivers. Kendall (1924) noted it from Athabasca Lake while Bajkov (1926) recorded it from several areas in Jasper Park.

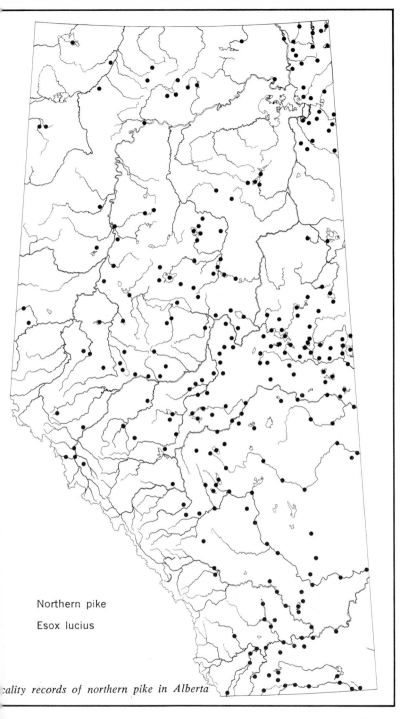

Northern pike

Esox lucius

cality records of northern pike in Alberta

117

MOONEYE FAMILY — HIODONTIDAE

Representatives of the mooneye family are confined to the fresh waters of North America. Two species are recognized, the mooneye *(Hiodon tergisus)* and the goldeye. The mooneye extends as far west as Saskatchewan; it has not been recorded in Alberta (see Appendix I).

The closest relatives to this family are the notopterids, a fresh-water group occurring in tropical Africa and parts of southern Asia. The mooneyes also bear a close relationship with the osteoglossids, a tropical group containing some of the largest fresh-water fish in the world. They are usually placed in the order Clupiformes, along with the salmon and pike families.

GOLDEYE

Hiodon alosoides (Rafinesque)

Hio don — hyoid tooth

alos oides — shad like

Goldeye female adults, 13 inches standard length, from confluence of Sturgeon and North Saskatchewan rivers.

DESCRIPTION

Color steel bluish dorsally, silvery or white laterally. Iris of eye yellowish or goldish. Fins without spots. Peritoneum silvery.

Body deep and highly compressed. Head blunt and strongly rounded dorsally; space between eyes about equal in length to vertical diameter of eyes; eyes large, adipose eyelids partially covering eyes anteriorly and posteriorly; mouth large (tip of maxilla extended past center of eye and much longer than eye diameter), terminal, and moderately oblique. No groove separating tip of upper jaw from snout. Teeth on shaft of vomer, palatines, tongue, and jaws. Gill membranes extended far forward, not attached to each other or to isthmus. Gular fold present (a membrane between the lower jaws, the only fish in Alberta with such a structure). Opercles and cheeks without scales. Origin of dorsal fin behind origin of anal fin. Lateral line complete and straight. Ventral keel sharp and smooth (i.e., knife-like rather than saw-like), extended from beneath pectoral fins to anal fin. Axillary process present above the pelvic fin base. Caudal fin strongly forked. Lateral-line scales 55-61; dorsal fin rays 9 or 10, anal fin rays 30-33; branchiostegal rays 7-10; gillrakers 15 or 16, short and knob-like.

Maximum length 18 inches and weight 3 pounds.

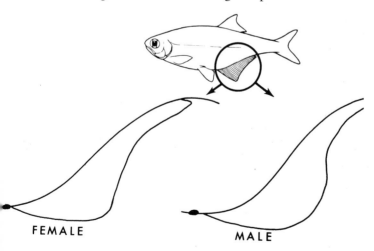

FEMALE   MALE

Sexual difference in anal fin shape in adult goldeye. In males the anterior rays of the anal fin are elongated, such that the anterior margin is convex while in females and immature specimens the rays are not elongated, such that the anterior margin is concave or nearly straight.

119

Alta: Meristic counts have been obtained as follows from the Peace River at 57° 45′N (4 specimens) and junction of the Sturgeon and North Saskatchewan rivers near Edmonton (6 specimens).

Scales

> Along lateral line: 57-60.
> Above lateral line: 6-7 (most at 7)
> Around caudal peduncle: 15-17

Gillrakers

> Upper arch: 5-6; lower arch: 9-10; total: 15-16

Rays

> Dorsal fin: 9-10 (most at 10)
> Anal fin: 31-33

Maximum length observed for Alberta is 18 inches fork length from the Athabasca River. Maximum weight is 4 pounds from the Bow River.

DISTRIBUTION

Northeastern British Columbia, through the Northwest Territories, to Quebec and Mississippi valley to Alabama. Absent from the Great Lakes.

Known in Alberta in Peace, Slave, Athabasca, North Saskatchewan, Red Deer, and South Saskatchewan rivers and in Lake Athabasca, Claire Lake, and other shallow lakes in the Athabasca delta area (see map on page 122).

BIOLOGY

Goldeye occur in lakes and rivers and appear to prefer water of high turbidity. They are a popular sport and commercial fish in some areas and are often taken by anglers in Alberta rivers. The commercial goldeye fishery in the western part of Lake Athabasca declined from 13,500 pounds in 1963 to only a few hundred pounds now taken incidently during the spring walleye fishery. Their food consists chiefly of insects, snails, crayfish, and fish. Spawning occurs in the spring, probably over rocky or gravelly bottoms in slow current. Lengthy river migrations occur. Paterson (1966) provides evidence that goldeye do not successfully reproduce in the Edmonton area and do not frequent the Edmonton area until they are 3 or 4 years old. The largest specimen noted in Alberta is believed to have been 12 years old.

120

ANGLING

Goldeye probably have not achieved the reputation of a fine game fish in Alberta that they rightly deserve. When taken on light tackle, this fish can provide sport comparable to some species of trout of equivalent size. They will take both wet and dry flies but most of the fish taken by anglers are caught on baits or small spinning lures. Favored places for goldeye fishing are in large turbid rivers near the mouths of small tributary streams or where a backwater meets an area of moderate current. The Peace, Athabasca, Pembina, North Saskatchewan, Red Deer, and South Saskatchewan rivers all have potentially good sport fisheries for goldeye. This species may be caught from the time of ice breakup throughout the open water season, with late May and June providing somewhat the best success.

HISTORICAL NOTE

First described by C. S. Rafinesque in 1819 from the Ohio River as *Amphiodon alveoides (=alosoides)*. Reported to Eigenmann (1895) as being present at Medicine Hat. Preble (1908) reported it to be common in the Athabasca and Slave rivers. Whitehouse (1919) noted it from the Red Deer River and refers to a report of it in the Peace River. Kendall (1924) recorded it from the Athabasca area under the cyprinid section. Bajkov (1926) noted it from near Jasper.

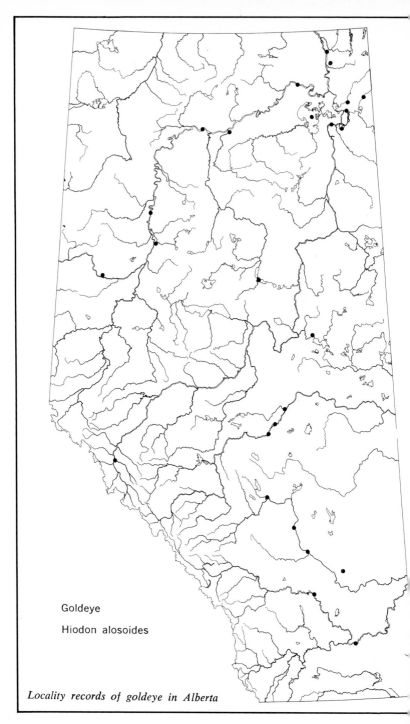

Goldeye

Hiodon alosoides

Locality records of goldeye in Alberta

MINNOW FAMILY - CYPRINIDAE

Representatives of the minnow family are found in North America, Africa, Europe, and Asia. Their greatest diversity is in southeast Asia. This fresh-water family contains about 2,000 species and is, perhaps, the largest of all fish families in the world. About 44 species occur in Canada, with 14 species native to Alberta.

Most minnows are small fish, seldom exceeding 6 inches in length. They spawn in the spring and summer. Many people erroneously refer to any small fish as a minnow but all species have small individuals and the term minnow refers only to members of one particular family. Minnows may serve as prey for game fish while other minnows may themselves be fish predators (squawfish) or cause detrimental effects to the environment of our native fish (carp). Many tropical minnows give pleasure in home aquaria.

Minnows, like suckers, lack teeth in their mouth. Instead, in both families, there is a series of teeth on the pharyngeal arch (fifth gill arch). Counts of these teeth are not required to name any Alberta minnow but this character is generally quite useful in verifying identifications. The arch lies adjacent to the shoulder girdle and may be easily removed (but with great care) through the opercular opening (see photograph on page 124). The teeth in each row are counted and given in a formula from left to right. A dash separates counts on the two sides. Thus, a count of 2,5-4,2 indicates that there are two teeth on the outer row, five teeth on the inner row of the left arch and four teeth on the inner row, two teeth on the outer row of the right arch. The teeth may be in one or two rows on each side in native Alberta minnows. The pharyngeal arch must be examined under magnification to ascertain the presence of a broken tooth or an old socket where a tooth once was. Counts on several specimens should preferably be made.

All minnows have the upper jaw margin formed by only the premaxillaries, 3 branchiostegal rays (1 epihyal and 2 cera-tohyal), and 30-46 vertebrae. Most have 17 branched rays in the caudal fin.

Most minnows are probably susceptible to the same parasites found in spottail shiners (see page 166).

Minnows are placed in the order Cypriniformes (=Ostariophysi), along with the sucker and catfish families. Members of this order have an air bladder which is connected to the inner ear by a series of bones called the Weberian apparatus. This modification of the anterior few vertebrae may permit these fish to "hear".

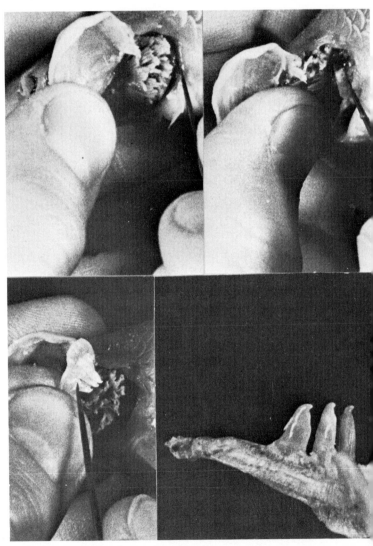

Steps involved in dissecting out the pharyngeal arch to count teeth (flathead chub shown).

KEY TO THE 14 SPECIES

Note—Seven species (carp, goldfish, peamouth, blackchin shiner, blacknose shiner, blacknose dace, and leopard dace) adjacent to or introduced and rare in Alberta are listed in Appendix I, not in key.

1 a	Barbel distinct and clearly visible at or near posterior end of upper jaw _____	2
1 b	Barbel absent (small and hidden barbels exist in *Semotilus*) _____	4

2 a (1) Premaxillaries nonprotractile (frenum present).
Rhinichthys cataractae - longnose dace

2 b Premaxillaries protractile (frenum absent) _____ 3

3 a (2) Tip of upper jaw extended distinctly forward past lower jaw; origin of dorsal fin opposite (vertically above) or in front of insertion of pelvic fins; barbel placed at end of upper jaw, at tip of maxilla; barbel length usually longer than ½ diameter of eye pupil; area between eyes flattened; scales above lateral line usually fewer than 9.
Platygobio gracilis - flathead chub

3 b Tip of upper jaw at most extended only slightly farther forward than lower jaw; origin of dorsal fin behind insertion of pelvic fins; barbel placed very slightly ahead of end of upper jaw; barbel length usually shorter than ½ diameter of eye pupil; area between eyes rounded; scales above lateral line usually more than 10.
Couesius plumbeus - lake chub

4 a (1) Anal fin with 10 or more rays; origin of dorsal fin behind insertion of pelvic fins _____ 5

4 b Anal fin with 9 or fewer rays; dorsal fin position variable _____ 6

5 a (4) Anal fin rays 10-12; scales above lateral line fewer than 9; color on side with silver and black tones only.
Notropis atherinoides - emerald shiner

5 b   Anal fin rays usually 13-17 (extremes 10-22); scales above lateral line more than 10; breeding males with yellow and crimson on side, some color on all adults.

Richardsonius balteatus - redside shiner

6 a (4)   Scales along lateral line more than 60; scales above lateral line 11 or more; origin of dorsal fin behind insertion of pelvic fins _____ 7

6 b   Scales along lateral line fewer than 55; scales above lateral line 11 or fewer; origin of dorsal fin even with or in front of insertion of pelvic fins _____ 10

7 a (6)   Scales along lateral line fewer than 76; lateral line complete (except in young); peritoneum silvery___ 8

7 b   Scales along normal position of lateral line more than 75; lateral line incomplete, pores not extending past dorsal fin; peritoneum black or brownish-black _____ 9

8 a (7)   Mouth large, generally extended past front of eye; scales above lateral line more than 14; depth of caudal peduncle less than length of dorsal fin base; barbel on upper jaw never present; young with black spot at base of caudal fin.

Ptychocheilus oregonensis - northern squawfish

8 b   Mouth of moderate size, not extended past front of eye; scales above lateral line fewer than 14; depth of cadual peduncle about equal to length of dorsal fin base; small barbel present ahead of end of upper jaw (not visible when mouth closed—often requires microscopic examination); young with blackish lateral band extending from gill cover to base of tail.

Semotilus margarita - pearl dace

9 a (7)   Mouth very oblique, not extended to front of eye; two distinct black lateral bands in adult; intestine long, usually with several loops or coils; pharyngeal teeth in one row, usually 0,5-5,0.

Chrosomus eos - northern redbelly dace

9 b   Mouth moderately oblique, usually extended to front of eye; only one distinct lateral band; intestine short, usually with a single coil; pharyngeal teeth in two rows, usually 2,5-4,2.

Chrosomus neogaeus - finescale dace

10 a (6)   Peritoneum blackish or black; intestine elongated, about twice standard length or more; pharyngeal teeth 0,4-4,0 _____ 11

10 b   Peritoneum silvery; intestine much less than twice standard length; pharyngeal teeth usually 1 or 2,4-4,2 or 1 _____ 13

11 a (10) Mouth terminal or nearly so; scales before dorsal fin crowded, in 21 or more rows and much smaller than those on rest of body; scales above lateral line 9 or more; anal fin usually with 7 rays; head of breeding males nearly black and with numerous nuptial tubercles and dorsal fin with a stout, blunt-tipped, anterior half-ray that is distinctly separated from the first principal ray.

Pimephales promelas - fathead minnow

11 b   Mouth distinctly subterminal; scales before dorsal fin not unusually crowded or smaller than those on rest of body, in 19 or fewer rows; scales above lateral line 7 or fewer; anal fin usually with 8 rays; head of breeding males not black and without tubercles and dorsal fin with the typical anterior half-ray slender and tightly bound to the first principal ray _____ 12

12 a (11) Dorsal fin rounded at tip; sides yellowish or brassy in life, dusky lateral band often present; dorsal fin rays outlined with melanophores; about 20 small radii in scales of adults (grooves radiating toward center of scale).

Hybognathus hankinsoni - brassy minnow

12 b   Dorsal fin somewhat pointed at tip; sides silvery in life, no dusky lateral band; dorsal fin rays not outlined with melanophores; about 10 distinct radii in scales of adult.

Hybognathus nuchalis - silvery minnow

13 a (10) A large conspicuous black spot (very rarely faint) on the base of the caudal fin; anal fin usually with 8 rays; upper jaw length usually shorter than diameter of eye.

Notropis hudsonius - spottail shiner

13 b   No large conspicuous black spot on the base of the caudal fin; anal fin usually with 7 rays; upper jaw usually longer than diameter of eye.

Notropis blennius - river shiner

Rhinichthys cataractae (Valenciennes)
Rhin ichthys - snout fish
    (referring to the long snout)
cataractae - of the cataract
    (Niagara waterfall)

Longnose dace adults, 3½ inches standard length, from Graburn Creek, Cypress Hills.

DESCRIPTION

    Color darkish dorsally, darkish to silvery laterally with mottling often present. Young with a distinct blackish lateral band from gill cover to tail and on snout but not extending across upper lip; band usually faint or absent in adults. Peritoneum somewhat silvery with much black mottling. A reddish-orange tinge occurs at the base of the pectoral, pelvic, and anal fins and on the upper lip and lower cheeks in breeding females, rather than in males as in the eastern range of the species (observed in Cypress Hills and Red Deer River tributaries).

129

Body rounded in section. Head conical and slightly rounded dorsally, space between eyes about 2½ times eye diameter; eyes small and placed entirely on upper half of head; mouth moderate in size (not extended to eye but much longer than eye diameter), markedly subterminal, and almost horizontal (almost sucker-like, with long snout); barbels conspicuous and placed at end of upper jaw; tip of upper jaw without a groove separating it from tip of snout (the only minnow known in Alberta with a frenum). Isthmus wide, more than ½ width of head. Origin of dorsal fin slightly behind insertion of pelvics. Lateral line complete and straight. Caudal fin moderately forked. Lateral-line scales 55-75; dorsal fin rays 8 and anal fin rays 7; pharyngeal teeth 2,4-4,2.

Maximum length about 6 inches.

Alta.: According to Nichols (1916), specimens from Banff Hot Springs have a lower number of lateral-line scales (50-60) than is typical for the species. A collection from the same site (NMC 58-226) examined by Mr. T. A. Willock, also had an unusually low number of lateral line scales, 56-59.

Meristic counts have been obtained as follows:

Scales
    Along lateral line (5 specimens in each population):
        Junction of Blindman and Red Deer Rivers: 65-68
        Graburn Creek, Cypress Hills: 59-73
    Above lateral line: 11-13
    Around caudal peduncle: 25-30

Gillrakers
    Upper arch: 1-2; lower arch: 4-6; total: 5-7
    Maximum length noted in Alberta is 4¼ inches fork length in Upper Kananaskis Reservoir.

DISTRIBUTION
British Columbia to Labrador, extending north in the Mackenzie River and south along the Rocky Mountains to northern Mexico, and south from the Great Lakes to North Carolina.

Widespread in Alberta in Peace, Athabasca, North Saskatchewan, Battle, Red Deer, South Saskatchewan, Bow, Oldman, and Milk drainages (see map on page 132).

BIOLOGY

Longnose dace occur in lakes, rivers, and small creeks, often with lake chub and usually on the bottom. Individuals can adjust their air bladder size to suit various currents. In swift rivers they tend to have a very reduced air bladder which increases their density and enables them to stay on the bottom. They feed primarily on aquatic insect larvae. Spawning occurs from early June to mid-August. A maximum age of 4 years has been reported for males and 5 years for females.

Fully ripe individuals have been taken in early August in Upper and Lower Kananaskis reservoirs. Longnose dace hybridize with lake chub in Upper Kananaskis Reservoir and are known to hybridize with redside shiners in British Columbia.

HISTORICAL NOTE

First described by A. Valenciennes (in Cuvier and Valenciennes) in 1842 from Niagara Falls as *Gobio cataractae*. First noted in Alberta by Eigenmann (1895) at Medicine Hat, Calgary, and Banff (Bow River and hot sulphur springs) as *Rhinichthys dulcis*.

Specimens collected at Cave and Basin Hot Spring in 1915 were described as a new subspecies, *Rhinichthys cataractae smithi,* by Nichols (1916). R. B. Miller's notes indicate that he had in his care a collection made from the same site July 27, 1924, under the name *Agosia nubilus*. The Cave and Basin population is now apparently extinct. Bajkov (1926) described and recorded the species from several lakes and creeks in Jasper National Park under the name *Agosia nubila*. The identification of minnows in the genus *Agosia,* as defined at that time, infers that the specimens lacked a frenum and thus might be *Rhinichthys falcatus* (leopard dace) or part of the *R. osculus* (speckled dace) complex. Both leopard and speckled daces are known from the Columbia River system in British Columbia. However, Nichols reported his type specimen to have "premaxillaries not proctractile" and only *R. cataractae* has been verified from the Jasper-Banff area.

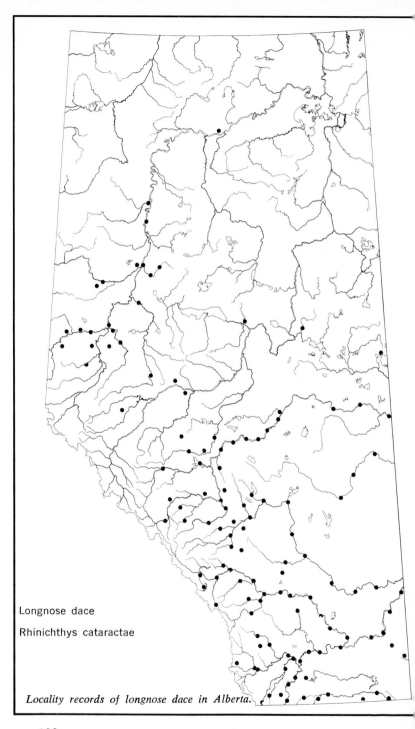

Longnose dace

Rhinichthys cataractae

Locality records of longnose dace in Alberta.

132

Platygobio gracilis (Richardson)
Platy gobio - broad, a gudgeon
 (a European minnow)
gracilis - slender

Flathead chub juveniles, 3½ inches standard length, from Peace River at Dunvegan.

DESCRIPTION

Color pale brownish dorsally, silvery laterally. Young with faint blackish lateral band fading out anteriorly. Peritoneum silvery with no black mottling.

Body slightly compressed. Head broad and flattened dorsally, space between eyes about 2 - 2½ times eye diameter; eyes small; mouth large (extended to front margin of eye and distinctly longer then eye diameter), subterminal, and slightly oblique; barbels conspicuous and placed at end of upper jaw. Isthmus moderate, less than ½ width of head. Origin of dorsal fin over or slightly in front of insertion of pelvics. Lateral line complete and slightly decurved. Dorsal, anal, and pectoral fins falcate (sickle-shaped). Caudal fin deeply forked. Lateral-line scales 45-59; dorsal and anal fin rays 8; pharyngeal teeth 2,4-4,2.

Breeding males with minute tubercles on top of head and on the fins.

Maximum length about 12 inches.

Alta: Meristic counts have been obtained as follows:

Scales

Along lateral line (5 specimens in each population):
Peace River at about 58°N: 52-56
North Saskatchewan at Edmonton: 49-51

Above lateral line: 7-8

Around caudal peduncle: 16-18

Gillrakers

Upper arch: 1-3; lower arch: 3-6; total: 4-7

Specimens up to 10 inches fork length have been taken at Edmonton, while Kendall (1924) reported them up to 12 inches fork length near Fort Chipewyan, Athabasca delta area.

DISTRIBUTION

Northwestern British Columbia to Manitoba and northward in the Mackenzie system and southward to New Mexico.

Widespread in Alberta in Peace, Athabasca, North Saskatchewan, Red Deer, South Saskatchewan, Oldman, and Milk drainages (see map on page 135).

BIOLOGY

In Alberta flathead chub occur primarily in large muddy rivers and are often very abundant. They frequent backwaters or river margins and are sometimes caught by fishermen on natural baits. Their diet is made up of insects and occasionally fish. Spawning probably occurs in July and August.

HISTORICAL NOTE

First described by Sir John Richardson in 1836 from Carleton House, Saskatchewan River, as *Cyprinus (Leuciscus) gracilis*. Placed in the genus *Hybopsis* by many recent workers. First noted in Alberta by Eigenmann (1895) at Medicine Hat. Preble (1908) found it abundant in the Athabasca River from Athabasca northward while Whitehouse (1919) reported it to be common in the vicinity of Red Deer. Bajkov (1926) recorded it in the Athabasca River in Jasper National Park.

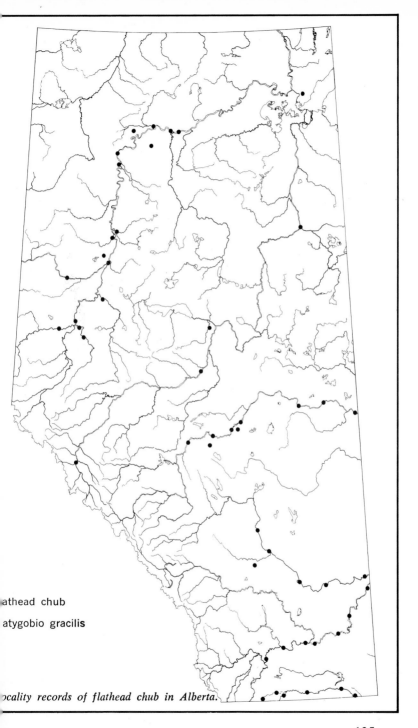

flathead chub

atygobio gracilis

locality records of flathead chub in Alberta.

Couesius plumbeus (Agassiz)

Couesius - after Dr. Elliot Coues,
    an ornithologist
plumbeus - lead colored

*Lake chub adults, about 2¾ inches standard length, from
Little Smoky River.*

DESCRIPTION

Darkish or greenish color dorsally, silvery laterally. Young
with a distinct black lateral band from gill cover to tail and
usually extended around snout and across upper lip, band often
present in adults posteriorly. Peritoneum silvery with only a few
black spots or light dusky appearance. Mature males have a
distinct reddish patch behind the pectoral fins.

Body rounded in section. Head conical and slightly rounded
dorsally, space between eyes about 1¾ times eye diameter; eyes
large; mouth large (extended to front margin of eye and about
equal in length to eye diameter), terminal, and slightly oblique;
barbels moderately conspicuous and placed very slightly ahead
of end of upper jaw. Isthmus narrow, about ¼ width of head.
Origin of dorsal fin over or behind insertion of pelvics. Lateral

line complete and decurved. Caudal fin moderately forked. Lateral-line scales 54 to 70; dorsal and anal fin rays 8; pharyngeal teeth 2,4-4,2.

Breeding males with tubercules on the head and pectoral fins (observed in several southern Alberta localities).

The lake chub is similar in general appearance to the pearl dace.

Maximum length about 6 inches.

Alta: Meristic counts have been obtained as follows:

Scales

Along lateral line (5 specimens in each population):

Little Smoky River: 56-64

Brazeau Reservoir: 60-70

Above lateral line: 11-14

Around caudal peduncle: 23-26

Gillrakers

Upper arch: 1-2; lower arch: 1-4; total: 3-5

Maximum length observed for Alberta is 5 inches fork length in Upper Kananaskis Reservoir.

DISTRIBUTION

British Columbia to Nova Scotia and northward in the Yukon and Mackenzie systems and southward to Colorado.

Widespread in Alberta in Hay, Slave, Peace, Athabasca, Beaver, North Saskatchewan, Battle, Red Deer, South Saskatchewan, Oldman, Bow, and Milk drainages (see map on page 138).

BIOLOGY

Lake chub occur in lakes, rivers, and small creeks and are often extremely abundant. They feed on crustaceans, aquatic insects, and algae. Spawning occurs from late June to mid-August. Maturity is probably reached when at age 3 or 4. Few live for more than 5 years.

Lake chub hybridize with longnose dace in Upper Kananaskis Reservoir.

HISTORICAL NOTE

First described by L. Agassiz in 1850 from Lake Superior as *Gobio plumbeus*. Formally placed in the genus *Hybopsis* (as *Hybopsis plumbea*) by some workers; many similarities exist with *Semotilus*. First noted in Alberta by Eigenmann (1895) at Medicine Hat and Calgary as *Couesius dissimilis*.

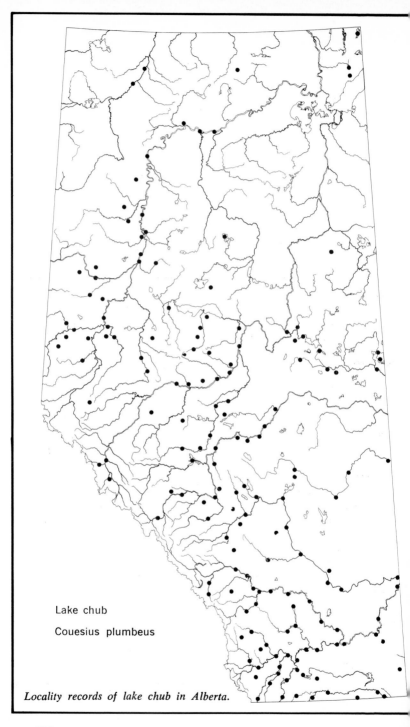

Lake chub

Couesius plumbeus

Locality records of lake chub in Alberta.

PEARL DACE

Semotilus margarita (Cope)
Semotilus - banner (dorsal fin) spotted
margarita - a pearl

Pearl dace adults, 3 inches standard length, from Freeman River drainage.

DESCRIPTION

Color darkish green or grey dorsally, dusky silver laterally. Young with a distinct brownish-black lateral band, often present posteriorly in adults. Peritoneum somewhat silvery with a few black spots. Males in breeding season usually with a bright red band below the lateral line.

Body slightly compressed. Head conical and moderately rounded dorsally, space between the eyes about 1½ times eye diameter; eyes large; mouth moderate (extended or almost extended to front margin of eye and about equal in length to eye diameter), very slightly subterminal (upper lip projecting slightly in front of lower lip), and slightly oblique; barbels flattened or flap-like (not slender as in other species), inconspicuous (not visible when mouth closed, may be absent on one side), and placed distinctly ahead of end of upper jaw. Isthmus narrow, about

139

¼ width of head. Origin of dorsal fin behind insertion of pelvics. Lateral line complete and decurved. Caudal fin moderately forked. Lateral-line scales 60-75; dorsal and anal fin rays 8; pharyngeal teeth 2,5-4,2.

The pearl dace is similar in general appearance to the lake chub.

Maximum length about 6 inches.

Male pearl dace from inlet to Obed Lake.

Alta: Meristic counts have been obtained as follows from Obed Lake (7 specimens).

Scales

    Along lateral line: 68-74
    Above lateral line: 11-13
    Around caudal peduncle: 25-28

Gillrakers

    Upper arch: 1-2; lower arch: 3-4; total: 4-6

Maximum lengths noted in Alberta are 4½ inches fork length in Running Lake, Whitemud drainage in the Clear Hills and 6 inches fork length from a small unnamed lake south of Fort Vermilion at 57° 55′ lat. and 115° 30′ long.

DISTRIBUTION

Lower Peace drainage of British Columbia to Nova Scotia and southward to Nebraska (in Northwest Territories south of Great Slave Lake).

Known from scattered headwater localities throughout Alberta in Peace, Athabasca, upper North Saskatchewan, upper Red Deer, upper Bow, and upper Oldman drainages (see map on page 142).

BIOLOGY

Pearl dace occur in lakes (usually along margins near cover) and in slow streams. They feed on aquatic insects and zooplankton. Spawning probably occurs from May to early summer.

HISTORICAL NOTE

First described by E. D. Cope in 1866 from the Conestoga River, Pennsylvania, as *Clinostomus margarita*. Formerly referred to as *Margariscus margarita nachtriebi*. First noted in Alberta by Bajkov (1926) from the Athabasca River and beaver dams near Jasper as a new subspecies, *Leuciscus nachtriebi athabascae*. Miller and Macdonald (1949) noted the species next from Goldeye and Obed lakes.

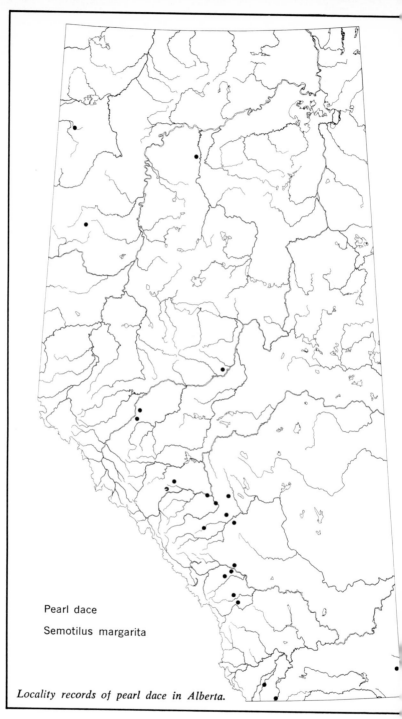

Pearl dace

Semotilus margarita

Locality records of pearl dace in Alberta.

142

Ptychocheilus oregonensis (Richardson)

Ptycho cheilus - fold lip (skin of mouth
    behind jaws is folded)

oregonensis - of Oregon

Squawfish juveniles, 3½ inches standard length, from Dunvegan, Peace River.

DESCRIPTION

Color pale brownish dorsally, silvery laterally. Belly often yellowish. Young with faint blackish lateral band fading out anteriorly. Distinct black spot at base of caudal fin in young and juveniles. Peritoneum silvery with few black spots. Breeding males have orangish fins and a white line below the lateral line.

Body slightly compressed. Head long, conical, and slightly rounded dorsally, space between eyes about 2 times eye diameter; eyes moderate; mouth large (extended past front margin of eye except in small fish and much longer than eye diameter), terminal to very slightly subterminal, and slightly oblique; barbels absent. Isthmus narrow, about ¼ width of head. Origin of dorsal fin slightly behind insertion of pelvics. Lateral line complete and decurved. Caudal fin deeply forked. Lateral-line scales 65-77 dorsal and anal fin rays 8-10; pharyngeal teeth usually 2,5-4,2.

Maximum length 25 inches.

Alta: Meristic counts have been obtained as follows from the Peace River.

Scales

Along lateral line: 65, 66, 67
Above lateral line: 15-16
Around caudal peduncle: 25-27

Gillrakers

Upper arch: 2; lower arch: 7; total: 9

A specimen obtained by F. Somerville at the town of Peace River was 17¼ inches fork length.

DISTRIBUTION

Coastal drainages from British Columbia to Oregon and Peace system of British Columbia and Alberta. Widespread in eastern British Columbia in Fraser and Columbia drainages.

Restricted in Alberta to the Peace system, downstream to the town of Peace River and possibly the Cadotte River (see map on page 145).

BIOLOGY

Squawfish are primarily lake inhabitants but are found only in the Peace River in Alberta. The young feed on insects and plankton while juveniles and adults feed extensively on fish. Spawning occurs from May to July. Sexual maturity is probably reached in the sixth year and the life span of an individual is as long as 20 years. In British Columbia squawfish hybridize with peamouth and redside shiners.

HISTORICAL NOTE

First described by Sir John Richardson in 1836 from the Columbia River as *Cyprinus (Leuciscus) oregonensis*. First official record in Alberta by R. B. Miller and M. J. Paetz on August 15, 1956 at Dunvegan, Peace River.

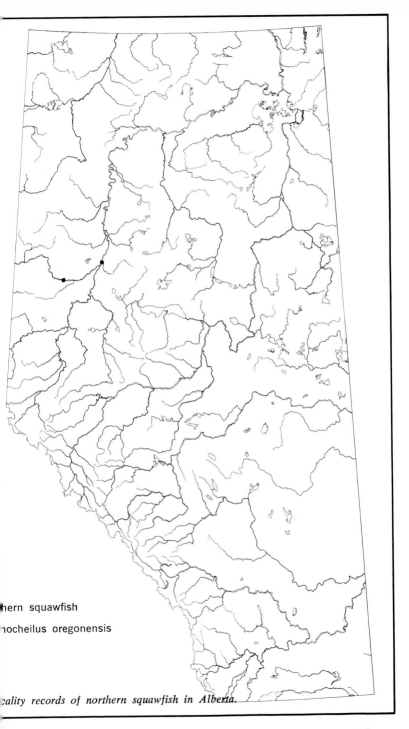

hern squawfish

nocheilus oregonensis

...cality records of northern squawfish in Alberta.

Richardsonius balteatus (Richardson)
Richardsonius - after Sir John Richardson
balteatus - girdled

Redside shiner juveniles, 2½ inches standard length, from Smoky River at Highway 34.

DESCRIPTION

Color dark olive or brownish dorsally, silvery laterally. Young and adults with a dark lateral band, fading out anteriorly. Peritoneum silvery with few to many black spots. Males brilliant at spawning time with yellow and vivid crimson on sides and belly.

Body deep and strongly compressed. Head short, conical, and strongly rounded dorsally, space between eyes about 1½ times eye diameter; eyes large; mouth moderate (extended or almost extended to front margin of eye and about equal in length to eye diameter), terminal or with lower lip extended slightly beyond upper lip, moderately oblique; barbels absent. Isthmus narrow, about ¼ width of head. Origin of dorsal fin well behind insertion of pelvics. Lateral line complete and strongly decurved. Caudal fin deeply forked. Lateral-line scales 52-67; dorsal fin rays 8-11 and anal fin rays 10-22; pharyngeal teeth 2,5-4,2.

Maximum length 7 inches.

Alta: Meristic counts have been obtained as follows:

Scales (Smoky River—15 specimens)

Along lateral line: 52-58

Above lateral line: 11-13

Around caudal peduncle: 18-20

Gillrakers

Upper arch: 1-2; lower arch: 6-7; total: 7-9

Anal fin ray frequency:

	13	14	15	16	17
Smoky River	1	2	11	1	—
Beaverlodge River	—	1	2	3	—
Peace R., Dunvegan	—	—	—	2	2
Economy Creek	1	1	2	1	—
Pinto Creek	—	—	1	3	1
Simonette River	1	1	7	4	1

Maximum length observed for Alberta is 4¼ inches fork length from Pinto Creek in the Wapiti drainage.

DISTRIBUTION

Coastal drainages from British Columbia to Oregon, eastward to Utah, and in Peace system of British Columbia and Alberta. Widespread in eastern British Columbia in Fraser and Columbia drainages.

Restricted in Alberta to the Peace system. Known from Wapiti R., Smoky R., Little Smoky R., Big Mountain Cr., Simonette R., Pinto Cr., Economy Cr., Beaverlodge R., and Peace River north to the Cadotte River and near Carcajou (see map on page 148).

BIOLOGY

In Alberta, redside shiners are known only from rivers while in British Columbia they commonly occur in both lakes and streams. In the Peace drainage of Alberta they are often very abundant. They feed on crustaceans and aquatic and terrestrial insects. Spawning occurs from June to July. Individuals probably live as long as 5 years. In British Columbia redside shiners hybridize with longnose dace, northern squawfish, and peamouth.

HISTORICAL NOTE

First described by Sir John Richardson in 1836 from the Columbia River as *Cyprinus (Abramis) balteatus*. Placed in the genus *Gila* by some recent workers. First taken in Alberta by R. B. Miller and R. C. Thomas on August 16, 1954 in Wapiti River and Big Mountain Creek.

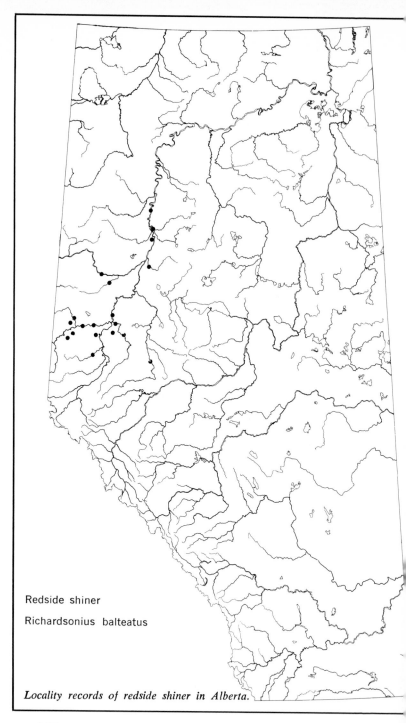

Redside shiner

Richardsonius balteatus

Locality records of redside shiner in Alberta.

Chrosomus eos Cope

Chro somus - colored body

eos - sunrise

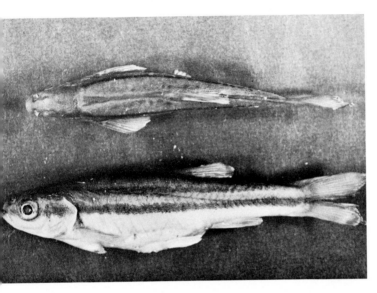

*Northern redbelly dace adults, 1¾ inches standard length, from
Summit Lake.*

DESCRIPTION

Color light brownish-olive dorsally, silvery or yellowish on
ventral area. Two blackish lateral bands present, the upper extended from the nape to the caudal peduncle (often broken
posteriorly), the lower extended from the snout to base of tail.
Between the two dark bands is a silvery-yellowish band. A thin
dark oblique line usually extends from the upper band anteriorly
to the lower band posteriorly, in a position beneath the dorsal fin.
Young with a dark spot on base of tail. Peritoneum brownish-
black with a faint trace of silver. Sides and belly yellow or red in
breeding males.

Body rounded in section. Head short, conical, and slightly
rounded dorsally, space between eyes about 1½ times eye diameter; eyes moderate; mouth small (not extended to front margin of
eye and slightly shorter than eye diameter), terminal or with

149

lower lip tending to project in front of upper lip, and very oblique; barbels absent. Isthmus moderate, between ⅓ and ¼ width of head. Origin of dorsal fin behind insertion of pelvics. Lateral line incomplete, often ending under the pectoral fin. Intestine elongate, usually 1 main loop and 2 coils. Caudal fin moderately forked. Lateral-line scales about 75-90 (so small that a microscope is usually required to see them); scales around caudal peduncle about 21-25; dorsal and anal fin rays usually 8; pharyngeal teeth 0,5-4,0 or 0,5-5,0; first arch gillrakers about 8-11.

Maximum length 3 inches. Maximum length observed for Alberta is 2½ inches fork length from Beauvais Lake.

DISTRIBUTION

Northeastern British Columbia and southwestern Northwest Territories to New Brunswick and southward to Wisconsin; in New Mexico.

Known from scattered localities throughout much of Alberta from Hay, Peace, Athabasca, North Saskatchewan, South Saskatchewan, Oldman, and Milk drainages (see locality records on page 151).

BIOLOGY

Northern redbelly dace occur in lakes and streams. They feed primarily on algae and zooplankton. Spawning occurs over aquatic plants. In eastern North America northern redbelly dace hybridize with finescale dace. Hybridization between these two species is also suspected in several Alberta lakes.

HISTORICAL NOTE

First described by E. D. Cope in 1861 from Susquehanna River, Pennsylvania, as *Chrosomus eos*. Placed in the genus *Phoxinus* by some recent workers. First reported from Alberta by Miller and Macdonald (1949) from Battle Creek (Cypress Hills) and Beauvais Lake.

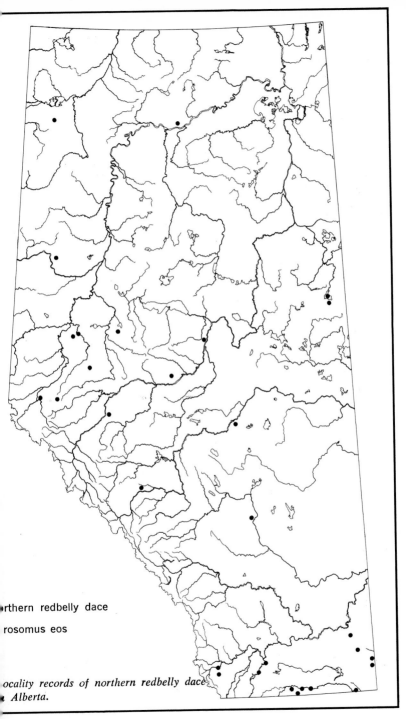

northern redbelly dace

Chrosomus eos

Locality records of northern redbelly dace in Alberta.

151

Chrosomus neogaeus (Cope)

neo gaeus - new world

Finescale dace adults, 2 inches standard length, from Summit Lake.

DESCRIPTION

Color dark brownish-olive dorsally, silvery on ventral area. A single dark lateral band extended from the gill cover to the tail, in the same position as the lower dark band in *C. eos*. Above this band is a silvery-yellowish band, above which there is only a faint trace of the upper darkish band present in *C. eos*. A thin dark oblique line usually extends from the upper dark area anteriorly to the lower band posteriorly, in a position beneath the dorsal fin. Young with the dark lateral band distinct and with a dark caudal spot. Peritoneum brownish-black to blackish with silvery sheen underneath (and much paler than in *C. eos*). Sides and belly yellow or red in breeding males.

Body rounded in section. Head moderate (longer than in *C. eos*), and slightly rounded dorsally, space between eyes about 1½ times eye diameter; eyes moderate; mouth moderate (extended or almost extended to front margin of eye and about equal in length to eye diameter), terminal and moderately oblique;

barbels absent. Isthmus moderate, between ⅓ and ¼ width of head. Origin of dorsal fin behind insertion of pelvics. Lateral line incomplete, ending under or before the dorsal fin. Intestine short, 1 main loop. Caudal fin moderately forked. Lateral-line scales about 80-100 (so small that a microscope is usually required to see them); scales around caudal peduncle about 34-37; dorsal and anal fin rays 8; pharyngeal teeth 2,5-4,2 or 2,5-5,2; first arch gillrakers about 8-10.

Maximum length 3 inches. Maximum length observed for Alberta is 3 inches fork length from Beauvais Lake.

DISTRIBUTION

Northeastern British Columbia, northern Alberta, and northward down the Mackenzie drainage; Manitoba to New Brunswick; Nebraska area.

Known in Alberta from only a few scattered localities in Hay, Peace, Simonette, lower Athabasca, upper North Saskatchewan, and Milk drainages (see map on page 154).

BIOLOGY

Finescale dace occur in lakes and sluggish creeks. It is usually larger than the redbelly dace in sympatric situations. In eastern North America finescale dace hybridize with northern redbelly dace. Hybridization between these two species is also suspected in several Alberta lakes.

HISTORICAL NOTE

First described by E. D. Cope in 1866 from New Hudson, Michigan, as *Phoxinus neogaeus*. Placed in the monotypic genus *Pfrille* or the polytypic genus *Phoxinus* by some recent workers. First taken in Alberta in the collection of R. E. Ayling, June 16, 1956, from Beauvais Lake. This species was not distinguished from *Chrosomus eos* in Alberta until the 1960's.

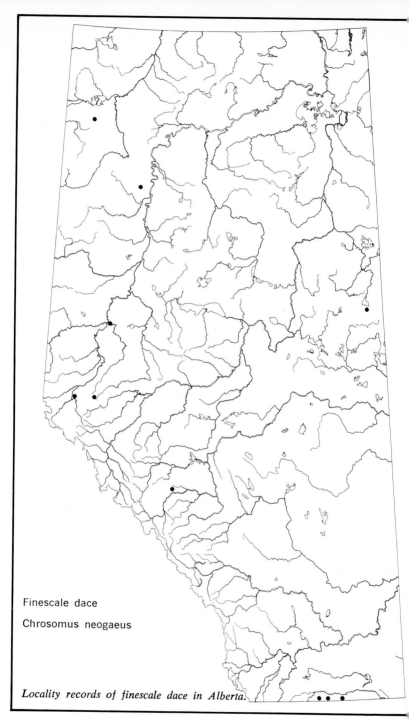

Finescale dace

Chrosomus neogaeus

Locality records of finescale dace in Alberta.

FATHEAD MINNOW

ʾimephales promelas Rafinesque
ʾime phales - fat head
ʾro melas - before black

ʾathead minnow, upper-typical of females and non-breeding individuals. Middle and lower-breeding males with tubercles, 2½ inches standard length, from Verdigris Lake.

DESCRIPTION

Color olive-yellow to straw-yellow dorsally and laterally, and yellow-silvery underneath (sides not glistening silvery as is characteristic of most Alberta minnows). Blackish lateral band from gill cover to tail (sometimes very faint, most distinct in young). Peritoneum blackish, with some silver showing through. Breeding males with black head and large black spot at anterior base of dorsal fin (may be diffuse and faint in immature).

Body slightly to moderately compressed. Head blunt in breeding males, conical in others, strongly rounded dorsally in breeding males, moderately so in others; distance between eyes about 1¾-3½ times eye diameter; eyes moderate to small; mouth small (not extended to front margin of eye and about equal in length to eye diameter), slightly subterminal to terminal, and slightly oblique; barbels absent. Isthmus moderate to wide, about

155

⅓-½ width of head. Origin of dorsal fin above or slightly in front of insertion of pelvics. Lateral line usually almost complete, faint in places, slightly decurved. Intestine long and coiled, several loops crossing ventral midline. Caudal fin moderately forked. Lateral-line scales 41-50; scales before the dorsal fin crowded and much smaller than those along the side; dorsal fin rays 8 and anal fin rays 7 (anal fin exceptionally small, especially in immature); pharyngeal teeth 0,4-4,0.

Breeding males with numerous horny tubercles, in 3 rows around the snout and usually 2 tubercles under the lower jaw; a thick puffed-out spongy area extending from the nape to front of dorsal fin; a conspicuous blunt half-ray, separated from the first principal ray by a membrane, at front of dorsal fin. Adult females have an enlarged urogenital structure.

Maximum length 3½ inches.

Alta: Meristic counts have been obtained from Verdigris Lake, Milk River drainage (10 specimens).

Scales

Along lateral line: 45-50
Above lateral line: 9-11
Around caudal peduncle: 19-21

Gillrakers

Upper arch: 2-3; lower arch: 10-12; total: 12-15

Maximum length observed for Alberta is 3 inches fork length in Muir Lake.

DISTRIBUTION

Alberta to Quebec to northeastern Mexico.

Widespread in central and southern Alberta in Athabasca, North Saskatchewan, Battle, Red Deer, Bow, South Saskatchewan, Oldman, and Milk drainages. Known from Pine Lake in Wood Buffalo National Park (see map on page 158). Recent collecting has revealed this species to be present in other waters of the Slave drainage west and south of Fort Smith.

BIOLOGY

Fathead minnows often occur in large numbers in muddy creeks, ponds, and lakes. Individuals are frequently found with brook sticklebacks and are quite tolerant to extremes in pH and salinity; often occurring in areas where other fish could not surive. The fathead minnow feeds primarily on algae but also takes zooplankton. The thick spongy pad in the breeding male is used to clean eggs which the female deposits on the underside of various objects. Spawning probably extends from June until August, with sexual maturity reached in one year.

HISTORICAL NOTE

First described by C. S. Rafinesque in 1820 from near Lexington, Kentucky, as *Pimephales promelas*. First noted from Alberta by Eigenmann (1895) at Medicine Hat.

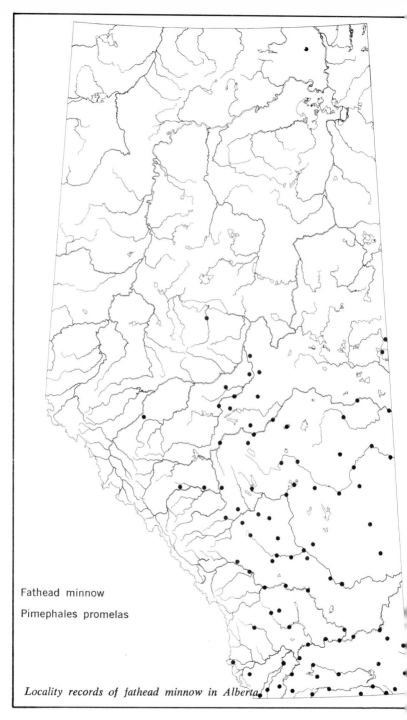

Fathead minnow

Pimephales promelas

Locality records of fathead minnow in Alberta.

EMERALD SHINER

Notropis atherinoides Rafinesque
Notropis - back keel (the keel was presumably
a deformity in a shriveled specimen).
atherin oides - silverside resemblance

Emerald shiner adults, 2¼ inches standard length, from Fort Saskatchewan, North Saskatchewan River.

DESCRIPTION

Color of body yellowish silver with bluish purple iridescence and somewhat transluscent. Shining silvery lateral band (appearing blackish in preserved specimens). Gill cover shiny silvery. Peritoneum silvery, with numerous small black spots. Breeding individuals devoid of color other than as noted above.

Body strongly compressed (but not as deep bodied as *Richardsonius*). Head conical and strongly rounded dorsally; distance between eyes about 1-1¼ times eye diameter; eyes large; mouth large (extended or almost extended to front margin of eye and equal or greater in length than eye diameter), terminal, and slightly oblique; barbels absent. Isthmus narrow, about ¼ width of head. Origin of dorsal fin behind insertion of pelvics. Lateral line complete and moderately decurved. Caudal fin moderately forked. Lateral-line scales 35-41; dorsal fin rays 8 and anal fin rays 9-13; pharyngeal teeth 2,4-4,2.

Breeding males, especially, with small tubercles on the pectoral fin.

159

Maximum length 4¼ inches.

Alta: Meristic counts have been obtained from several localities.

Scales

Along lateral line: 35-41

Above lateral line: 6-8

Around caudal peduncle: 13-14

Gillrakers

Upper arch: 1-3; lower arch: 8-9; total: 9-12

The gillrakers are longer and more distinct than on most other Alberta minnows.

Anal fin ray frequency.

	10	11	12
Salt River (59°58'N, 112°21'W)	—	8	2
Lesser Slave Lake	2	8	—
Cold Lake	1	9	—
North Sask. R., near Edmonton	—	6	4
Pigeon Lake	8	2	—

Maximum length observed for Alberta is 4¼ inches fork length from Big Island, North Saskatchewan River, nead Edmonton.

DISTRIBUTION

Fort Nelson, British Columbia to Quebec and New York to Texas.

Widespread in much of Alberta in Petitot, Slave, Peace, Athabasca, North Saskatchewan, Beaver, Red Deer, South Saskatchewan, lower Bow, and Oldman drainages (see map on page 161).

BIOLOGY

Emerald shiners are usually most common in large rivers but in Alberta they are also common in many lakes. They tend to be surface swimming and feed predominantly on zooplankton. Spawning probably occurs from June to August with a 3 year maximum life span.

HISTORICAL NOTE

First described by C. S. Rafinesque in 1818 from Lake Erie as *Notropis atherinoides*. It is the type species for the unusually large North American genus *Notropis*, which contains about 97 species. First noted in Alberta by Eigenmann (1895) at Medicine Hat. Recorded from Lake Athabasca by Kendall (1924).

160

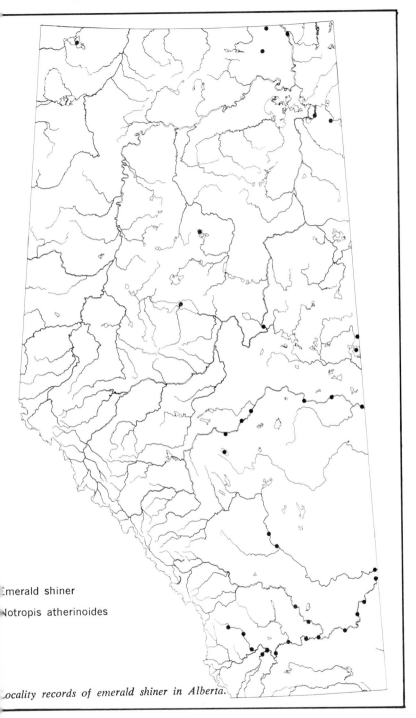

Emerald shiner

Notropis atherinoides

Locality records of emerald shiner in Alberta.

Notropis blennius (Girard)
blennius - blenny (an eel-like marine fish).

River shiner adults, 2¼ inches standard length, from North Saskatchewan River at Fort Saskatchewan.

DESCRIPTION

Color olive-straw to light brown and silvery dorsally. Silvery lateral band (a darkish band appears in preserved specimens). No caudal spot. Peritoneum silvery with few or no black spots.

Body moderately compressed. Head conical and slightly rounded dorsally; distance between eyes about 1½ times eye diameter; eyes moderate; mouth moderate (usually not extended to front margin of eye but longer than eye diameter), slightly subterminal, and silghtly oblique; barbels absent. Isthmus narrow, about ¼ width of head. Origin of dorsal fin about even with or slightly in front of insertion of pelvic fins. Lateral line complete and decurved. Caudal fin moderately forked. Lateral-line scales 34-37; dorsal fin rays 8 and anal fin rays usually 7; pharyngeal teeth 1 or 2,4-4,2 or 1.

162

Breeding males with tiny tubercles on the pectoral fin.

Maximum length 5 inches.

Alta: Meristic counts have been obtained from the North Saskatchewan River, near Edmonton.

Scales

Along lateral line: 34-36 (most have 36)
Above lateral line: 5-6
Around caudal peduncle: 11-12

Gillrakers

Upper arch: 2-3; lower arch: 4-6; total: 6-8

Anal fin rays

17 specimens had 7 rays while 2 had 8 rays.

Maximum length noted in Alberta is 3 inches fork length in the North Saskatchewan River at Edmonton.

DISTRIBUTION

Alberta to eastern Manitoba and Oklahoma to Pennsylvania.

Sporadic in central and southern Alberta. Occur in the North Saskatchewan (near Edmonton and downstream), Red Deer, South Saskatchewan, and Oldman rivers (see map on page 164).

BIOLOGY

The river shiner is commonest in large streams overy sandy and gravel bottoms. They probably spawn in July and August.

HISTORICAL NOTE

First described by C. F. Girard in 1856 from the Arkansas River, Arkansas, as *Alburnops blennius*. First noted in Alberta by Eigenmann (1895) at Medicine Hat as *Notropis jejunus*. It was further collected in 1914 from Morrin, Red Deer drainage (McAllister, 1962).

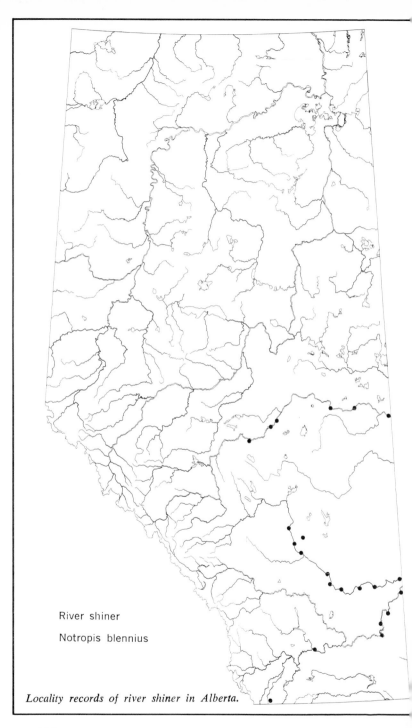

River shiner

Notropis blennius

Locality records of river shiner in Alberta.

Notropis hudsonius (Clinton)
hudsonius - after the Hudson River

Spottail shiner adults, 2¼ inches standard length, from Beaver Lake.

DESCRIPTION

Color bluish-green dorsally, silvery laterally. Preserved specimens have a dark lateral band which is not evident in living fish (except for scattered melanophores). Distinct black caudal spot usually present. Peritoneum silvery with a few small black spots.

Body moderately compressed. Head conical and moderately rounded dorsally; distance between eyes about 1-1¼ times eye diameter; eyes large; mouth small (usually not extended to front margin of eye and shorter than eye diameter), slightly subterminal, and slightly oblique; barbels absent. Isthmus narrow, about ¼ width of head. Origin of dorsal fin even with or slightly ahead of insertion of pelvics. Lateral line complete and decurved. Caudal fin moderately forked. Lateral-line scales 36-40; dorsal fin rays 8 and anal fin rays usually 8; pharyngeal teeth usually 1 or 2,4-4,2 or 1.

Breeding males with tiny tubercles on the pectoral fin.

Maximum length 5¾ inches

Alta: Meristic characters have been obtained as follows:

Scales (Beaver Lake)
Along lateral line: 36-40 (most have 38)
Above lateral line: 6
Around caudal peduncle: 12

Gillrakers (four lakes)
Upper arch: 1-2; lower arch: 3-7; total: 4-9

Anal fin rays (six scattered localities)
2 had 7 rays, 54 had 8 rays, and 1 had 9 rays

Maximum length observed for Alberta is 4 inches fork length from Lac Ste. Anne.

DISTRIBUTION

Alberta and the Northwest Territories to Quebec with southward extension to Kansas and Georgia.

Widespread in Alberta in Petitot, Slave, Peace, Athabasca, North Saskatchewan, Beaver, Red Deer, South Saskatchewan, Bow, and Oldman drainages (see map on page 167).

BIOLOGY

The spottail shiner is common in lakes and streams. Large schools are often found in pelagic situations. They feed on plankton, aquatic insects, and bottom fauna. Their life span is 4 years and spawning probably occurs from June to August. Larvae of the large tapeworm *Ligula intestinalis,* often occur in the spottail shiner. *Neascus,* trematode larvae which produce "black spot". in the skin, and other trematode larvae in the brain are also frequently found. The latter can be quite pathogenic to the fish.

HISTORICAL NOTE

First described by DeWitt Clinton in 1824 from the Hudson River, New York, as *Clupea hudsonia.* First noted in Alberta by Eigenmann and Eigenmann (1893) and Eigenmann (1895) at Medicine Hat as *Notropis scopiferus.* One small specimen taken at Fort Chipewyan, Lake Athabasca, in 1914 was described as a new species, *Opsopoeodus borealis* (Harper and Nichols, 1919). Spottail shiners collected in Lake Athabasca in 1920 were referred to the subspecies *Notropis hudsonius selene* (Kendall, 1924).

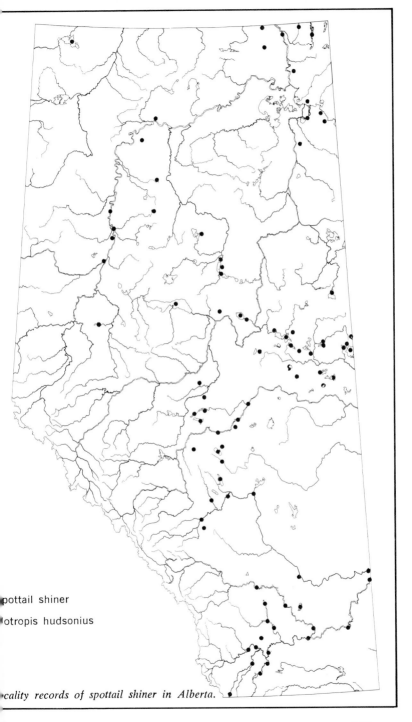

spottail shiner

Notropis hudsonius

Locality records of spottail shiner in Alberta.

Hybognathus hankinsoni Hubbs
Hybo gnathus - protuberant jaw
hankinsoni - after Dr. T. L. Hankinson,
    an ichthyologist

Brassy minnow adults, 2¼ inches standard length, from Halfbreed Creek, Milk River drainage near Aden.

DESCRIPTION

Color olive-green dorsally, brassy-yellow to dull silvery laterally. Darkish lateral band extended from gill cover to tail, often indistinct anteriorly. Dorsal, pectoral, and pelvic fin rays outlined with melanophores. Peritoneum jet black to dusky black.

Body moderately compressed. Head conical and moderately rounded dorsally, distance between eyes about 2-2½ times eye diameter; eyes moderate; mouth small (not extended to front margin of eye and about equal in length to eye diameter), subterminal (snout distinctly produced beyond lower jaw), and slightly oblique; barbels absent. Isthmus very narrow, less than ¼ width of head. Origin of dorsal fin in front of insertion of pelvics. Anterior tip of dorsal and pectoral fins rounded. Lateral line complete and slightly decurved. Scales with about 20 radii on posterior margin (may be difficult to locate) in adults. Intestine long, with numerous coils. Caudal find moderately forked. Lateral-line scales 35-39; dorsal fin rays 8 and anal fin rays usually 8; pharyngeal teeth 0,4-4,0.

Maximum length 4 inches

Alta: Meristic counts have been obtained from Halfbreed Creek near Aden (10 specimens).

Scales

Along lateral line: 35-38
Above lateral line: 6-7 (most at 6)
Around caudal peduncle: 16

Gillrakers

Upper arch: 2-4; lower arch: 7-8; total: 9-11

The gillrakers are longer and more distinct than on most other Alberta minnows.

Maximum length observed for Alberta is 3¼ inches fork length from Halfbreed Creek near Aden.

DISTRIBUTION

Alberta and Colorado to New York; scattered localities in British Columbia near New Westminster and Prince George.

Known in Alberta only in Milk River drainage (tributaries to the Milk River within Alberta, Lost River, and Lodge Creek —see map on page 170).

BIOLOGY

The brassy minnow in Alberta occurs in slow currents of the Milk drainage, including "alkali" streams. They probably spawn in late spring and summer. Individuals with ripe eggs have been found in July in the Milk drainage.

HISTORICAL NOTE

First described by C. L. Hubbs in 1929 (holotype not designated by Hubbs, lectotype designated in 1954 by R. M. Bailey from Dead River, Michigan) as *Hybognathus hankinsoni*. First noted from Alberta by McAllister (1962) from specimens collected July 9, 1961, in Lodge Creek (southeastern-most Alberta). Willock (1968) and Henderson and Peter (1969) reported additional finds from the Milk drainage and Violet Scott collected one adult in 1968 in the Lost River southeast of Comrey.

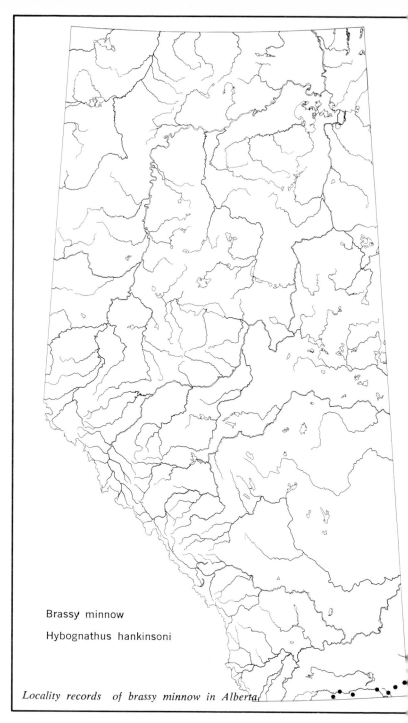

Brassy minnow

Hybognathus hankinsoni

Locality records of brassy minnow in Alberta.

Hybognathus nuchalis Agassiz
nuchalis - pertaining to the nape
   (which is streamlined).

Silvery minnow adult, 3½ inches standard length, from Milk drainage, east of Milk River town.

DESCRIPTION

Color brownish-yellow dorsally, silvery laterally. Lateral band absent (dusky spots may be present). Dorsal, pectoral, and pelvic fin rays not outlined with melanophores. Peritoneum dusky black, some silver showing through.

Body moderately compressed. Head conical and moderately rounded dorsally, distance between eyes about 2 times eye diameter; eyes moderate; mouth small (not extended to front margin of eye and about equal in length to eye diameter), subterminal, and slightly oblique; barbels absent. Isthmus very narrow, less than ¼ width of head. Origin of dorsal fin in front of (sometimes only slightly so) insertion of pelvics. Anterior tip of dorsal and pectoral fins pointed. Lateral line complete and decurved. Scales with about 10 distinct radii on posterior margin in adults. Intestine long, with numerous coils. Caudal fin moderately forked. Lateral-line scales 35-41; dorsal fin rays 8 and anal fin rays usually 8; pharyngeal teeth 0,4-4,0.

171

Maximum length 6 inches

Alta: Meristic counts have been obtained from the Lost River at its junction with the Milk River (about 1 mile south of the Alberta border in Montana, 10 specimens).

Scales

Along lateral line: 36-38

Above lateral line: 5-6

Around caudal peduncle: 13-14 (most at 14)

Gillrakers

Upper arch: 2-3; lower arch: 7-8; total: 9-11

The gillrakers are longer and more distinct than on most other Alberta minnows.

Maximum length noted in Alberta is 4 inches fork length from near Milk River townsite, Milk River.

DISTRIBUTION

Alberta and southern Quebec and from Texas to Georgia.

Known in Alberta only in the Milk River near Milk River and Aden and the South Saskatchewan River at Medicine Hat (see map on page 173).

BIOLOGY

The silvery minnow usually occurs in relatively clear water. It is presumed to be intolerant of turbid water.

HISTORICAL NOTE

First described by L. Agassiz in 1855 from Quincy, Illinois, as *Hybognathus nuchalis*. It is the type species of the genus. First collected in Alberta by Grant Campbell on May 13, 1961 (but not identified as this species until 1969) from Milk River south of Pendant d'Oreille. Further collected by Henderson and Peter (1969) in 1963 from the South Saskatchewan River at Medicine Hat (1 specimen) and by Willock (1968) in 1966 from the Milk River east of Milk River townsite.

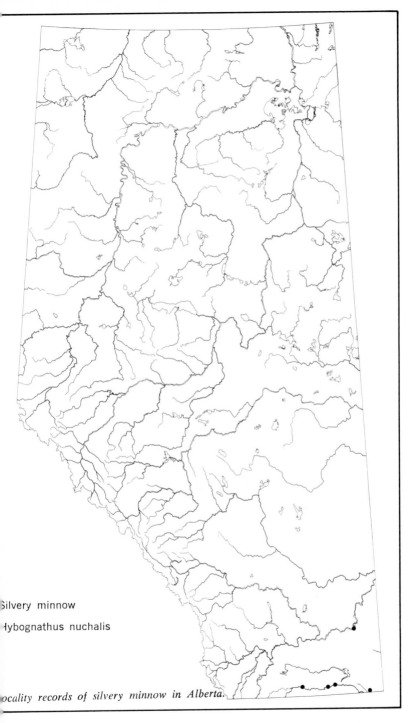

Silvery minnow

Hybognathus nuchalis

locality records of silvery minnow in Alberta.

SUCKER FAMILY — CATOSTOMIDAE

Representatives of the sucker family are found in North and Central America, eastern Siberia, and China. Their greatest diversity occurs in the United States. This fresh-water family contains about 70 species. About 17 species occur in Canada with 7 species in Alberta.

In some lakes suckers may reach relatively large sizes, often exceeding 15 inches in length. They generally feed on small animals (insects, snails, worms, etc.) and algae on the bottom on lakes and rivers, for which their protrusible subterminal mouth is well adapted. Spawning occurs in the spring and early summer. Adult males usually develop conspicuous tubercles on the anal fin and lower lobe of the caudal fin at spawning time. The sucker and minnow families are similar in several characters and are closely related.

Suckers lack teeth on the jaws but possess numerous comb-like pharyngeal teeth (see section on minnows for dissecting out the pharyngeal arch). The upper jaw margin is formed by the premaxillaries and the maxillaries. Suckers have 3 branchiostegal rays (1 epihyal and 2 ceratohyal) and 30-50 vertebrae. All have a broad isthmus, usually more than ⅓ width of head. The origin of the dorsal fin is in front of the pelvic fin insertion. Most Alberta species have 7 anal fin rays, *Carpiodes* often has 8 rays. Most have 16 branched caudal fin rays. The intestine is usually longer than 2 times the standard length. There are no pyloric caeca and the stomach is not externally differentiated from the rest of the alimentary canal. Females, on the average, are longer than males; considerable overlap occurs, however. Mature individuals may be sexed with considerable reliability in any season by examining the pelvic fins. In males, the 3rd ray is shorter than the 7th while in females (and immature individuals) the 3rd ray is longer than the 7th.

KEY TO THE 7 SPECIES

1 a	Dorsal fin rays more than 21; dorsal fin base contained less than 4 times in standard length; lateral-line scales usually fewer than 39.

Carpiodes cyprinus - quillback

1 b	Dorsal fin rays fewer than 19; dorsal fin base contained more than 4 times in standard length; lateral-line scales usually more than 39 _____ 2

a (1)   Lateral-line scales fewer than 48; scales above lateral line fewer than 8; lips plicate, with papilla-like elements in *Moxostoma anisurum* _____   3

b   Lateral-line scales more than 54; scales above lateral line more than 8; lips papillose _____   4

a (2)   Dorsal fin usually with 15 or 16 rays; lateral-line scales usually fewer than 43; dorsal fin rounded at front tip and with rounded outer margin; posterior margin of lower lip forms an angle at midline, not a straight line; body scales without dark spots at base; caudal fin olive or slate-colored in life.

Moxostoma anisurum - silver redhorse

b   Dorsal fin usually with 12 or 13 rays; lateral-line scales usually more than 42; dorsal fin pointed at front tip and with a falcate (sickle shaped) outer margin; posterior margin of lower lip forms a straight line; body scales on upper side each with a dark spot at base; caudal fin reddish in life.

Moxostoma macrolepidotum- northern redhorse

a (2)   Scales around caudal peduncle more than 21, above lateral line usually more than 15, and along lateral line usually more than 79; dorsal fin usually with 9 to 11 rays; peritoneum blackish or black _____   5

b   Scales around caudal peduncle fewer than 21, above lateral line usually fewer than 15, and along lateral line usually fewer than 80; dorsal fin usually with 11 to 15 rays; peritoneum silvery or dusky _____   6

a (4)   Large notch at each corner of mouth between upper and lower lips; cleft in midline of lower lip shallow, with 3 or more rows of papillae crossing in front; edge of lower jaw with a sharp-edged cartilaginous sheath; lateral-line scales usually fewer than 90; small fleshy struts connecting inner rays of pelvic fins to body.

Catostomus platyrhynchus - mountain sucker

b   No distinct notch between upper and lower lips; cleft in midline of lower lip deep, usually no papillae crossing cleft; lower jaw without cartilaginous sheath; lateral-line scales more than 90; no fleshy struts connecting inner rays of pelvic fins to body.

Catostomus catostomus - longnose sucker

6 a (4)   Dorsal fin with 10 to 12 rays (rarely 13); scales above lateral line 9 to 11; ratio of distance between front of dorsal fin and front of pelvic fin to depth of caudal peduncle (narrowest area between dorsal fin and tail) 1.9 to 2.5 (accurate only in specimens between 2 and 10 inches standard length).

Catostomus commersoni - white sucker

6 b   Dorsal fin with 13 to 16 rays (rarely 12); scales above lateral line usually 12 to 14; ratio of distance between front of dorsal fin to front of pelvic fin to depth of caudal peduncle 2.6 to 3.4.

Catostomus macrocheilus - largescale sucker

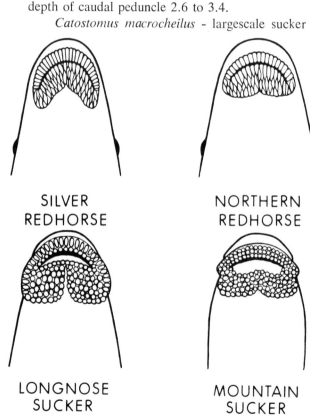

SILVER
REDHORSE

NORTHERN
REDHORSE

LONGNOSE
SUCKER

MOUNTAIN
SUCKER

Ventral view of the lips of 4 suckers showing the differences in structure used in identification.

arpiodes cyprinus (Lesueur)
arpiodes - carp-like
yprinus - carp

Quillback adult, 17 inches fork length, from the Red Deer River.

DESCRIPTION

Color tan dorsally, silvery laterally.

Body deep and strongly compressed. Head subtriangular and strongly rounded dorsally. Mouth small, horizontal, and slightly subterminal. Lips thin and weakly plicate. No small knob at tip of lower jaw (unlike other members of the genus). Anterior fontanelle (opening through skull bones between nostrils and eyes on midline of head) present throughout life (as is the posterior fontanelle). Dorsal fin highly falcate anteriorly; anterior rays elongated. Air bladder with 2 chambers. Lateral-line scales 33-42; dorsal fin rays 22-30.

Maximum length 26 inches and weight 12 pounds.

Alta: One specimen obtained from the Red Deer River, east of Red Deer near Nevis, in 1968, was 17 inches fork length and had 36 scales along the lateral line, 8 scales above the lateral line, 18 scales around the caudal peduncle, and 27 principal dorsal fin rays.

DISTRIBUTION

Alberta to southern Quebec and eastern Missouri to Virginia

Known from central and southern Alberta from the North Saskatchewan, Battle, Red Deer, lower Bow, and South Saskatchewan rivers (see map on page 179).

BIOLOGY

Over their range quillbacks occur in lakes and large rivers (both clear and turbid). In Alberta they have been recorded from sluggish and usually turbid rivers but not from lakes. Individuals are sometimes in the mouths of smaller tributaries of the North Saskatchewan (i.e., Sturgeon) and Red Deer rivers. They are bottom feeders and individuals live up to at least 10 years. Nothing is known of their spawning habits in Alberta.

HISTORICAL NOTE

First described by C. A. Lesueur in 1817 from tributaries of Chesapeake Bay as *Catostomus cyprinus*. It is the type species for the genus *Carpiodes*. First noted from Alberta by Eigenmann (1895) at Medicine Hat as *Carpiodes velifer*.

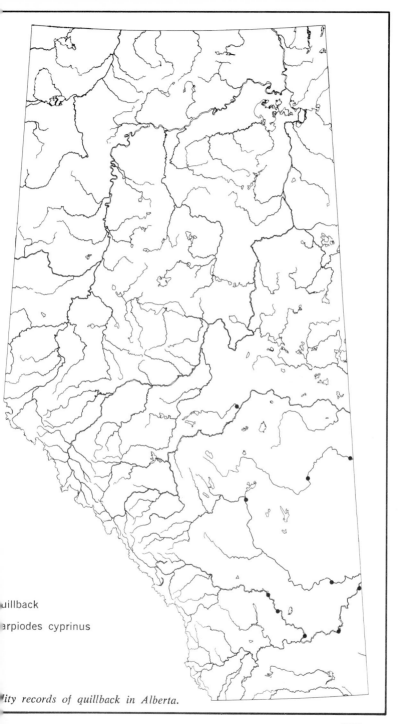

uillback

arpiodes cyprinus

ity records of quillback in Alberta.

Moxostoma anisurum (Rafinesque)
Moxo stoma - to suck, mouth
anis urum - unequal tail

Silver redhorse young, 1 inch standard length, from the North Saskatchewan River.

DESCRIPTION

Color bronzy-olive dorsally, silvery laterally and sometimes with goldish reflections. No dark spots on scales in adult. Fins clear or slate-colored. Young with 2 or 3 black lateral blotches. Peritoneum silvery, with a few black spots.

Body slightly compressed. Head conical, moderately rounded dorsally, and slightly longer than in *M. macrolepidotum*. Mouth moderate in size and subterminal. Hind margin of lower (posterior) lip forming a deeply incised angle (V-shaped, not a straight line, see page 176); lower lip relatively small and thin, plicae (elongated folded ridges) of lips broken up into papilla-like elements (small conical fleshy projections). Distal margin of dorsal fin rounded outwardly in adults, straight in young. Air bladder divided into 3 chambers. Lateral line complete and straight. Lateral-line scales 38-44 (usually 40-42); dorsal fin rays 14-18 (usually 14-16).

Maximum length 25 inches and weight 8 pounds.

180

DISTRIBUTION

Alberta to southern Quebec and Missouri to northern Alabama.

Known in Alberta only from the North Saskatchewan River at Fort Saskatchewan and the South Saskatchewan River at Medicine Hat (see map on page 182).

BIOLOGY

The silver redhorse frequents large rivers, especially pools or areas of slow gradient, and, less commonly, lakes. They usually spawn in clear water in the late spring. Maturity is reached at age 5. They are bottom feeders, consuming mainly immature insects. Young-of-the-year have been taken with northern redhorse young-of-the-year at Fort Saskatchewan. Nothing is known of the habits of the silver redhorse in Alberta.

HISTORICAL NOTE

First described by C. S. Rafinesque in 1820 from the Ohio River as *Catostomus anisurus*. It is the type species for the genus *Moxostoma*. First noted in Alberta by Henderson and Peter (1969) from nine specimens collected in 1963 at Medicine Hat. Specimens were collected later by Colin Paterson from Fort Saskatchewan, September 26, 1963 (but not identified until 1969).

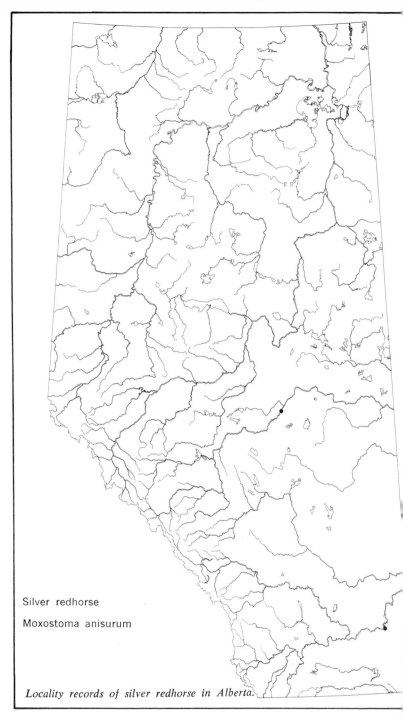

Silver redhorse

Moxostoma anisurum

Locality records of silver redhorse in Alberta.

182

NORTHERN REDHORSE
northern shorthead redhorse

Moxostoma macrolepidotum (Lesueur)
macro lepidotum - large scaled

Northern redhorse male adults, 13½ inches standard length, from the confluence of the Sturgeon and North Saskatchewan River.

DESCRIPTION

Color olivaceous dorsally, golden to silvery sheen laterally. Scales in adult with dark spots at their bases. Fins with reddish or orangish color. Young with 2 or 3 black lateral blotches. Peritoneum silvery, with a few black spots.

Body slightly compressed. Head subconical, moderately rounded dorsally, and slightly shorter than in *M. anisurum*. Mouth small and subterminal. Hind margin of lower (posterior) lip in juveniles and adults forming a straight line (inwardly curved in young—see page 176); lower lip moderate in size and thick; lips plicate (elongate folded ridges, occasionally broken into papilla-like elements posteriorly). Distal margin of dorsal fin flacate in adults, almost straight in young. Air bladder divided into 3 chambers. Lateral line complete and straight. Lateral-line scales 40-47; dorsal fin rays 11-15 (usually 12 or 13).

Maximum length 24 inches and weight 6 pounds.

183

Alta: The following meristic counts have been obtained from the North Saskatchewan River near Edmonton, including from the mouth of the Sturgeon River (6 specimens).

Scales
> Along lateral line: 44-46
> Above lateral line: 6-7
> Around caudal peduncle: 12-14

Rays
> Dorsal fin: 12-13

Gillrakers
> Total: 20-23

Maximum length noted in Alberta is 14 inches fork length from the North Saskatchewan River near Edmonton.

DISTRIBUTION

Alberta to Quebec and Oklahoma to New York.

Known from scattered localities in central and southern Alberta in North Saskatchewan, Battle, Red Deer, lower Bow, Oldman, and South Saskatchewan rivers and their immediate tributaries (see map on page 185).

BIOLOGY

The northern redhorse is found in large streams, especially near riffles or other areas of fast water, and lakes. They usually spawn in clear creeks in the spring, slightly before the silver redhorse, starting at water temperatures of about 52°F. Maturity is reached at age 3. They are bottom feeders, consuming mainly immature insects. Young-of-the-year have been taken with silver redhorse young-of-the-year at Fort Saskatchewan. Little is known of the habits of the northern redhorse in Alberta.

HISTORICAL NOTE

First described by C. A. Lesueur from the Delaware River in 1817 as *Catostomus macrolepidotus*. The occurrence of the northern redhorse in Alberta has been known for some time, certainly as early as 1951 by R. B. Miller. Specimens were taken in 1956 by M. J. Paetz from the Red Deer River near Steveville and from the mouth of the Sturgeon River near Fort Saskatchewan. Known previously from Alberta as *Moxostoma aureolum*.

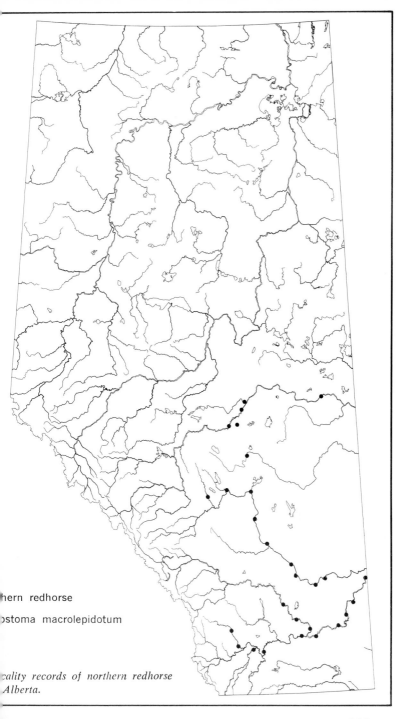

hern redhorse

ostoma macrolepidotum

cality records of northern redhorse
Alberta.

185

Catostomus catostomus (Forster)
Cato stomus - inferior mouth

Longnose sucker juveniles, 3½ inches standard length, from Peace River at Dunvegan.

DESCRIPTION

Color dark olive-slate dorsally and laterally, white ventrally. Spawning males with black band along lateral line above which is a bright red band; head and back blackish. Spawning females often develop a rosy tinge above the lateral line. Young often with 3 black lateral blotches (sometimes faint or absent in Alberta). Peritoneum dusky black to black.

Body rounded in section. Head conical and slightly rounded dorsally; snout rounded. Mouth moderate in size and distinctly subterminal (snout projecting well beyond upper lip, except in very young). Lower lips thick and covered with papillae; midline cleft deep, often with no papillae crossing in front (see page 176). Anterior fontanelle absent, posterior fontanelle (median opening in skull between frontal and parietal bones) long and relatively narrow. Air bladder with 2 chambers. Length of intestine shorter than 4 times standard length. Lateral line complete and straight. Young and juveniles with caudal peduncle deeper and body depth shallower than in largescale suckers. Lateral-line scales 91-115; scales above lateral line 16-21; scales around caudal peduncle 25-29; dorsal fin rays 9-11.

Maximum length 25 inches and weight 7 pounds.

Alta: Gillraker counts have been obtained as follows:

Total: 25-27

Maximum length noted in Alberta is 19 inches fork length from Lesser Slave Lake.

Mature longnose sucker from Sherburn Reservoir.

DISTRIBUTION

Eastern Siberia through the Northwest Territories to Nova Scotia and Idaho to New York.

Known throughout Alberta in Hay, Slave, Peace, Athabasca, Beaver, North Saskatchewan, Red Deer, Bow, Oldman, South Saskatchewan, and Milk drainages (see map on page 189).

BIOLOGY

The longnose sucker is found in rivers and lakes (most often in deep lakes). They usually spawn from April to June, shortly before white and largescale suckers. Spawning usually occurs in creeks but beach spawning is not uncommon (and is necessary in many Alberta lakes). Average size females produce about 20,000-

187

30,000 eggs. The young are frequently found in large schools along lake shores. Maturity is reached at about age 5. They are bottom feeders, consuming molluscs, crustaceans, immature insects, and worms. Longnose suckers are known to hybridize with the white and mountain sucker in the United States. The former cross suspected to occur in Alberta. Longnose suckers are frequently infected with the very large larvae of a tapeworm, *Ligula,* which occurs in the body cavity, and occasionally with "black spot" *(Neascus),* a trematode larvae, which encyst in the skin and stimulate the fish to deposit black pigment around them.

HISTORICAL NOTE

First described by J. R. Forster in 1773 from streams about Hudson Bay as *Cyprinus catostomus.* It is the type species for the genus *Catostomus.* First noted from Alberta by Eigenmann (1895) at Medicine Hat, Calgary, and Banff as *Catostomus catostomus* and additionally at Medicine Hat as *C. griseus.* It is probably the longnose sucker that Vick (1913) refers to as being near the Vermilion lakes at Banff (under the highly erroneous spelling for the white sucker, *Cutostonus Commersone).* Noted by Kendell (1924) from Rivière Coupée, near Fort Chipewyan. Bajkov (1926) described it from 4 Jasper Park lakes as a new sub-species, *C. catostomus lacustris.* As noted by Rawson and Elsey (1950), this distinction seems unwarranted.

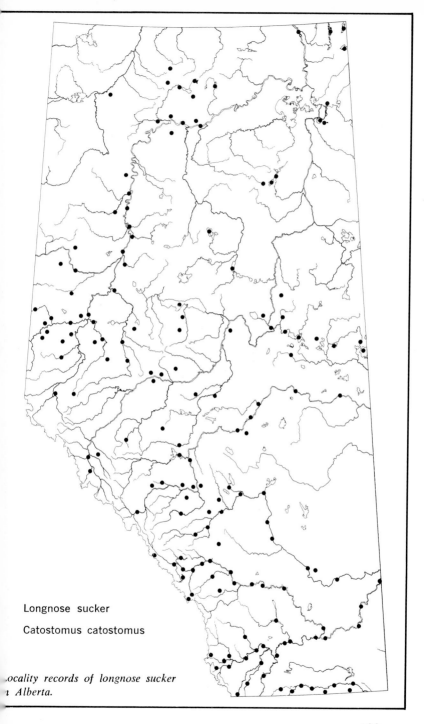

Longnose sucker

Catostomus catostomus

Locality records of longnose sucker
in Alberta.

189

Catostomus commersoni (Lacépède)
commersoni - after Philebert Commerson

White sucker juveniles, 6½ inches standard length, from Lac Ste. Anne.

DESCRIPTION

Color blackish or greyish dorsally, shading to silver laterally and ventrally. Anterior margin of pectoral and pelvic fins usually white. Spawning males with distinct black lateral band, above which is a pale olive-green band. No bright reddish band has been observed in Alberta although it has been noted for eastern specimens. Spawning females tend to resemble the immature in color. Young with 3 black lateral blotches. Peritoneum silvery to light dusky.

Body rounded in section. Head subconical and flattened (or slightly depressed medially) to slightly rounded dorsally (squarish in cross section); snout blunt. Mouth moderate in size and slightly subterminal. Lower lips thick and covered with papillae; midline cleft deep, usually with no papillae (2 rows at most) crossing in front. Anterior fontanelle absent, posterior fontanelle moderately long and wide. Air bladder with 2 chambers. Lateral line complete and straight. Young and juveniles with caudal peduncle deeper and

190

body depth shallower than in largescale suckers; ratio of distance between origin of dorsal fin and insertion of pelvic fin to depth of caudal peduncle 1.9-2.5 in individuals less than 10 inches fork length. Area in front of dorsal fin rounded. Lateral-line scales 55-85 (usually 58-68); scales above lateral line 9-11; scales around caudal peduncle 16-20; dorsal fin rays 10-13 (usually 11 or 12); gillrakers 20-27.

Maximum length 30 inches and weight 8 pounds.

Alta: Gillraker counts have been obtained as follows:

Total: 24-27

Maximum lengths noted in Alberta are 20¾ inches fork length (4¾ pounds) from Lesser Slave Lake and 21¾ inches fork length (4 pounds) from Sturgeon Lake, west of Valleyview.

White sucker from Wolf Lake (Beaver drainage).

DISTRIBUTION

British Columbia through the southern Northwest Territories to Nova Scotia and New Mexico to northern Georgia.

Known throughout Alberta in Hay, Slave, Peace, Athabasca, Beaver, North Saskatchewan, Battle, Red Deer, Bow, Oldman, South Saskatchewan, and Milk drainages (see map on page 193).

191

BIOLOGY

The white sucker is found in rivers and shallow and deep lakes. They are exceptionally tolerant to a wide diversity of environments. Spawning usually occurs from late April to June, shortly after longnose suckers, starting at water temperatures of about 50°F. Creeks (clear or turbid) are generally utilized for spawning but beach spawning in lakes is not uncommon (and is necessary in many Alberta lakes). Maturity is reached at about age 5 with a life span of up to 13 years. They are bottom feeders, consuming molluscs, immature insects, and algae. The young, after the yolk sac is absorbed, feed near the surface for a short period. In the early life stage the mouth is terminal and feeding occurs mostly on plankton. White suckers hybridize with the largescale sucker in British Columbia and with longnose and mountain suckers in the United States. The first two crosses are suspected to occur in Alberta.

HISTORICAL NOTE

The description of B.G.E.C. Lacépède in 1803 of *Cyprinus commersonnii* is probably this species. Apparently the collections of Commerson from the East Indies were confused with those of another worker. The type locality is unknown. First noted from Alberta by Eigenmann (1895) at Medicine Hat and Calgary. Noted from the Athabasca Lake area by Kendell (1924).

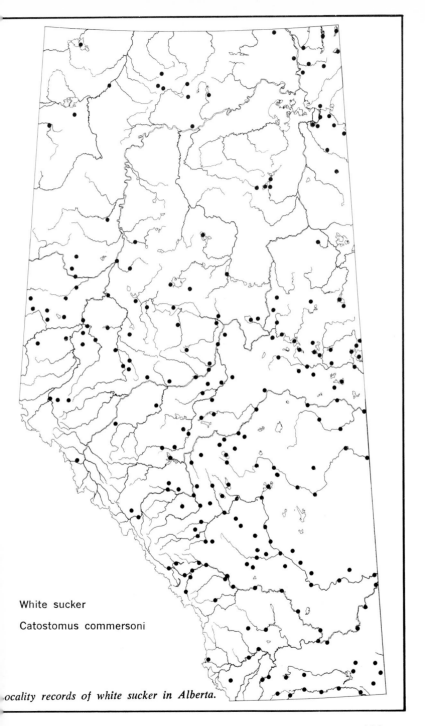

White sucker
Catostomus commersoni

Locality records of white sucker in Alberta.

Catostomus macrocheilus Girard
macro cheilus - large lip

Largescale sucker juveniles, 3½ inches standard length, from Peace River at Dunvegan.

DESCRIPTION

Color dark olive to black dorsally and laterally, white or yellowish ventrally. Anterior margin of pectoral and pelvic fins usually dark, rarely white. Spawning individuals with a golden tinge dorsally and laterally and with a black lateral band above which is an iridescent light olive-green band. A yellow stripe lies below the black band (all color differences are much more distinct in males than females). Young usually with 3 faint black lateral blotches (may be absent or moderately distinct). Peritoneum dusky silvery to light dusky black.

Body rounded to slightly compressed. Head subconical and slightly rounded dorsally; snout blunt. Mouth moderate in size and slightly subterminal. Lower lip thick and covered with papillae; midline cleft deep, usually with no papillae crossing in front. Anterior fontanelle absent, posterior fontanelle moderately long and wide. Air bladder with 2 chambers. Lateral line complete and straight. Young and juveniles with caudal peduncle narrower and body depth greater than in longnose, white, and mountain suckers; ratio of distance between origin of dorsal fin and insertion of pelvic fin to depth of caudal peduncle 2.6-3.3 in individuals over 2 inches fork length. Small ridge in front of dorsal fin. Lateral line scales 62-81; scales above lateral line 11-15; scales around caudal peduncle about 17; dorsal fin rays 12-17 (usually 13-15); gill-rakers 25-32.

Maximum length 24 inches.

DISTRIBUTION

Coastal streams from British Columbia to Oregon and Peace system of British Columbia and Alberta. Widespread in eastern British Columbia in Fraser and Columbia drainages.

Restricted in Alberta to the Peace River system. Known from Peace River at Dunvegan, Simonette River, Wapiti River, Pinto Creek and Big Mountain Creek (see map on page 196). No adults have been recorded in Alberta, only young and juveniles up to 4⅛ inches fork length.

BIOLOGY

The largescale sucker is found in rivers and deep lakes (known in Alberta only from rivers). They usually spawn in May and June, shortly after the longnose sucker. Spawning generally occurs in creeks (clear or turbid), starting at water temperatures of about 50°F. Maturity is reached at age 5. They are bottom feeders, consuming mainly molluscs, immature insects, and algae. The young feed extensively on diatoms, rotifers, and cladocerans and occur near the surface for a short period in their early life when the mouth is terminal. Largescale suckers hybridize with white suckers in British Columbia and hybrids of this cross are also suspected in Alberta from Pinto Creek and Simonette River.

HISTORICAL NOTE

First described by C. F. Girard from Astoria, Oregon, in 1856 as *Catostomus macrocheilus*. First taken in Alberta by R. B. Miller and M. J. Paetz on August 15, 1956, at Dunvegan, Peace River.

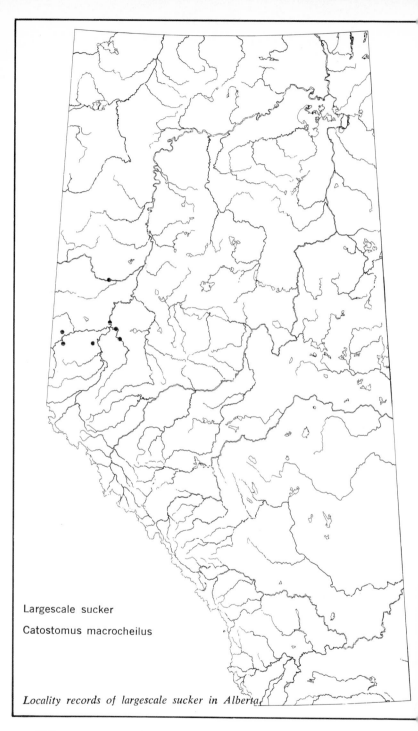

Largescale sucker

Catostomus macrocheilus

Locality records of largescale sucker in Alberta.

Catostomus platyrhynchus (Cope)
platy rhynchus - flat snout

Mountain sucker juveniles, 2½ inches standard length, from North Fork Milk River.

DESCRIPTION

Color dark greenish or dusky brownish dorsally and laterally, finely speckled with black, light yellowish ventrally. Darkish lateral band usually present from snout to base of tail. Breeding males with red or orange lateral band above the blackish band. Young with 3 black lateral blotches. Caudal interradial membranes sparsely pigmented. Peritoneum jet black or dusky (with some silver showing through).

Mature male mountain sucker from the Sheep River, Highwood drainage.

Body rounded in section. Head flattened to slightly rounded and conical. Mouth moderate in size and subterminal. Lower lip flat, thick, and broad; covered with papillae; midline cleft shallow, with 3-5 rows of papillae crossing in front. Distinct notch at each corner of mouth between upper and lower lip (see page 176). Edge of lower jaw with a cartilaginous sheath. Anterior fontanelle absent, posterior fontanelle usually reduced to a narrow slit. Membranous stays connecting inner rays of pelvic fins to body; pelvic axillary process distinct (fleshy projection with free end originating dorsal to the first pelvic rays—it is absent or indistinct in other Alberta suckers). Air bladder small, with 2 chambers. Length of intestine usually long, longer than 5 times standard length and extensively coiled. Lateral line complete but not distinct.

198

Lateral-line scales 70-100; scales above lateral line 15-20; scales around caudal peduncle about 23; dorsal fin rays 9-12 (usually 10 or 11); gillrakers 23-37.

Maximum length 8 inches.

Maximum known length in Alberta is 5 inches fork length from Threepoint Creek (N. Fork Sheep River).

DISTRIBUTION

Alberta and southwestern Saskatchewan to Utah and northwestern Nebraska; isolated populations in western United States and lower Fraser, Similkameen, and North Thompson rivers in British Columbia.

Known from Alberta in North Saskatchewan, Red Deer, Bow, Oldman, upper South Saskatchewan, and Milk drainages (see map on page 200).

BIOLOGY

The mountain sucker is most commonly found in mountain streams, often in swift waters at high altitudes (up to about 8000 feet in the United States), in both clear and turbid waters. Feeding occurs on algae and diatoms; some invertebrates are also consumed. The long intestine and cartilaginous sheath in the mouth adapt the species for eating algae in streams. They spawn in late spring and summer. Maturity is reached by age 2 and the life span of individuals is probably not longer than 4 years. Mountain suckers have been found to hybridize with longnose and white suckers in Wyoming and South Dakota.

HISTORICAL NOTE

First definitely described by E. D. Cope from Provo River, Utah, in 1874 as *Minomus platyrhynchus*. First taken in Alberta by R. B. Miller and C. Ward on August 8, 1950, from the North Fork Milk River, near Del Bonita. Formerly known from Alberta as *Pantosteus jordani*. *Pantosteus* is now considered a subgenus of the genus *Catostomus*.

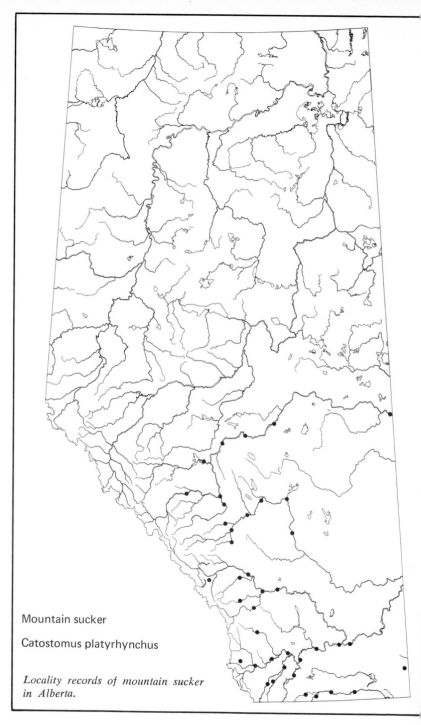

Mountain sucker

Catostomus platyrhynchus

Locality records of mountain sucker in Alberta.

FRESHWATER CATFISH FAMILY — ICTALURIDAE

Representatives of the fresh-water catfish family are confined to North and Central America. Members of other catfish families, some of which are marine, occur in South America, Africa, Asia, and parts of Europe and Australia. The greatest abundance of catfish in the family Ictaluridae occur in the United States in the Mississippi drainage. This fresh-water family contains about 30 species. Seven species occur in Canada with one in Alberta.

Individuals of some species in the United States exceed 4 feet in length and may weigh more than 100 pounds while individuals of other species seldom exceed 3 inches. Several species are important as sport fish. As a group, catfish generally feed at night on bottom-dwelling insects and snails. Spawning occurs in the spring and early summer; males guard the nest.

This family is characterized in having 8 sensory barbels on the head, 8-13 branchiostegal rays, 37-53 vertebrae, a spinous ray on the dorsal fin and on each pectoral fin, an adipose fin, and a naked skin. Members of the madtom genus *(Noturus),* of which the Alberta species is a member, have a venom gland which connects to the pectoral spines and a painful wasplike sting can be inflicted.

Noturus flavus Rafinesque

Noturus - black tail, in reference to the connection of the adipose fin with the caudal fin

flavus - yellow

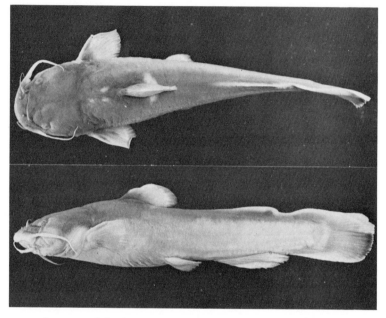

Stonecat adult, 6¼ inches standard length, from Milk River, west of Wild Horse.

DESCRIPTION

Color yellowish-brown dorsolaterally, creamy ventrally. Peritonium silvery.

Body rounded in section. Head broad and flattened dorsally; space between eyes about 5 times eye diameter; eyes very small; mouth wide (about as wide as distance between eyes and ending well in front of eye) and subterminal; 8 long barbels, 4 under the chin, 2 at the corner of the mouth (supported by the maxillae), and 2 in front of the nostrils. Teeth on upper (premaxillae) and lower jaw numerous and short; the band on the premaxillae extends backward and to the side. Gill membranes extending forward and narrowly joined to each other. Pelvic spines smooth, without serrations. Origin of dorsal fin far in front of insertion of pelvics. Lateral line faint anteriorly and straight. Adipose fin low and joined to the caudal fin by a small fleshy ridge (no posterior free end, only a notch); caudal fin somewhat rounded (straight posterior edge). Dorsal fin with 1 spine and about 6 soft rays and anal fin with 15-18 soft rays; gillrakers distinct, about 8; branchiostegal rays 9.

Maximum length 12 inches. Maximum length noted in Alberta is 9 inches fork or total length from west of Wildhorse, Milk River.

DISTRIBUTION

Alberta and southern Quebec and southward from Oklahoma to Tennessee.

Known in Alberta only from the Milk River (see map on page 204).

BIOLOGY

The stonecat is adaptable to many habitats. It is commonest over rocky bottoms in currents or riffles of large streams, both turbid and clear. It is occasionally caught by fishermen.

HISTORICAL NOTE

First described by C. S. Rafinesque in 1818 from the Ohio River as *Noturus flavus*. It is the type species for the genus. Eigenmann (1895) noted verbal reports of the species from the Medicine Hat vicinity (probably from Milk drainage) while the first specimens were recorded by Nursall and Lewin (1964), caught June 20, 1962, west of Wildhorse, in the Milk River. Willock (1968) noted additional specimens from the Milk.

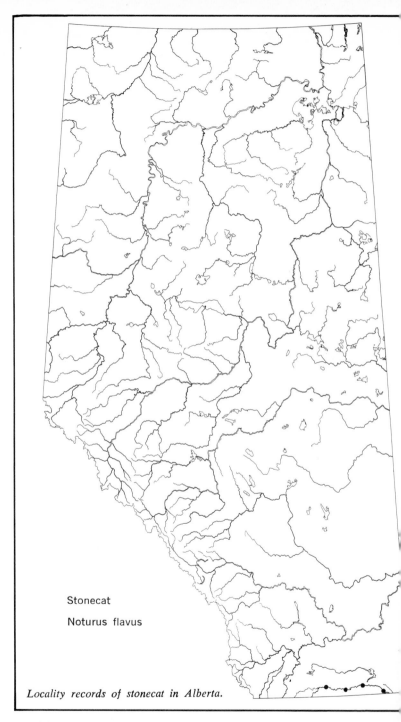

Stonecat

Noturus flavus

Locality records of stonecat in Alberta.

CODFISH FAMILY — GADIDAE

Representatives of the codfish family are found in the fresh waters of North America and Eurasia and in marine waters of North and South America, Eurasia, Africa, and New Zealand. Their greatest abundance occurs in the North Atlantic Ocean. The family contains about 58 species, only one of which is confined to fresh water. Many of the marine species constitute an important commercial group. Unlike the freshwater species, most marine forms have 3 dorsal and 2 anal fins.

The burbot is the only member of the order Gadiformes in Alberta.

BURBOT
maria
ling

Lota lota (Linnaeus)
Lota - from an old French name (Lotte)
used by the 16th century French
zoologist G. Rondelet.

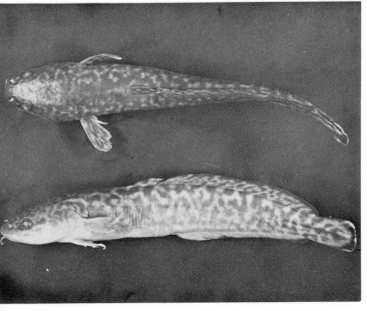

Burbot young, 5¾ inches standard length, from Wandering River.

DESCRIPTION

Color dark olive-brown dorsally with darkish markings on back, sides, and median fins (most pronounced on young). Yellow or dusky below. Peritoneum silvery with some black spots occasionally present.

Body rounded in section and very elongate. Head broad and flattened dorsally; space between eyes about 2-3½ times eye diameter; eyes moderate in size; mouth wide (wider than distance between eyes and extended as far or almost as far back as the front margin of eye) and very slightly subterminal (upper jaw only slightly produced forward beyond the lower jaw); one long median barbel under lower jaw, one short barbel at each anterior nostril; upper lip separated from snout by a complete groove. Teeth numerous, short, and in bands; on premaxillae, head of vomer, and lower jaw. Gill membranes extended forward and broadly joined to each other. Pectoral fin base almost vertical and located ½ way up body. Second pelvic fin ray elongated. Pelvics far forward, their insertion lying in front of the pectoral fin base. Body and most of head covered with very small cycloid scales (often requiring microscopic examination to see; body superficially appearing naked). Lateral line complete (but often faint) and oblique. Caudal fin strongly rounded. Scales along lateral line about 220; scales above lateral line about 23; dorsal fin rays 9-15 in the first short fin and 61-90 in the longer fin and anal rays 52-75; gillrakers about 7-10; branchiostegal rays 7 or 8, all on the ceratohyal; vertebrae about 60-64.

Maximum length about 40 inches and weight about 14 pounds. Maximum length noted for Alberta is 29½ inches fork or total length from Lesser Slave Lake.

DISTRIBUTION

Northern portions of the Northern Hemisphere. In North America from Alaska to northeastern Quebec and Oregon to Missouri.

Common throughout most of Alberta in Petitot, Hay, Slave, Peace, Athabasca, North Saskatchewan, upper Battle, upper Red Deer, upper Bow, upper Oldman, and Milk drainages (see map on page 208).

BIOLOGY

Burbot occur in the cold parts of lakes and both in large and small streams. Their main food consists of fish and aquatic insects

206

larvae but they have also been found to prey heavily on whitefish eggs. They spawn during the winter and early spring. Maturity is normally reached in their third year. Large females may contain over 1,000,000 eggs. Burbot are occasionally caught by sport fishermen but are seldom eaten. When skinned, however, it is a tasty fish. The liver is extremely high in vitamin A and D and is comparable with medicinal cod liver oil. Burbot are sometimes incorrectly referred to as catfish in Alberta.

HISTORICAL NOTE

First described by C. Linnaeus in 1758 (well known before that time, however) from Europe as *Gadus lota*. First mentioned to be in Alberta by Eigenmann (1895) on reports from Calgary. Whitehouse (1919) noted it from Sylvan Lake, Red Deer River, and Peace River as *Lota maculosa*.

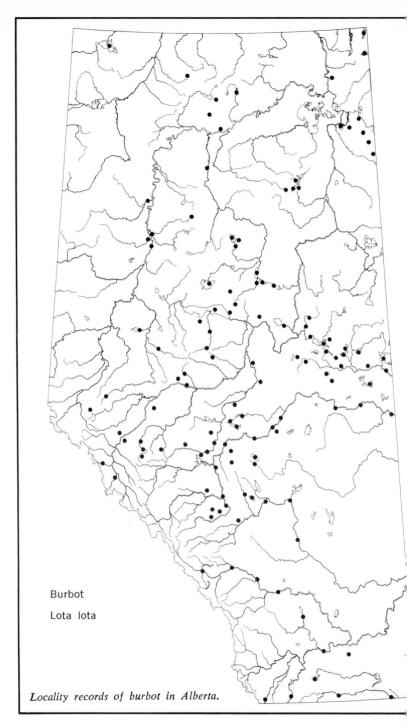

Burbot

Lota lota

Locality records of burbot in Alberta.

TROUT-PERCH FAMILY — PERCOPSIDAE

Representatives of the trout-perch family are confined to the fresh waters of North America. Two species are recognized, the sand roller *(Percopsis transmontana* — in the Columbia River System of the United States) and the trout-perch. Both are small fish, seldom exceeding 5 inches in length.

Members of this family possess some characters of the trout-like fish as well as some characters of the perch-like fish. The closest relative of the family is the pirate perch *(Aphredoderus sayanus),* a fresh water fish in eastern United States.

The trout-perch is the only member of the order Percopsiformes in Alberta.

TROUT-PERCH

Percopsis omiscomaycus (Walbaum)
Perc opsis - perch appearance
omisco maycus - a vernacular name

Trout-perch adults, 2 inches standard length, from Simonette River.

DESCRIPTION

Color pale yellow and silvery, somewhat transluscent in life, with 8-13 dark blotches along lateral line. Small blotches above and sometimes below lateral line. Peritoneum silvery with a few black spots.

Body slightly compressed, somewhat triangular in section. Head conical and slightly rounded dorsally; space between eyes about 1⅓ times eye diameter; eyes moderate in size; mouth moderate in size (not extended back nearly as far as front margin of eye) and slightly subterminal; upper lip not separated from snout by a continuous groove (narrow frenum present); front margin of snout rounded. Extremely small teeth in bands confined to premaxillae and lower jaw. Gill membranes extended forward and very narrowly joined, if at all, to each other and to the isthmus. Pectoral fin base oblique (almost at a 45° angle) and on lower half of body. Origin of dorsal fin over or slightly ahead of insertion of pelvic fins; posterior third or so of pectoral fin extended past pelvic fin insertion; origin of adipose fin behind basal end of anal fin. Scales cycloid anteriorly and ctenoid posteriorly. Lateral line complete and straight. Caudal fin deeply forked. Lateral-line scales 44-52; dorsal fin usually with 2 short weak spines and 9 or 10 soft rays; anal fin usually with 1 short weak spine and 6 or 7 soft rays; pelvic fin with 1 small weak spine-like ray and 7 or 8 soft rays; branchiostegal rays usually 6 (1 epihyal and 5 ceratohyal); vertebrae usually 33 or 34.

Maximum length about 6 inches.

Alta: Meristic counts have been obtained as follows from Peace River drainage (6 specimens).

Scales

Along lateral line: 46-52
Above lateral line: 7-8
Around caudal peduncle: 17-20

Gillrakers

Upper arch: 1-3; lower arch: 7-8; total 8-11, short and stumpy.

Maximum length noted for Alberta is 3¼ inches fork length from the Oldman River.

DISTRIBUTION

Alaska and northeastern British Columbia (lower Peace and Liard drainages) to Quebec and from Kansas to West Virginia.

Common in Alberta in Hay, Slave, Peace, Athabasca, Beaver, North Saskatchewan, Battle, Red Deer, Bow, Oldman, and South Saskatchewan drainages (see map on page 212).

BIOLOGY

Trout-perch occur in deep lakes and slow rivers. Inshore movements at night are commonly noted in lakes. Their man food consists of aquatic insects and crustaceans. Spawning occurs during spring and summer in small streams and along beaches of lakes. Some spawning occurs in individuals as young as age 1. They live as long as 4 years. In Manitoba, individuals have been found to harbor the larval stage of the tapeworm *Triaenophorus stizoste-ion,* which occurs in walleye in the adult stage. Trout-perch are a common forage fish.

HISTORICAL NOTE

First described by J. J. Walbaum (through T. Pennant) in 1792 from specimens collected in the Hudson Bay area as *Salmo miscomaycus* (originally not in binomial form, however; first description of species in 1784). First reported in Alberta by Eigenmann (1895) at Medicine Hat as *Percopsis guttatus.* No other early reports exist.

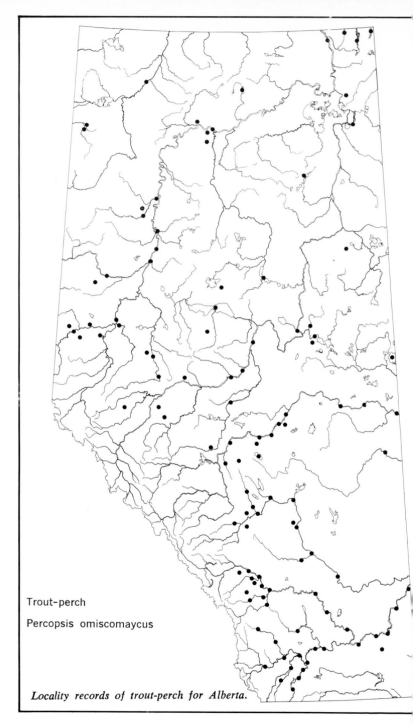

Trout–perch

Percopsis omiscomaycus

Locality records of trout-perch for Alberta.

STICKLEBACK FAMILY — GASTEROSTEIDAE

Representatives of the stickleback family occur in fresh water and along coastlines in the Northern Hemisphere. Some coastal members are anadromous, spawning in fresh water but spending much of their life in the ocean, while others are fully marine. The family contains 5 genera and about 8 well-defined species. Six species occur in Canada with 2 in Alberta.

Sticklebacks are small fish that spawn in the spring and early summer. They have been extensively studied by zoologists, especially the threespine stickleback *(Gasterosteus aculeatus)*. In particular, their nest building activity for reproduction has received much attention. Males build a nest in which the female lays eggs. The male then guards the nest, fans the eggs with his pectoral fins, and cares for the young for a short while after they hatch.

All sticklebacks have 3 branchiostegal rays (1 epihyal and 2 ceratohyal), a series of isolated spines preceding the soft dorsal fin, paired pelvic spines (see description of *Culaea* and *Pungitius* for exceptions), and a single spine in the anal fin.

Sticklebacks are closely related to the small coastal Pacific family of tubesnouts, Aulorhynchidae. With this family, sticklebacks are usually placed in the order of Gasterosteiformes.

KEY TO THE 2 SPECIES

a   Isolated dorsal spines usually 5 or 6, in a straight line; caudal peduncle deeper than wide, without a lateral keel; caudal fin posterior margin rounded.
Culaea inconstans - brook stickleback

b   Isolated dorsal spines 7 to 11, divergent from the midline; caudal peduncle wider than deep, with a lateral keel; caudal fin posterior margin lunate (concave).
Pungitius pungitius - ninespine stickleback

Culaea inconstans (Kirtland)
Culaea - a name coined in 1950
inconstans - variable (referring to the
number of spines and rays).

Brook stickleback adults, 2 inches standard length, from Sousa Creek, Hay drainage.

DESCRIPTION

Color dark olive with pale mottling laterally. Dorsal and anal fin membranes with well-developed melanophores. Breeding males black. Peritoneum silvery with numerous black spots.

Body moderately compressed. Head conical and flattened dorsally; distance between the eyes about equal to diameter of eyes; eyes large; mouth moderate in size (tip of maxilla not quite extended to anterior margin of eye), slightly supraterminal (lower lip projecting forward past upper lip), and moderately oblique. Continuous groove separating upper lip from snout. Teeth small, confined to upper and lower jaws. Gill membranes extended forward and joined to each other. Opercular opening not extended distinctly above upper edge of pectoral fin. Pectoral fin base almost vertical, mostly on lower half of body. Insertion of pelvic spines under front half of pectoral fin; the majority or a high proportion of individuals lack the pelvic skeleton in several populations in Alberta (e.g., in Redwater River and Astotin and Muir

214

kes near Edmonton and Pine Lake in Wood Buffalo National
ark) and Saskatchewan. Lateral line complete and with a row
f 30-36 small circular bony scutes (visible only when stained).
audal peduncle deeper than it is wide. Caudal fin slightly rounded
convex). Series of 4-7 (usually 5 or 6) non-divergent isolated
ines in front of the soft dorsal fin. Dorsal fin soft rays 8-13 and
nal fin with 1 short spine and 7-12 soft rays. Gillrakers 10-15.

Maximum length 3½ inches fork length (from Astotin Lake,
lk Island National Park, Alberta).

DISTRIBUTION

Lower Peace system of British Columbia to New Brunswick
nd Nebraska to Maine; northeastern New Mexico.

Widespread in Alberta from Hay, Slave, Peace, Athabasca,
Iorth Saskatchewan, Beaver, Red Deer, Bow, Oldman, South
askatchewan and Milk drainages (see map on page 216). Recent
ollecting has found it not to be uncommon in Slave drainage,
est of Fort Smith.

BIOLOGY

Brook sticklebacks occur in small clear streams, bogs, beaver
ams, and lakes. It is the most abundant fish in many small lakes
nd ponds and is frequently associated with the fathead minnow.
ndividuals have a high tolerance to low oxygen and they some-
mes occur in areas where other fish could not survive. Tornado -
ain storms in Alberta have been known to deposit this fish in
arge numbers in farmers fields. Brook sticklebacks feed primarily
n small aquatic insects and crustaceans. Adults occur close to or
ithin aquatic vegetation and tend to be highly territorial. Young
nd adults in Alberta have been observed in schools. Spawning
akes place in late spring and early summer. The male builds a
est of aquatic material about 1½ inches in diameter which is
eld together by a thread-like substance secreted from the kidney.
'he nest is built on rooted aquatic plants or submerged tree
ranches and is guarded vigorously by the male. Nests can be
asily observed along the shoreline of many Alberta lakes in June.
Iany populations are heavily infected with larval tapeworm of
ne genus *Schistocephalus* in the body cavity which may account
or more than ⅓ of the fish's weight.

HISTORICAL NOTE

First described by J. P. Kirtland in 1841 from Trumbull
County, Ohio, as *Gasterosteus inconstans*. First reported in Alberta
y Eigenmann (1895) at Calgary as *Eucalia inconstans*.

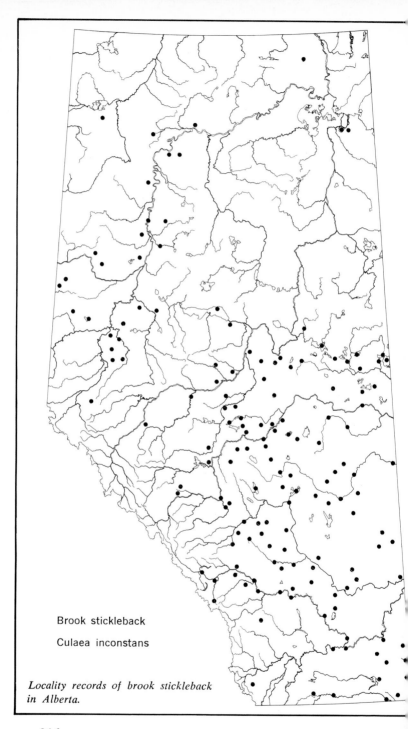

Brook stickleback

Culaea inconstans

Locality records of brook stickleback in Alberta.

ungitius pungitius (Linnaeus)
ungitius - pricking

Ninespine stickleback adults, 2 inches standard length, from Pine Lake, Wood Buffalo National Park.

ESCRIPTION

Color pale green or grey dorsally, silvery with darkish bars terally, silvery ventrally. Dorsal and anal fin membranes with w or no melanophores. Breeding males with black breast and hite pelvic fin membranes. Peritoneum silvery with few to any black spots.

Body moderately compressed. Head conical and flattened orsally; distance between the eyes about equal to eye diameter; yes large; mouth moderate in size (tip of maxilla not quite xtended to anterior margin of eye), slightly supraterminal (lower p projecting forward past lower lip), and moderately oblique. ontinuous groove separating upper lip from snout. Teeth small, onfined to upper and lower jaws. Gill membranes extended forward and joined to each other. Opercular opening extended distnctly above upper edge of pectoral fin. Pectoral fin base almost ertical, mostly on lower half of body. Insertion of pelvic spines nder front half of pectoral fin; about ¼ of the individuals lack

217

all or most of the pelvic skeleton in Pine Lake, Wood Buffalo National Park. Lateral line complete and with 6-16 bony scutes on the caudal peduncle, a few scutes are occasionally present behind the pectoral skeleton. Caudal peduncle wider than it is deep. Caudal fin somewhat lunate (concave). Series of 7-11 divergent isolated dorsal spines in front of the soft dorsal fin (extremes of 6-10 occur in Pine Lake but most have 8 or 9 spines). Dorsal fin soft rays 9-11 and anal fin with 1 spine and 7-10 soft rays. Gillrakers 11-15.

Maximum length 3 inches.

Maximum length observed for Alberta is 2½ inches fork length from Pine Lake, Wood Buffalo National Park.

DISTRIBUTION

Circumpolar in the Northern Hemisphere from tidal and inland waters. Ranges in North America along the northern coastline from the Aleutian Islands to New Jersey; penetrates inland from Fort Nelson, British Columbia, to western Quebec and extends south to Minnesota and Indiana.

Known in Alberta from a few localities in Petitot, Hay, Slave, Peace, Athabasca, and Beaver drainages (see map on page 219).

BIOLOGY

Ninespine sticklebacks occur in streams, lakes, and coastal marine water. In Alberta, this species occurs only in deep cold lakes. They feed predominantly on small aquatic insects and crustaceans. Adults do not have as strong an affinity for rooted aquatics as does the brook stickleback, and they tend to school in open water (often in deeper zones).

HISTORICAL NOTE

First described by C. Linnaeus in 1758 (well-known before this time, however) from Europe as *Gasterosteus pungitius*. First collected in Alberta by R. B. Miller and M. J. Paetz in Cold Lake on September 2, 1952. Some workers incorrectly recognize the generic name *Pygosteus* as having priority over *Pungitius*.

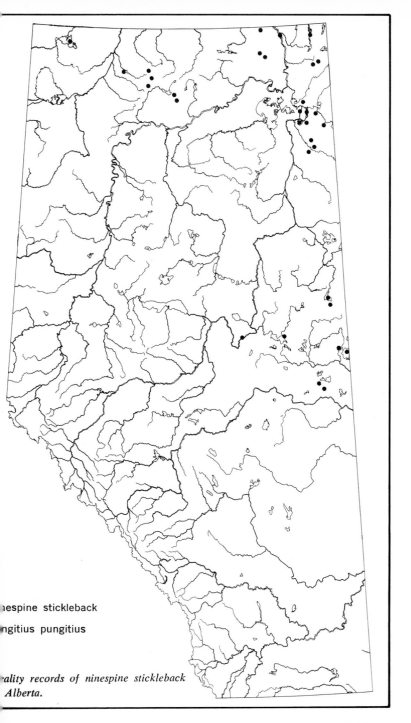

nespine stickleback

ngitius pungitius

ality records of ninespine stickleback
Alberta.

PERCH FAMILY — PERCIDAE

Representatives of the perch family occur in fresh water throughout most of the Northern Hemisphere. They are not native west of the Rocky Mountains in North America. Small bottom-dwelling forms, called darters, make up the vast majority of the species in the family. Their greatest abundance is in the eastern half of the United States. The family contains about 110 species. Fourteen species occur in Canada with 4 in Alberta.

Members of the perch family have 5-8 branchiostegal rays (usually 2 epihyal and 5 ceratohyal), 31-50 vertebrae, two separate dorsal fins (one spinous, one soft rayed), pelvic fins each with 1 spine and 5 branched rays, anal fin with 1 or 2 spines, and 2 nostrils on either side of the head.

Perch are placed in the largest and most diversified of all fish orders, the Perciformes, which comprises numerous families of marine fish. They are close relatives of the sea basses (Serranidae) and sunfish (Centrarchidae).

KEY TO THE 4 SPECIES

Note: One species (Johnny Darter) of doubtful occurrence in Alberta, diagnosed in Appendix I, not in key.

1 a   First dorsal fin with 8-10 spines; posterior end of upper jaw usually not extended past front of eye; preopercle with smooth edge; caudal fin posterior margin rounded; premaxillaries non-protractile.
Etheostoma exile - Iowa darter

1 b   First dorsal fin with 12-15 spines; posterior end of upper jaw extended well past front of eye; preopercle with strongly serrated (rough) edge; caudal fin forked; premaxillaries protractile _____ 2

2 a (1)   Teeth small and relatively uniform in size; pelvic fins so close together that the inner edges of their bases almost touch; and anal fin with 6 to 8 soft rays.
Perca flavescens - yellow perch

2 b   Several large teeth present, together with relatively short ones; distance between pelvic fins almost equal to the width of the base of either fin; anal fin with 12 to 14 soft rays _____ 3

3 a (2) First dorsal fin with oblique rows of round, black spots (not evident in young under 6 inches); first dorsal fin without prominent black blotch on posterior end; second dorsal fin with 17 to 20 rays; pyloric caeca 3 to 9 (useful in fish as short as 1 inch), the longest caeca much shorter than length of stomach; lower lobe of caudal fin without white tip.

Stizostedion canadense - sauger

3 b First dorsal fin with only obscure mottlings; first dorsal fin with prominent black blotch on posterior end (not always prominent on young under 6 inches); second dorsal fin with 19 to 23 rays; pyloric caeca 3, each about as long as stomach; lower lobe of caudal fin with white tip.

Stizostedion vitreum vitreum - walleye

IOWA DARTER

Etheostoma exile (Girard)

Etheo stoma - etymology uncertain, stated by author of type species to mean various mouths

exile - slim

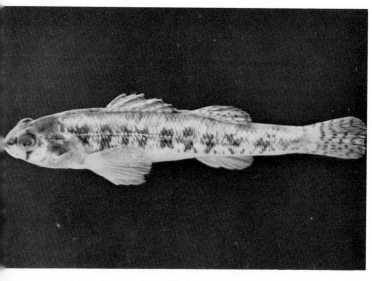

Iowa darter adult, 1½ inches standard length, from Red Creek, Milk drainage.

DESCRIPTION

Color pale olivaceous dorsally, about 8 dark saddle bands laterally. Breeding males vividly colored with 9-12 dark blue blotches on side alternating with brick red blotches. Lower sides orange-yellow. Spinous dorsal fin with blue and orange markings. Peritoneum silvery with numerous black spots.

Body moderately compressed and slender. Head subconical and flattened dorsally; distance between the eyes about equal to diameter of eyes; eyes large; mouth moderate in size (tip of maxilla extended past front margin of eye), very slightly subterminal, and horizontal to slightly oblique; upper lip not separated from snout by a continuous groove (i.e., frenum present); front margin of snout rounded. Cheeks fully scaled. Teeth very small, in bands confined to upper and lower jaws. Gills membranes extending forward and narrowly joined to each other (nearly separate). Pectoral fin base strongly oblique (sloping forwards at top) to almost vertical, mostly on lower half of body. Distance between inner rays of pelvic fins less than width of base of either fin. Lateral line complete (fewer than 35 pores and ending before or under the second dorsal fin). Caudal fin slightly rounded (convex). Lateral-line scales (along normal position) 50-65. First dorsal fin usually with 8-10 spines and second dorsal fin with 10-12 soft rays; anal fin with 2 spines (the first larger than the second) and 7 or 8 soft rays.

Maximum length 2½ inches.

Alta: Meristic counts have been obtained from Wabamun Lake as follows:

Gillrakers:
Upper arch: 1-3;
lower arch: 5-7;
total: 7-10

Pyloric caeca: 3-4

Maximum length observed for Alberta is 2⅜ inches fork length from Cold Lake.

DISTRIBUTION

Alberta to Quebec and Colorado to Ohio.

Known in Alberta from Slave (Pine Lake only), Peace, Athabasca, Beaver, North Saskatchewan, upper Battle, upper Red Deer, Bow, and Milk drainages (see map on page 224).

BIOLOGY

The Iowa darter occurs in lakes and clear slow streams, particularly in shallow water around aquatic vegetation. They spend most of their time on the bottom and feed primarily on aquatic insects. Spawning occurs in the spring; eggs are laid on stones, often in crevices.

HISTORICAL NOTE

First described by C. F. Girard in 1859 from a tributary of the upper Missouri River as *Boleichthys exilis*. First noted in Alberta by Miller and Macdonald (1949) from Battle Creek, Cypress Hills, and Beauvais Lake from specimens collected August, 1947 and July, 1949, respectively, and from a collection made in Muriel Lake by R. B. Miller in July, 1948. Known previously in Alberta as *Poecilichthys exilis*.

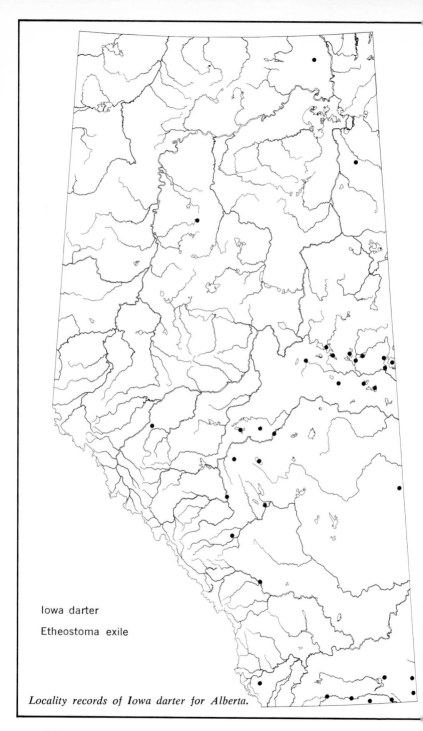

Iowa darter

Etheostoma exile

Locality records of Iowa darter for Alberta.

Perca flavescens (Mitchill)
Perca — the ancient name for the
    European perch, meaning dusky
flavescens — yellowish

Yellow perch juveniles.

DESCRIPTION

Color greenish-olive or golden yellow dorsally, golden yellow laterally with 6-9 broad dark vertical bands, and white ventrally. Darkish blotch on hind end of spinous dorsal. Peritoneum silvery with few black spots.

Body moderately compressed. Head conical and rounded dorsally; distance between eyes about 1¼ times eye diameter; eyes large; mouth moderate in size (tip of maxilla extended past front margin of eye), terminal, and slightly oblique. Continuous groove separating upper lip from snout; front margin of snout rounded. Cheeks fully scaled. Opercles with a sharp spine. Teeth small (no canines), in bands on upper jaw, vomer, palatines, and lower jaw. Pseudobranch rudimentary. Gill membranes extended forward and not joined to each other or to isthmus. Pectoral fin base strongly oblique (sloping forwards at top) to

225

almost vertical; on lower half of body. Distance between inner rays of pelvic fins less than width of base of either fin. Ctenoid scales covering body. Lateral line arched upward and on dorsal half of body, curving down to midline on the caudal peduncle (generally following the dorsal contour), usually ending at base of caudal fin. Caudal fin moderately forked. Lateral-line scales 54-60. First dorsal fin with 12-14 spines, second dorsal fin with 1 or 2 spines and 12-14 soft rays; anal fin with 2 strong spines and 6-8 soft rays. Larvae have about 16-21 myomeres between the anus and caudal fin.

Maximum length 13 inches and maximum weight 1⅓ pounds.

Alta: Meristic counts have been obtained from Lac Ste. Anne as follows: Gillrakers. Upper arch: 4-7; lower arch: 12-16; total: 17-22

Pyloric caeca: 3

Maximum lengths noted for Alberta are 11½ inches fork length from Lac Ste. Anne, 12½ inches fork length (1¼ pounds) from Sturgeon and Beaver lakes, and 15 inches fork length (2¼ pounds) from Tucker Lake. Stunting is common in Alberta and in some lakes few perch exceed 6 inches in length.

Yellow perch showing characteristic color.

DISTRIBUTION

The yellow perch occurs from Alberta to Nova Scotia and northern Missouri to western Pennsylvania to South Carolina. It has been introduced outside this range (e.g., Okanagan and Kootenay drainages in British Columbia). A close relative, *Perca fluviatilus* Linnaeus, occurs in Europe and Asia.

Known in Alberta from Peace, Slave, Athabasca, Beaver, North Saskatchewan, upper Battle, Red Deer, Bow, and Oldman drainages (see map on page 229).

BIOLOGY

The yellow perch is common in lakes, ponds, and large slow-moving streams. They usually occur in loose schools. Nursall and Pinsent (1969) have noted young perch to swim in schools with spottail shiners of similar size in Beaver Lake. Older perch, as well as other predators, swam below these schools, occasionally feeding on shiners. In general, perch feed predominately on plankton during their first year and later on aquatic insects, crustaceans, snails, and, to a limited extent, small fish. Sexual maturity is usually reached in the 3rd year with a life span seldom exceeding 7 years. They spawn in the spring, usually after the walleye. Eggs are laid in long ribbon-like gelatinous bands. Perch are a popular sport fish in some areas at all seasons of the year but they are of limited commercial value in Alberta. The role of perch as a forage fish for larger game species is very important.

Larvae of the large tapeworm *Ligula intestinalis* often occur in the body cavity of perch. They are also susceptible to a trematode larvae of the genus *Neascus,* which cause black-spotted cysts in the skin; *Tetracotyle,* another trematode larvae which resemble tiny sand grains in the flesh; and the larvae of *Triaenophorus nodulosus,* which produce cysts in the liver. On rare occasions the flesh of very large perch may contain the larvae of *Diphyllobothrium latum,* which can infect humans.

ANGLING

Yellow perch are probably our commonest game fish in terms of numbers of fish caught and total angling time spent. The ease with which they are caught as well as their general abundance and excellent table qualities may account for this. Most perch fishing takes the form of still-fishing from small boats using casting or spinning tackle and small baited hooks. Earthworms and leeches are most frequently used as baits although bacon rind and salmon eggs are also popular. Perch are slowly gaining some recognition by fly fishermen. An assortment of wet flies may be used when exploring this method.

HISTORICAL NOTE

The first acceptable description of the yellow perch was by S. L. Mitchill in 1814 from near New York City as *Morone flavescens*. Its conspecificity with the European yellow perch is open to question, and some workers have proposed the designation *Perca fluviatilus flavescens* for the American yellow perch. First noted in Alberta by Whitehouse (1919) from Pine and Sylvan lakes near Red Deer.

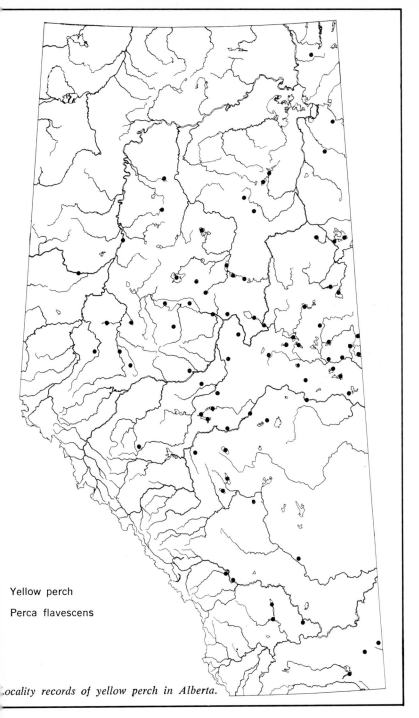

Yellow perch

Perca flavescens

Locality records of yellow perch in Alberta.

Stizostedion canadense (Smith)
Stizo stedion — to prick, a little breast
(sharp pointed throat)
canadense — of Canada

Adult sauger

DESCRIPTION

Color golden olive dorsally, somewhat silver-yellow laterally, white ventrally. Usually 3 or 4 dusky vertical bars on body, 2 or 3 oblique rows of dusky half-moon spots on spinous dorsal fin (except in very young). Black spot at base of pectoral fin, no white tinge on anterior tip of anal fin or on lower lobe of caudal fin. Peritoneum silvery with few black spots.

Body somewhat rounded in section (moderately compressed in young). Head conical and flattened dorsally, distance between the eyes about 1-1½ times eye diameter; eyes large; mouth long (tip of maxilla extended to or past center of eye), terminal (upper jaw slightly produced in young fish), and slightly oblique. Continuous groove separating upper lip from snout; front margin of snout rounded. Most of cheeks covered with ctenoid scales. Opercle with a sharp spine. Teeth on upper and lower jaws, palatines, and head of vomer; sharp long canine-like teeth on jaws and palatines, present on young as small as 1 inch. Pseudo-branch well developed. Gill membranes extended forward and not joined to each other or to isthmus. Pectoral fin base strongly oblique (sloping forward at top) and on lower half of body. Pelvic fin insertion under front third of pectoral fin. Distance between inner rays of pelvic fins about equal to width of base of either fin. Ctenoid scales covering body. Lateral line almost straight, beginning on upper half of body and at center on caudal peduncle, extended well onto the caudal fin. Caudal fin moderately forked. Lateral-line scales about 80-90. First dorsal fin with 10-14 spines, second dorsal fin with 1 weak spine and 17-22 soft rays (usually 18 or 19); anal fin with 2 weak spines and 11-13 soft rays. Pyloric caeca 3-9, each shorter than stomach length.

Maximum length 30 inches and maximum weight 8 pounds.

Alta: Gillraker counts have been obtained from 1 specimen from Whitemud Creek as follows: upper arch 6 and lower arch 15.

The maximum length noted in Alberta is 13½ inches fork length from Whitemud Creek.

DISTRIBUTION

Alberta to southern Quebec and eastern Texas to West Virgina.

Known in Alberta from North Saskatchewan, Red Deer, Bow, St. Mary, and Milk rivers (or at the mouth of a smaller tributary — see map on page 233).

BIOLOGY

Sauger occur in both lakes and rivers; present in Alberta, however, only in rivers. They appear to be tolerant of silty waters. Feeding occurs mostly on bottom – dwelling fishes and aquatic insects. They spawn in the spring, starting at a water temperature of about 43°F. The diameter of ripe sauger eggs (1.0-1.5 mm) has been reported to be much smaller than ripe walleye eggs. In Alberta, due to its rarity, the sauger is not a sport or commercial fish of any value. Sauger hybridize with walleye in the eastern United States.

ANGLING

Sauger have not attained a notable status in the province's sport fishery. They do, however, provide some angling in the larger silty rivers of central and southern Alberta. The angling methods suggested for walleyes are also used for sauger. In fact, most fishermen are unfamiliar with the differences between the two species, and class the sauger in their catch as walleyes. Casting with spoons or spinners using a slow retrieve in the backwaters of rivers or near the mouths of tributaries will frequently produce sauger. The Milk River and the lower reaches of the Red Deer River are among the better sauger waters in the province.

HISTORICAL NOTE

First described by C. H. Smith in 1836 from the Great Lakes region of Canada as *Lucioperca canadensis*. First collected in Alberta by G. F. Sternberg in 1915 from the Red Deer River and 1916 at Morrin in the Red Deer drainage (McAllister, 1962). Whitehouse (1919) speculated upon their occurrence in Alberta while Paetz (1958) was the first to report their presence in the province from the Red Deer and Milk rivers.

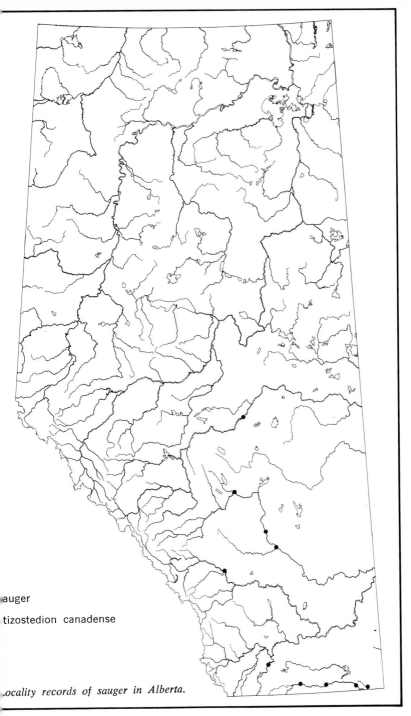

Sauger

Stizostedion canadense

Locality records of sauger in Alberta.

233

Stizostedion vitreum vitreum (Mitchill)
vitreum — glassy (pertaining to the eye)

*Walleye young, 2¾ inches standard length
from Hay River, N.W.T.*

DESCRIPTION

Color yellow-olive dorsally, brassy silvery laterally with numerous yellowish spots, white ventrally. Usually 6-8 indistinct oblong dusky vertical bars on body, large dusky blotch near hind end of spinous dorsal fin (except in very young), no definite spots in rows. Black spot at base of pectoral fin, white tinge on anterior tip of anal fin and lower lobe of caudal fin. Peritoneum silvery with few black spots.

Body somewhat rounded in section (moderately compressed in young). Head conical and flattened dorsally, distance between the eyes about ¾-1 times eye diameter; eyes large; mouth large (tip of maxilla extended past center of eye), terminal (upper jaw slightly produced in young fish), and slightly oblique. Continuous groove separating upper lip from snout; front margin of snout rounded. Cheeks scaleless or with only a few ctenoid scales. Opercle with a sharp spine. Teeth on upper and lower jaws, palatines, and head of vomer; sharp long canine-like teeth on jaws and palatines, present on young as small as 1 inch. Pseudo-branch well developed. Gill membranes extended forward and not joined to each other or to isthmus. Pectoral fin base strongly oblique (sloping forward at top) and on lower half of body. Pelvic fin insertion under front third of pectoral fin. Distance between inner rays of pelvic fins about equal to width of base of either fin. Ctenoid scales covering body. Larvae with about 22-29 myomeres between the anus and caudal fin. Lateral line almost straight, beginning on upper half of body, curving down to midline posteriorly and extended well onto the caudal fin. Caudal fin moderately forked. Lateral-line scales about 80-90. First dorsal fin with 10-14 spines, second dorsal fin with 1 weak spine and 19-23 soft rays; anal fin with 2 weak spines and 12 or 13 soft rays. Pyloric caeca 3, each about as long as the stomach.

Maximum length 36 inches and maximum weight about 25 pounds.

Alta: Gillraker counts have been obtained from 5 specimens from Lac Ste. Anne as follows: upper arch: 6-8; lower arch: 7-14; total: 16-21.

The maximum length noted in Alberta is 28 inches fork length from the Medicine River west of Innisfail.

Adult walleye

DISTRIBUTION

Northeastern British Columbia to Quebec and Nebraska to northern Georgia. Introduced outside this range.

Known in Alberta from Petitot, Hay, Slave, Peace, Athabasca, Beaver, North Saskatchewan, lower Battle, lower Red Deer, lower Bow, and South Saskatchewan drainages (see map on page 238).

BIOLOGY

Walleye occur in both lakes and rivers; present in Alberta, however, predominantly in lakes. They feed mostly on fish and aquatic invertebrates. Spawning occurs in streams or on lake bottoms in early spring near temperatures of about 40°F, usually before suckers and perch. Individuals may live to be at least 13 years old. They are important in the sport and commercial fishery and have an excellent tasting white flesh. Walleye are unfortunately called pickerel by most Albertan fisherman (the true pickerel is a member of the pike family). Walleye are known to hybridize with sauger in eastern United States.

At least three types of tapeworms, including *Triaenophorus stizostedionis* obtained from eating infected trout-perch, occur as adults in the walleye intestine. They are also host to a variety of other parasites, including the larvae of the broad tapeworm, *Diphyllobothrium* (= *Dibothriocephalus*) *latum* which was studied by Anthony (1967) in Iosegun Lake. These larvae, which are found in the flesh, are the only fish parasites in Alberta known to infect humans (where they occur in the adult form in the small intestine). Proper cooking, of course, eliminates all danger.

ANGLING

Walleye are probably more highly prized by fisherman for their eating qualities than for their sporting qualities. They are, however, a good game fish. They are taken most frequently on casting or spinning tackle using artificial lures such as feathered or hair jigs, spoons, and spinners. During the winter, still-fishing with bait or jigs fished with an up and down motion is often productive. The preferred fishing time for walleye is in the late afternoon or evening when the light is fading. They are frequently taken along rocky or sandy shoals of lakes during the spring and summer, although in late fall and early winter they are

236

frequently found in deeper water. In the more turbid streams of the province, still-fishing with bait is the commonly accepted method of angling for this species.

HISTORICAL NOTE

First described by S. L. Mitchill in 1818 from Cayuga Lake, New York, as *Perca vitrea*. First noted in Alberta by Whitehouse (1919) from various localities along the Red Deer River. Kendall (1924) noted it from Lake Athabasca.

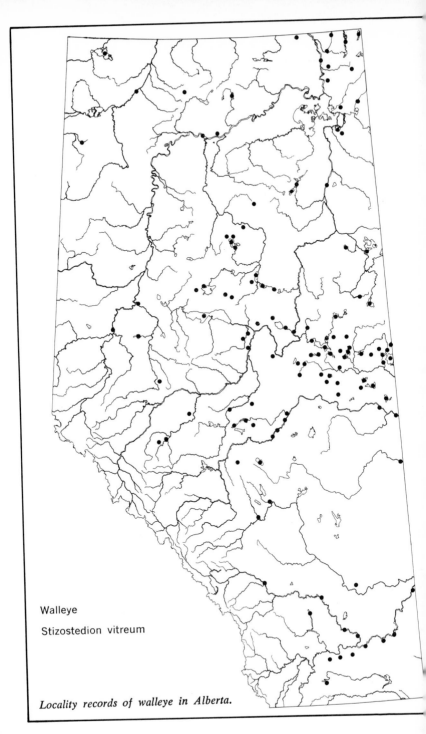

Walleye

Stizostedion vitreum

Locality records of walleye in Alberta.

SCULPIN FAMILY — COTTIDAE

Representatives of the sculpin family occur in the oceans and fresh waters throughout most of the Northern Hemisphere. In addition, two marine species have been found near New Zealand. Most species are marine and their greatest diversity is along the North Pacific coastline. The large freshwater genus, *Cottus,* is found throughout much of the Northern Hemisphere. This family contains about 85 marine and freshwater species in North America. Many more occur in Eurasia, especially in Japan and Lake Baikal. Seven species occur in fresh water in Canada with 3 in Alberta.

Most sculpins are small fish but a few marine species reach lengths of over 2 feet. They are generally bottom dwelling fish in cool waters.

Members of the sculpin family have 5-7 branchiostegal rays (usually 1 epihyal and 5 ceratohyal), about 31-39 vertebrae, 4-10 pyloric caeca, and two separate dorsal fins (the first weakly spinous, the second soft-rayed). The pelvic fin has a slender spiny splint bound by a membrane to the first soft-ray and not apparent without dissection or staining. The body is naked or provided with prickles or with a few scales and the air bladder is usually absent in the adult.

Sculpins are sometimes placed in the order Perciformes or split from that order, together with rockfish and greenlings, and placed in the order Scorpaeniformes.

KEY TO THE 3 SPECIES

Note—Three species adjacent to but not recorded from Alberta (prickly sculpin, torrent sculpin, and fourhorn sculpin) in Appendix I, not in key.

1 a   One pore on midline at tip of chin; upper spine on opercle very long and curved upward and inward; lateral line extending onto caudal peduncle (in specimens over 1½ inches); head wide and flat; distinct prickles usually covering most of body.
         Cottus ricei — spoonhead sculpin

1 b   Two pores bordering midline at tip of chin; upper spine on opercle not long and only slightly curved; lateral line not extending onto caudal peduncle; head rounded in profile; prickles small and not covering most of body _____ 2

2 a (1)　No teeth on palatine bones; first dorsal fin with 7 to 10 spines; anal fin with 9 to 13 soft rays; caudal peduncle length (distance from basal end of anal fin to end of hypural plate) more than postorbital distance (from end of eye to bony edge of operculum).

Cottus cognatus — slimy sculpin

2 b　Teeth on palatine bones; first dorsal fin with 7 or 8 spines; anal fin with 11 to 14 soft rays; caudal peduncle length less than postorbital distance.

Cottus bairdi — mottled sculpin

MOTTLED SCULPIN

Cottus bairdi Girard
Cottus — an old name for the common European fresh-water sculpin
bairdi — after S. F. Baird, American ichthyologist

Adult mottled sculpin, 2¾ inches standard length, from North Fork of the Milk River, west of Del Bonita.

DESCRIPTION

Color dark brown dorsally. Three darkish bands under the second dorsal fin, broad darkish bands on pectoral and caudal

240

fins. Peritoneum silvery with few black spots. Breeding males with darkish central band on the first dorsal fin.

Body rounded in section. Head subconical and slightly depressed between the eyes; distance between the eyes about ½-1 times eye diameter; eyes large; mouth moderate in size (tip of maxilla extended past front margin of eye), terminal, and horizontal to slightly oblique. Continuous groove separating upper lip from snout. Posterior nostrils semitubular. Teeth on upper and lower jaws, vomer, and usually on palatines. About 11 pores in each side along underneath of lower jaw; two pores on tip of chin, each on either side of midline. Short preopercular spine covered with skin but visible without dissection (two other spines hidden from view). Gill membranes joined to a moderately wide isthmus, about ¼ width of head (shallow posterior fold may be present). Pectoral fin base strongly oblique (sloping backwards at top). Pelvic fin insertion under front third of pectoral fin. Prickles usually confined to a patch behind the pectoral fin. Lateral line incomplete, extended past the center of the second dorsal fin but usually absent from the caudal peduncle. Caudal fin slightly rounded (convex). Lateral-line pores 23-38. First dorsal fin with 7 or 8 spines and second dorsal fin with 16-19 soft rays. Anal fin rays 11-15. Pectoral fin rays 13-16. Pelvic

Mottled sculpin from Milk drainage.

241

fin with 1 weak spine and 4 soft rays. Last ray of anal fin branched.

Maximum length 5 inches.

Maximum length noted from Alberta is 4 inches fork or total length from St. Mary River.

DISTRIBUTION

Similkameen and Kettle drainages of British Columbia to New Brunswick and Alabama to Virginia.

Known in Alberta from upper Oldman, North Fork Milk, and upper South Fork Milk drainages (see map on page 243).

BIOLOGY

Mottled sculpins occur in slow moving streams. They feed on aquatic insects, crustaceans, and small fish. They probably spawn from April to June.

HISTORICAL NOTE

First described by C. F. Girard in 1850 from the Mahoning River, Ohio, as *Cottus bairdii*. First definitely noted in Alberta by Henderson and Peter (1969) and Willock (1969 a, b) from Oldman and Milk drainages. Bajkov (1926) described a sculpin with palatine teeth from the Athabasca and Maligne rivers near Jasper as *Cottus punctulatus* (Gill), the speckled Rocky Mountain bullhead (currently considered a subspecies of *C. bairdi),* which may be the mottled sculpin and thus represent the first Alberta record and an important range extension. The mottled sculpin has been confused with the slimy sculpin in the past in Alberta.

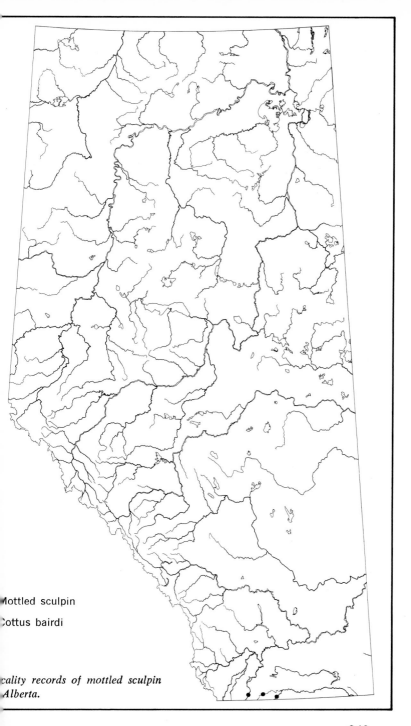

Mottled sculpin

Cottus bairdi

Locality records of mottled sculpin
in Alberta.

Cottus cognatus Richardson
cognatus — related (to the
   European species *Cottus gobio*).

Adult slimy sculpin, 2¼ inches standard length, from a tributary of the Cutbank River.

DESCRIPTION

Color dark brown or greyish-yellow mottling dorsally and laterally. Two or three darkish bands under the second dorsal fin, dark brown bars on pectoral and caudal fins. Peritoneum silvery with few black spots. Breeding males with spinous dorsal black and lined with orange.

Body rounded in section. Head subconical and slightly depressed between the eyes; distance between the eyes about ½-1 times eye diameter; eyes large; mouth moderate in size (tip of maxilla extended past front margin of eye), terminal, and horizontal to slightly oblique. Continuous groove separating upper lip from snout. Posterior nostrils not tubular. Teeth on upper and lower jaws and vomer but very seldom on palatines. About 10 pores on each side along underneath of lower jaw; two pores on tip of chin, each on either side of midline. Short

244

preopercular spine covered with skin but visible without dissection (other spines hidden from view). Gill membranes joined to a moderately wide isthmus, about ¼ width of head. Pectoral fin base strongly oblique (sloping backwards at top). Pelvic fin insertion under front third of pectoral fin. Prickles indistinct and found only behind the pectoral fin base. Lateral line incomplete, ending below or before middle of second dorsal fin. Caudal fin slightly rounded (convex). Lateral-line pores 12-25. First dorsal fin with 7-10 spines and second dorsal fin with 15-19 soft rays (usually 16 or 17). Anal fin rays 10-13. Pectoral fin rays 12-15 (usually 13 or 14). Pelvic fin with 1 weak spine and 3 or 4 soft rays. The slimy sculpin shows much geographic variation in number of pelvic fin rays and presence or absence of branching in the last anal ray; generally, 4 pelvic rays and branched last anal ray predominate in British Columbia while to the east 3 pelvic rays and an unbranched last anal ray are common. This variation has been little studied from Alberta specimens.

Maximum length almost 5 inches.

Maximum length noted from Alberta is 3½ inches fork or total length from Cold and Christina lakes.

DISTRIBUTION

Eastern Siberia and Alaska to New Brunswick and Washington to Virginia.

Known in Alberta from Petitot, Hay, Slave, Peace, Athabasca, and Beaver drainages (see map on page 246). The Red Deer drainage record from Sylvan Lake, based on an early report by D. S. Rawson, is considered questionable.

BIOLOGY

Slimy sculpins occur in lakes and cool rocky streams. They feed on aquatic insects, crustaceans, small fish, and plant material. Spawning probably occurs in the spring with the male guarding the eggs.

HISTORICAL NOTE

First described by Sir J. Richardson in 1836 from Great Bear Lake as *Cottus cognatus*. First noted in Alberta by Kendall (1924) from Popular Point, Lake Athabasca.

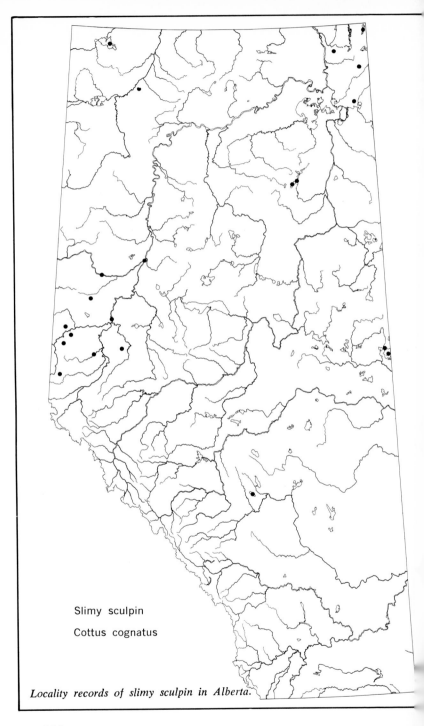

Slimy sculpin

Cottus cognatus

Locality records of slimy sculpin in Alberta.

Cottus ricei (Nelson)
ricei — after its discoverer
   Mr. F. L. Rice

*Spoonhead sculpin adult, 3¼ inches standard length,
from North Saskatchewan River.*

DESCRIPTION

Color light brown or greenish-brown dorsally with dark markings. Darkish bands on pectoral and caudal fins. Peritoneum silvery with few or no black spots.

Body rounded in section. Head very depressed, broad and flat; distance between the eyes 1-¼ times eye diameter, eyes moderate in size; mouth small (tip of maxilla usually not quite extended to anterior margin of eye), terminal, and slightly oblique. Continuous groove separating upper lip from snout. Posterior nostrils semitubular. Teeth on upper and lower jaws and on vomer but not on palatines. About 10 pores on each side along underneath of lower jaw plus a median pore at tip of chin. Preopercular spines 2-4, the uppermost elongate and curved inward and upward, the others concealed by skin. Gill membranes joined to a broad isthmus, about ⅓ or more width

247

of head. Pectoral fin base strongly oblique (sloping backwards at top). Pelvic fin insertion under front third of pectoral fin. Prickles usually over entire body (appearing as small dense white bumps or as spines), sometimes nearly absent. Lateral line slightly decurved under the first dorsal fin and usually complete. Caudal fin slightly rounded (convex). Lateral-line pores 33-36. First dorsal fin with 7-10 spines and second dorsal fin with 16-19 soft rays. Anal fin rays 11-16 (usually 12 or 13). Pectoral fin rays 14-16.

Maximum length 4½ inches fork or total length (from Oldman River, Alberta).

DISTRIBUTION

Northeastern British Columbia to western Quebec with northward extensions to the mouth of the Mackenzie River.

Known in Alberta from Peace, Athabasca, North Saskatchewan, upper Red Deer, Bow (near Calgary), and upper Oldman drainages (see map on page 249). One specimen is known from Milk drainage (collected by R. B. Miller and J. C. Ward, August 8, 1950, from the North Fork Milk River, near Del Bonita). Recent collecting has turned them up in Slave drainage west and south of Fort Smith.

BIOLOGY

Spoonhead sculpin occur in muddy rivers and in large lakes. Near Fort Smith they have been found in clear "salty" rivers. They probably spawn in the spring.

HISTORICAL NOTE

First described by E. W. Nelson in 1876 from Lake Michigan at Evanston as *Cottopsis ricei*. First noted in Alberta by Eigenmann and Eigenmann (1892) and Eigenmann (1895) at Calgary (Bow River) as a new species, *Cottus onychus*.

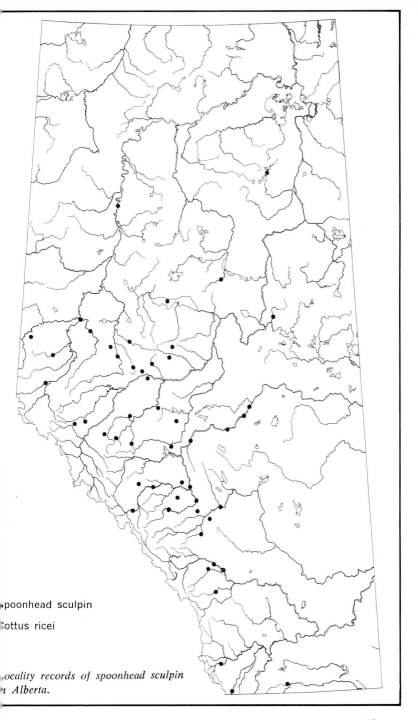

spoonhead sculpin

Cottus ricei

Locality records of spoonhead sculpin in Alberta.

249

Exotic species, species of questioned status, unsuccessful introductions, and species in adjacent areas.

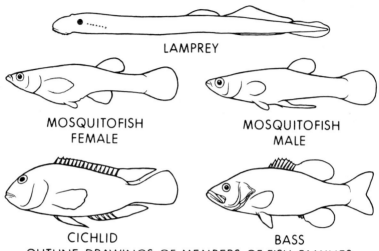

LAMPREY

MOSQUITOFISH FEMALE

MOSQUITOFISH MALE

CICHLID

BASS

OUTLINE DRAWINGS OF MEMBERS OF FISH FAMILIES MENTIONED ONLY IN APPENDIX I.

Petromyzontidae. Distinguished from other families in lacking jaws, lacking paired fins, and having 7 pairs of external gill openings.

Lampetra japonica—Arctic lamprey, occur in the Northwest Territories a short distance from the Alberta border in the Slave River at Fort Smith and in the Hay River. They are almost certain to get within the Alberta border in the Slave River.

Salmonidae

Coregonus nigripinnis—blackfin cisco, reported in Lake Athabasca, Alberta (Dymond and Pritchard, 1930). The presence of this species in Alberta cannot be accepted without verification.

Oncorhynchus keta—chum salmon, reported by N. S. Novakowski a short distance from the Alberta border in the Northwest Territories at Fort Smith (1957-1959). Distinguished from other *Oncorhynchus* in having 19-26 gillrakers, 140-186 pyloric caeca, absence of distinct black spots on back and fins, and young with 6-10 oval parr marks scarcely extending below the lateral line.

Oncorhynchus kisutch—coho salmon, stocked as yearlings in Cold Lake, May, 1970; eggs were obtained from Alaska. Distinguished from other *Oncorhynchus* in having 19-25 gillrakers, 45-80 pyloric caeca, black spots on back and usually on upper lobe of caudal fin, and young with long narrow parr marks which extend well above and below the lateral line, a reddish brown tail fin, and an anal fin with a concave margin and the first rays elongate and white, followed by a dark stripe.

Prosopium coulteri—pygmy whitefish, occur in the Kickinghorse River at Field and in the Peace River drainage, British Columbia. Distinguished from other *Prosopium* in having fewer than 70 lateral-line scales, fewer than 21 gillrakers, snout blunt and rounded, 16-20 horizontal scale rows around the caudal peduncle, and fork length usually less than 6 inches.

Prosopium cylindraceum—round whitefish, occur in Liard drainage of British Columbia, Slave River in the Northwest Territories, and the Saskatchewan portion of Lake Athabasca. Attempts to find this species in the shallower Alberta portion of Lake Athabasca have failed. Kendall (1924) reported it in Lake Athabasca as *Prosopium quadrilaterale*. Distinguished from other *Prosopium* in having black or brown spots on top of head and on adipose fin, fewer than 21 gillrakers, base of adipose fin about equal to eye diameter, and 24-26 horizontal scale rows around the caudal peduncle.

Salmo salar—Atlantic salmon, introduced into Sawback Creek (1959), Cascades River (1959), and Lake Minnewanka (1915, 1963) in Banff National Park, and into Moab (1961), Celestine (1962), Pyramid (1917, 1961), and Patricia (1962) lakes in Jasper National Park. Reproduction is not known to occur and individuals from these stockings are probably no longer alive. Distinguished from other *Salmo* in having the caudal fin deeply forked, no distinct black spots on the caudal and adipose fins, few or no spots below the lateral line, teeth on shaft of vomer in adults weakly developed, and young with reddish spots on lateral line between parr marks (similar to brown trout young) but without orangish adipose fin.

Salvelinus alpinus—Quebec red trout (this variety of *S. alpinus,* the Arctic charr, is given specific status by some, namely *S. marstoni),* introduced into Upper and Lower Block lakes (1957) and Third Vermilion Lake (1959) in Banff National Park. Reproduction is not definitely known to occur. This charr, from Quebec, is related to the Dolly Varden and is characterized by the red coloration on the lower body. See discussion of brook trout for introduction of hybrids between these two species.

Stenodus leucichthys—inconnu, occur in British Columbia in the Liard drainage, and in Northwest Territories in Slave River near Fort Smith and Hay River. Distinguished from other Coregoninae in having lower jaw projecting beyond upper jaw (cisco-like), very short teeth on the jaws and prevomer-palatines, two flaps on each nostril, fewer than 25 gillrakers, and anal fin with 13-17 rays.

Hiodontidae

Hiodon tergisus—mooneye, occur in southwestern Saskatchewan and may be expected to occur in the South Saskatchewan drainage of Alberta. Distinguished from *H. alosoides* in having the dorsal fin with 11 or 12 principal rays and originating in front of the anal fin origin, iris of eye silvery without gold color, and height of eye more than half post-orbital length of head.

Cyprinidae

Carassius auratus—goldfish, several releases have been made in Alberta. They occur in many garden ponds; Henderson Lake, in Lethbridge, has a population. Distinguished from other cyprinids in having about 18 dorsal fin rays preceded by a spinous ray, 5 anal fin rays preceded by a spinous ray, no barbels on upper jaw, fewer than 32 lateral-line scales, and pharyngeal teeth in one row of 4-4.

Cyprinus carpio—carp, occur in neighboring Saskatchewan and Montana. Distinguished from other cyprinids in having more than 16 dorsal fin rays preceded by a spinous ray, 5 anal fin rays preceded by a strong toothed spine, two barbels on each side of upper jaw, pharyngeal teeth in 3 rows of 1,1,3-3,1,1, and length up to 25 inches.

Mylocheilus caurinus—peamouth, occur close to Alberta in eastern British Columbia in Peace, Fraser, and Columbia drainages. Reported in Alberta in checklist of Scott and Crossman (1969, p. 18) and at Athabasca on the Athabasca River by McPhail and Lindsey (1970) on the basis of 1 specimen. This 3 inch standard length juvenile was supposedly seined, along with individuals representing 7 species well-known from the area, May 2, 1957, by G. Hartman, R. Miller, and M. Warren. The specimen is deposited at The University of British Columbia (BC57-347). Recent collecting, the known distribution of the species, and conversation with the senior collector, Dr. Gordon Hartman, leads us to doubt the validity of the Athabasca record. Although the species might be expected from the Peace River of Alberta, all collecting has failed to find it. Distinguished from other cyprinids in having a small barbel at end of upper jaw, front of dorsal fin opposite or in front of pelvic fin insertion, upper jaw extended forward slightly over the small horizontal mouth, more than 68 lateral-line scales, lateral line complete, pharyngeal teeth 1,5-5,1, tip of dorsal fin somewhat pointed, two dark lateral bands in juveniles and adults, and fork length up to 14 inches.

Notropis heterodon — blackchin shiner, Eigenmann and Eigenmann (1893) and Eigenmann (1895) described the species *Notropis jordani* (= *N. albeolus* of Eigenmann and Eigenmann) from Medicine Hat on the basis of 1 individual. It was regarded as allied to *N. heterodon*. Probably represents a species known to Alberta. *N. heterodon* is not known closer to Alberta than North Dakota and southern Ontario.

Notropis heterolepis—blacknose shiner, occur in Saskatchewan, previously reported from Alberta. Distinguished from other cyprinids in the Alberta area in having black lateral band extending around snout but not on lower jaw, lateral line incomplete, pharyngeal teeth 0,4-4,0, and mouth almost horizontal and slightly subterminal.

Rhinichthys atratulus—blacknose dace, specimens reported from Minnewanka Reservoir by Rawson (1939) are most likely hybrids of *Couesius plumbeus* and *Rhinichthys cataractae*.

Rhinichthys falcatus—leopard dace, occur in Fraser and Columbia drainage in British Columbia. Distinguished from other cyprinids in having the upper lip protractile (no frenum), barbel at corner of mouth, and membranous stays at pelvic fin base.

Poeciliidae. Distinguished from other families in having third anal ray unbranched (usually requires magnification to determine), no lateral line, and males with a modified rod-like anal fin (employed as an intromittent organ). This is the only live-bearing group in Alberta.

Gambusia affinis—mosquitofish, introduced into outflow of Cave and Basin Hotspring, Banff, in 1924 for mosquito control where they survive in good numbers today (Mail, 1954; McAllister, 1969); also known from Vermilion lakes. Distinguished from other poeciliids in Alberta in having 6-9 dorsal fin rays, 30-32 lateral-line scales, spots on caudal fin, and origin of dorsal fin behind origin of anal fin.

Poecilia latipinna—sailfin molly, taken in the marsh at the outflow of Cave and Basin Hotsprings, one mile south-west of Banff, in 1968, probably introduced by local aquarists (McAllister, 1969). Distinguished from other poeciliids in Alberta in having 13-15 dorsal fin rays, 26-28 lateral-line scales, and origin of dorsal fin in front of origin of anal fin.

Poecilia reticulata—guppy, taken in large numbers in the marsh at the outflow of Cave and Basin Hotspring, Banff, in 1968, probably introduced by local aquarists (McAllister, 1969). Distinguished from other poeciliids in Alberta in having 7 or 8 dorsal fin rays, 26-28 lateral-line scales, no spots on caudal fin, and origin of dorsal fin even with or behind origin of anal fin.

Xiphophorus helleri—green swordtail, taken in the marsh at the outflow of Cave and Basin Hotspring, Banff, in 1968, probably introduced by local aquarists (McAllister, 1969). Distinguished from other poeciliids in Alberta in having 11-14 dorsal fin rays, 26-30 lateral-line scales, origin of dorsal fin in front of origin of anal fin, and lower rays of caudal fin in mature males forming an elongate spike.

Cichlidae. Distinguished from other families in having three or more anal spines, only one nostril opening on each side of head, single long dorsal fin with spines and soft rays, vomer and palatines without teeth, and lateral-line interrupted (offset below the soft dorsal fin).

Cichlasoma nigrofasciatum—zebra cichlid, taken in the marsh at the outflow of Cave and Basin Hotspring, Banff, in 1968, probably introduced by local aquarists (McAllister, 1969). This species is very closely related to the popular aquarium fish, the Jack Dempsey.

Centrarchidae. Distinguished from other families in having three or more anal spines and teeth on the vomer.

Micropterus sp.—In 1908 bass were introduced into Lake Minnewanka near Banff and into Sylvan, Gull, Pine, Buffalo, and Cooking lakes in central Alberta. In 1924 bass were introduced into Ministik Lake, southeast of Edmonton. Several years later, largemouth bass, *Micropterus salmoides,* were liberated into Pigeon, Wabamun, and Lac la Nonne, all west of the Edmonton area. In these introductions, yearling and two year old bass were used, some were later angled, but there was never any evidence of reproduction.

Percidae

Etheostoma nigrum—Johnny darter, occur in Saskatchewan, previously reported from Alberta. We lack definite records. Distinguished from other *Etheostoma* in having protractile premaxillaries (no frenum), single anal spine (instead of two), and a complete lateral line extending on the caudal peduncle.

Cottidae

Cottus asper—prickly sculpin, occur in Peace, Fraser, and lower Columbia drainage, British Columbia. Distinguished from other cottids in having one pore at tip of chin, distinct dark oval spot at back of first dorsal fin, upper spine on opercle not long and only slightly curved, head rounded in profile, more than 14 soft rays in anal fin, and teeth on palatine bones.

Cottus rhotheus—torrent sculpin, occur in Columbia and Kootenay drainage, British Columbia. Distinguished from other cottids in having two pores at tip of chin, lateral line complete, fewer than 14 soft rays in anal fin, and teeth on palatine bones.

Myoxocephalus quadricornis — fourhorn or deepwater sculpin, occur in Northwest Territories (as close to Alberta as Great Slave Lake) and Saskatchewan. Distinguished from other cottids in having the dorsal fins widely separated, gill-membranes free from isthmus and joined to each other, skin mostly naked but with tubercles scattered over much of body, and usually 11-15 soft dorsal rays (all elements).

APPENDIX II

Features of some Alberta Lakes[1]

	Location	Surface Area - Sq. Mi.	Elevation	Maximum Depth - Ft.	Average Depth - Ft.	Summer Surface pH	No. of[2] Native Fish
Liard drainage							
Bistcho	NW High Level	147	1,812	23	12	7.6	8
Peace drainage							
Utikuma	N Lesser Slave	106	2,115	18	9	8.0	?
South Wabasca	NE Lesser Slave	19.5	1,790	10	5	7.3	6
North Wabasca	NE Lesser Slave	38.4	1,785	52	19	7.3	9
Legend	NW Fort McMurray	6.6	2,590	36	19	6.9	6
Athabasca drainage							
Amethyst	SW Jasper	1.8	6,450	69	24	7.2	0
Maligne	SE Jasper	8.4	5,460	315	132	7.8	0
Lesser Slave	NE Valleyview	460	1,892	60	?	?	?
Calling	N Athabasca	52	1,949	58	?	7.0	?
Lac La Biche	E Athabasca	87	1,922	75	24	7.9	11
Namur	NW Fort McMurray	16.9	2,375	92	43	7.1	5
Unnamed	15 mi. NE Namur L.	5.4	2,250	210	52	7.5	?
Athabasca[3]	N Fort McMurray	890	700	54	?	7.7	21
Beaver drainage							
Beaver	E Athabasca	12.8	2,005	50	22	8.2	8
Whitefish	NE St. Paul	11.6	1,894	140	43	9.5	10
Moose	W Bonnyville	14.9	1,748	65	19	8.8	10
Cold	NE St. Paul	144	1,756	330	?	?	15

Appendix 11 (Continued)

Features of some Alberta Lakes[1]

	Location	Surface Area - Sq. Mi.	Elevation	Maximum Depth - Ft.	Average Depth - Ft.	Summer Surface pH	No. of[2] Native Fish
North Saskatchewan drainage							
Swan	W Red Deer	0.8	3,950	38	20	7.7	4
Wabamun	W Edmonton	32.6	2,371	35	18	8.5	7
Lac St. Anne	NW Edmonton	21.8	2,370	35	16	?	9
Astotin	E Edmonton	2.2	2,335	23	10	9.0	1
Battle drainage							
Pigeon	SW Edmonton	37.0	2,770	32	14	?	9
Red Deer drainage							
Snowflake	N Banff	0.03	7,625	42	20	8.0	0
Sylvan	W Red Deer	16.5	3,080	60	31	?	?
Gull	NW Red Deer	32.2	2,960	27	16	?	?
Bow drainage							
Boulder	N Lake Louise	0.03	8,200	?	?	?	0
Bow	NW Banff	1.3	6,500	148	58	8.0	3
Minnewanka[4]	E Banff	8.3	4,840	325	170	8.2	7
Upper Kananaskis[4]	W Calgary	3.3	5,583	340	163	8.0	0
Lower Kananaskis[4]	W Calgary	2.5	5,469	138	47	8.1	5
Oldman drainage							
Waterton	SW Cardston	3.7	4,190	443	227	7.8	12

1 Information from numerous sources, mostly from papers listed in Bibliography. Data in some cases is approximate only.
2 The five lakes without native fish have had successful introductions.
3 That portion of lake in Alberta only.
4 The reservoir at high water level.

Discharge of major Alberta rivers in cubic feet per second[1]

River and Locality	Approx. lat N.	long W.	Average Discharge	Maximum Discharge	Minimum Discharge
Slave at Fitzgerald	59°52'	111°35'	131,000	315,500	18,600
Peace at Peace Point	59°07'	112°26'	80,700	421,000	9,600
Peace at Peace River	56°15'	117°19'	63,400	514,000	6,350
Athabasca below McMurray	56°47'	111°24'	22,900	147,000	3,410
Athabasca at Hinton	53°25'	117°35'	6,600	53,100	250
Beaver at Cold Lake	54°21'	110°13'	936	21,600	13
North Saskatchewan at Edmonton	53°32'	113°29'	7,760	164,000	220
North Saskatchewan near Rocky Mountain House	52°23'	114°56'	5,090	129,700	404
Red Deer at Drumheller	51°28'	112°42'	1,950	40,000	54
Battle Near Unwin, Saskatchewan	52°57'	109°53'	301	9,970	0
Bow at Calgary	51°03'	114°03'	3,280	41,100	123
Bow at Banff	51°10'	115°34'	1,430	14,100	128
Oldman near Lethbridge	49°42'	112°52'	3,290	135,000	134
South Saskatchewan at Medicine Hat	50°03'	110°41'	7,440	144,300	360
Milk River at eastern crossing of International Boundary	49°00'	110°35'	170	6,680	0

Total average inflow of water into province from British Columbia, Montana, Saskatchewan, and the Northwest Territories is about 53,500 cubic feet per second.

Total average outflow of water from the province into Northwest Territories, Saskatchewan, Montana, and British Columbia is about 151,000 cubic feet per second.

The average yearly flow in acre feet for the following rivers is: Slave River at Fitzgerald — 94,520,000; Peace River at Peace River — 45,460,000; North Saskatchewan at Edmonton — 5,705,000; Bow River at Calgary — 2,382,000; Bow River at Banff — 1,043,000. The highest discharge is usually in June or July while the lowest discharge is usually between January and March.

---

[1] This information was generously supplied by Mr. Jim R. Card of the Alberta Water Resources Division. Data were obtained by the Water Survey of Canada, Department of Energy, Mines, and Resources. It has been somewhat simplified in form. The length of time that the various stations have been measured varies from 9 to 58 years. The average discharge is the average for a year for the period the station has been measured. The minimum and maximum discharges are the mean daily values for the period the station has been measured. For conversion, 1 cubic foot per second equals 0.54 million Imperial gallons per day (1mgd = 1.85cfs.).

BIBLIOGRAPHY

ANDERSON, R. S. 1968a. The limnology of Snowflake Lake and other high altitude lakes in Banff National Park, Alberta. Ph.D. Thesis. Dept. of Biology, University of Calgary, Calgary, Alberta. 218 pp.

ANDERSON, R. S. 1968b. The zooplankton of five small mountain lakes in southwestern Alberta. Natl. Mus. of Canada Nat. Hist. Papers, No. 39:1-19.

ANDERSON, R. S. 1970a. Physical and chemical limnology of two mountain lakes in Banff National Park, Alberta. J. Fish. Res. Bd. Canada, 27(2):233-249.

ANDERSON, R. S. 1970b. *Diaptomus (Leptodiaptomus) Connexus* Light 1938 in Alberta and Saskatchewan. Canadian J. Zool. 48(1):41-47.

ANDREKSON, A. 1949. A study of the biology of the cutthroat trout in the Sheep River with special reference to Gorge Creek. M.Sc. Thesis. Dept. of Zoology, University of Alberta, Edmonton, Alberta. 74 pp.

ANTHONY, D. D. 1967. Taxonomy and ecology of *Diphyllobothrium* in Alberta and British Columbia. Ph.D. Thesis. Dept. of Zoology, University of Alberta, Edmonton, Alberta. 212 pp.

ARAI, H. and R. H. KUSSAT. 1967. Observations on the distribution of parasites of certain catostomid fishes of the Bow River, Alberta. Canadian J. Zool., 45(6):1287-1290.

BAILEY, R. M. (Chairman). 1970. A list of common and scientific names of fishes from the United States and Canada. Amer. Fish Soc. Spec. Publ. 6, 3rd ed.

BAILEY, R. M. and M. O. ALLUM. 1962. Fishes of South Dakota. Misc. Publ. 119. Mus. Zool., University of Michigan, Ann Arbor. 131 pp.

BAJKOV, A. 1926. Reports of the Jasper Park lakes investigations, 1925-26. I. The Fishes. Contrib. Can. Biol., 3(1):379-404.

BISHOP, F. G. 1967. The Arctic grayling of Great Slave Lake. M.Sc. Thesis. Dept. of Zoology, University of Alberta, Edmonton, Alberta. 166 pp.

BISHOP, F. 1969. A summary of fishes collected in the Peace River area 1968. Alberta Fish and Wildlife Division. Survey Report 5, 9 pp.

CARL, G. C., W. A. CLEMENS, and C. C. LINDSEY. 1967. The fresh-water fishes of British Columbia. B.C. Prov. Museum, Handbook 5, 4th ed. 192 pp.

CLIFFORD, H. F. 1969. Limnological features of a northern brown-water stream, with special reference to the life histories of the aquatic insects. Amer. Midl. Nat., 82:578-597.

CLIFFORD, H. F. 1970. Analysis of a northern mayfly (Ephemoptera) population, with special reference to allometry of size. Canadian J. Zool. 48(2):305-316.

CROSS, F. B. 1967. Handbook of fishes of Kansas. Misc. Publ. 45, Mus. Nat. Hist., University of Kansas, Lawrence. 357 pp.

CUERRIER, J.-P. 1954. The history of Lake Minnewanka with reference to the reaction of lake trout to artificial changes in environment. Canadian Fish Cult., 15:1-9.

CUERRIER, J.-P., J. A. KEITH, and E. STONE. 1967. Problems with DDT in fish culture operations. Naturaliste Can., 94:315-320.

CUERRIER, J.-P. and F. M. SCHULTZ. 1957. Studies of lake trout and common whitefish in Waterton Lakes, Waterton Lakes National Park, Alberta. Wildl. Manag. Bull., 3(5):1-41.

DYMOND, J. R. 1943. The Coregonine fishes of northwestern Canada. Trans. Royal Can. Instit. 24: part II:171-231.

DYMOND, J. R. and A. L. PRITCHARD. 1930. Some ciscoe or lake herrings of western Canada. Contrib. Can. Biol. and Fish. N.S. 5(17):469-474.

EIGENMANN, C. H. 1895. Results of explorations in western Canada and the northwestern United States. Bull. U.S. Fish Comm., 14:101-132.

EIGENMANN, C. H. and R. S. EIGENMANN. 1892. New fishes from western Canada. Amer. Nat., 26:961-964.

EIGENMANN, C. H. and R. S. EIGENMANN. 1893. Preliminary descriptions of new fishes from the north-west. Amer. Nat., 27:151-154.

FILLION, D. J. B. 1964. The benthic fauna of three mountain reservoirs in Alberta. M.Sc. Thesis. Dept. of Zoology, University of Alberta, Edmonton, Alberta. 160 pp.

GARDINER, B. G. 1966. Catalogue of Canadian fossil fishes. Royal Ontario Museum Contrib. 68, University of Toronto Press. 154 pp.

GILMOUR, W. M. 1950. A study of the lower Bow River trout with special reference to taxonomy. M.Sc. Thesis. Dept. of Zoology, University of Alberta, Edmonton, Alberta. 59 pp.

GOLDBERG, E., J.-P. CUERRIER, and J. C. WARD. 1967. Lactate dehydrogenase isozymes, vertebrae and caeca numbers in an isolated, interbreeding population of splake trout. Naturaliste Can., 94:297-304.

HARPER, F. and J. T. NICHOLS. 1919. Six new fishes from northwestern Canada. Bull. Amer. Mus. Nat. Hist., 41:263-270.

HARTLAND-ROWE, R. 1964. Factors influencing the life histories of some stream insects of Alberta. Verk. Int. Verein. Limnol. 15:917-925.

HARTLAND-ROWE, R. and R. S. ANDERSON. 1968. An Arctic fairy shrimp (*Artemiopsis stefanssoni* Johansen 1921) in southern Alberta, with a note on the genus *Artemiopsis*. Canadian J. Zool. 46(3):423-425.

261

HAUGEN, G. N. 1969. Life history, habitat and distribution of the lake sturgeon *Acipenser fulvescens* in the South Saskatchewan River, Alberta. M.Sc. Thesis, Montana State University, Bozeman. 27 pp.

HAUPTMAN, A. W. 1958. Winter conditions in three lakes with special reference to dissolved oxygen. M.Sc. Thesis. Dept. of Zoology, University of Alberta, Edmonton, Alberta. 58 pp.

HOFFMAN, G. L. 1967. Parasites of North American freshwater fishes. Univ. Calif. Press. 486 pp.

HUBBS, C. L. and K. F. LAGLER. 1964. Fishes of the Great Lakes region. University Mich. Press, Ann Arbor. 213 pp.

JOHNSTON, P. F. 1966. Succession and distribution of Ostracoda in highway borrow pit ponds of central Alberta. M.Sc. Thesis. Dept. of Zoology, University of Alberta, Edmonton, Alberta. 115 pp.

KENDALL, W. C. 1924. An annotated list of a collection of fishes made by Francis Harper in the Athabasca region in 1920, to which is appended a list of species collected by Dr. R. T. Morris in the district between Lake Winnipeg and Hudson Bay in 1905. Contrib. Can. Biol., 1(23):421-439.

KEREKES, J. 1965. A comparative limnological study of five lakes in central Alberta. M.Sc. Thesis. Dept. of Zoology, University of Alberta, Edmonton, Alberta. 165 pp.

KEREKES, J. and J. R. NURSALL. 1966. Eutrophication and senescence in a group of prairie-parkland lakes in Alberta, Canada. Verh. Internat. Verein. Limnol. 16:65-73.

KUSSAT, R. H. 1966. Bottom fauna studies in relation to the biology of certain fishes of the Bow River. M.Sc. Thesis. Dept. of Biology, University of Calgary, Calgary, Alberta. 76 pp.

KUSSAT, R. H. 1969. A comparison of aquatic communities in the Bow River above and below sources of domestic and industrial wastes for the city of Calgary. Canadian Fish Cult. 40:3-31.

LIN, C. K. 1968. Phytoplankton succession in Astotin Lake, Elk Island National Park, Alberta. M.Sc. Thesis. Dept. of Botany, University of Alberta, Edmonton, Alberta. 148 pp.

LINDSEY, C. C. 1964. Problems in zoogeography of the lake trout, *Salvelinus namaycush*. J. Fish Res. Bd. Canada, 21(5):977-994.

MacDONALD, W. H. 1958. Fishing in Alberta, Canada. Dept. Lands and Forests, Gov. of Alberta. 36 pp.

MacKAY, W. C. 1967. Plasma glucose levels in the northern pike, *Esox lucius* and the white sucker, *Catostomus commersonii,* and renal glucose reabsorption in the white sucker. M.Sc. Thesis. Dept. of Zoology, University of Alberta, Edmonton, Alberta. 77 pp.

MAIL, G. A. 1954. The mosquito fish *Gambusia affinis* (Baird and Girard) in Alberta. Mosquito news, 14(3):120.

MANGAN, U. M. 1951. Survival of hatchery-reared cutthroat trout in an Alberta stream. M.Sc. Thesis. Dept. of Zoology, University of Alberta, Edmonton, Alberta. 51 pp.

McALLISTER, D. E. 1962. The brassy minnow, river shiner and sauger new to Alberta. Canadian Field-Nat., 76(2):124-125.

McALLISTER, D. E. 1969. Introduction of tropical fishes into a hot spring near Banff, Alberta. Canadian Field-Nat., 83(1):31-35.

McALLISTER, D. E. and E. J. CROSSMAN. 1970. Guide to the freshwater sport fishes of Canada. Natl. Mus. Nat. Sciences. Queen's Printer, Ottawa. (In Press.)

McHUGH, J. L. 1940. Food of the Rocky Mountain whitefish *Prosopium williamsoni* (Girard). J. Fish. Res. Bd. Canada, 5(2):131-137.

McHUGH, J. L. 1941. Growth of the Rocky Mountain whitefish. J. Fish. Res. Bd. Canada, 5(4):337-343.

McPHAIL, J. D. 1963. Geographic variation in North American ninespine sticklebacks, *Pungitius pungitius*. J. Fish. Res. Bd. Canada, 20(1):27-44.

McPHAIL, J. D. and C. C. LINDSEY. 1970. Freshwater fishes of northwestern Canada and Alaska. Bull. Fish. Res. Bd. Canada. (In Press.)

MILLER, R. B. 1945a. Effect of *Triaenophorus* on growth of two fishes. J. Fish. Res. Bd. Canada, 6(4):334-337.

MILLER, R. B. 1945b. Studies on cestodes of the genus *Triaenophorus* from fish of Lesser Slave Lake, Alberta. IV. The life of *Triaenophorus crassus* Forel in the second intermediate host. Canadian J. Research, D, 23:105-115.

MILLER, R. B. 1946. Effectiveness of a whitefish hatchery. J. Wildl. Manag., 10(4):316-322.

MILLER, R. B. 1947. The effects of different intensities of fishing on the whitefish populations of two Alberta lakes. J. Wildl. Manag., 11(4):289-301.

MILLER, R. B. 1948. A note on the movement of the pike, *Esox lucius*. Copeia, 1948 (1):62.

MILLER, R. B. 1949a. The status of the hatchery. Canadian Fish. Cult., 4(5):19-24.

MILLER, R. B. 1949b. Problems of the optimum catch in small whitefish lakes. Biometrics, 5(1):14-26.

MILLER, R. B. 1950a. Observations on mortality rates in fished and unfished ciscoe populations. Trans. Amer. Fish. Soc., 79:180-186.

MILLER, R. B. 1950b. Recognition of trout in Alberta. Can. Fish Cult., 6:1-3.

MILLER, R. B. 1952a. The role of research in fisheries management in the prairie provinces. Canadian Fish Cult., 12:1-7.

MILLER, R. B. 1952b. The relative strength of whitefish year classes as affected by egg plantings and weather. J. Wildl. Manag., 16(1):39-50.

MILLER, R. B. 1953. The regulation of trout fishing in Alberta. Canadian Fish Cult., 14:1-6.

MILLER, R. B. 1954a. Effect of the Pocaterra power development on Lower Kananaskis Lake. Rept. to Alberta Dept. Lands and Forests. 11 pp.

MILLER, R. B. 1954b. Movements of cutthroat trout after different periods of retention upstream and downstream from their homes. J. Fish. Res. Bd. Canada, 11(5):550-558.

MILLER, R. B. 1955. Trout management research in Alberta. Trans. 20th North Amer. Wildl. Conf., 242-252.

MILLER, R. B. 1956a. The collapse and recovery of a small whitefish fishery. J. Fish. Res. Bd. Canada, 13(1):135-146.

MILLER, R. B. 1956b. The management of the fish resources of Cold Lake. Mimeo. 10 pp.

MILLER, R. B. 1957. Permanence and size of home territory in stream-dwelling cutthroat trout. J. Fish. Res. Bd. Canada, 14(5):687-691.

MILLER, R. B. 1958a. Inventory of fisheries research in Alberta, Alberta Resources Conference. Queen's Printer, Edmonton.

MILLER, R. B. 1958b. The role of competition in the mortality of hatchery trout. J. Fish. Res. Bd. Canada, 15(1):27-45.

MILLER, R. B. 1962. A cool curving world. Longmans, Toronto.

MILLER, R. B. and W. A. KENNEDY. 1948. Pike (Esox lucius) from four northern Canadian lakes. J. Fish. Res. Bd. Canada, 7(4):190-199.

MILLER, R. B. and W. H. MacDONALD. 1949. Preliminary biological surveys of Alberta watersheds 1947-1949. Gov. of the Prov. of Alberta, Dept. Lands and Forests. 139 pp.

MILLER, R. B. and M. J. PAETZ. 1953. Preliminary biological surveys of Alberta watersheds 1950-1952. Gov. of the Prov. of Alberta, Dept. Lands and Forests. 114 pp.

MILLER, R. B. and M. J. PAETZ. 1959. The effects of power, irrigation, and stock water developments on the fisheries of the South Saskatchewan River. Canadian Fish Cult., 25:1-14.

MILLER, R. B. and R. C. THOMAS. 1957. Alberta's "pothole" trout fisheries. Trans. Amer. Fish. Soc., 86:261-268.

MOORE, G. A. 1968. Fishes. In Vertebrates of the United States. McGraw-Hill Book Co., 2nd ed., 21-165.

NELSON, J. S. 1965. Effects of fish introductions and hydroelectric development on fishes in the Kananaskis River system, Alberta. J. Fish. Res. Bd. Canada, 22(3):721-753.

NELSON, J. S. 1966. Hybridization between two cyprinid fishes, *Hybopsis plumbea* and *Rhinichthys cataractae,* in Alberta. Canadian J. Zool., 44:963-968.

NELSON, J. S. 1968. Hybridization and isolating mechanisms between *Catostomus commersonii* and *C. macrocheilus* (Pisces: Catostomidae). J. Fish. Res. Bd. Canada, 25(1):101-150.

NELSON, J. S. 1969. Geographic variation in the brook stickleback, *Culaea inconstans,* and notes on nomenclature and distribution. J. Fish. Res. Bd. Canada, 26(9):2431-2447.

NELSON, J. S. and F. M. ATTON. 1970. Geographic variation in the presence and absence of the pelvic skeleton in the brook stickleback, *Culaea inconstans* (Kirtland), in Alberta and Saskatchewan. Manuscript.

NICHOLS, J. T. 1916. On a new race of minnow from the Rocky Mountains Park. Bull. Amer. Mus. Nat. Hist., 35(8):69.

NURSALL, J. R. 1949. Ecological changes in the bottom fauna in the first two years of the Barrier Reservoir. M.A. Thesis, University of Saskatchewan, Saskatoon. 47 pp.

NURSALL, J. R. 1952. The early development of a bottom fauna in a new power reservoir in the Rocky Mountains of Alberta. Canadian J. Zool., 30:387-409.

NURSALL, J. R. and V. LEWIN. 1964. The stonecat, *Noturus flavus,* newly recorded in Alberta. Canadian Field-Nat., 78(2):128-129.

NURSALL, J. R. and M. E. PINSENT. 1969. Aggregations of spottail shiners and yellow perch. J. Fish. Res. Bd. Canada, 26(6):1672-1676.

O'BRIAN, D. E. 1969. Osteology of *Kindleia fragosa* Jordan (Holostei: Amiidae), from the Edmonton Formation (Maestrichtian) of Alberta. M.Sc. Thesis. Dept. of Geology, University of Alberta, Edmonton, Alberta. 118 pp.

PAETZ, M. J. 1957. The management of trout streams of the East slopes of the Rocky Mountains in Alberta. M.Sc. Thesis. Dept. of Zoology, University of Alberta, Edmonton, Alberta. 58 pp.

PAETZ, M. J. 1958. The sauger—a newly discovered game fish in Alberta. Land Forests Wildl. 1(3):24 and 26.

PAETZ, M. J. 1959. An inventory of the stream sport fisheries of Alberta. Alberta Resources Conference. Queen's Printer, Edmonton. 24 pp.

PAETZ, M. J. 1967. The anglers domain. pp. 248-255. *In* W. G. Hardy (Ed.), Alberta, A Natural History. M. G. Hurtig, Edmonton.

PATERSON, C. G. 1966. Life history notes on the goldeye, *Hiodon alosoides* (Rafinesque), in the North Saskatchewan River in Alberta. Canadian Field.-Nat., 80(4):250-251.

PATERSON, C. G. 1966. The limnology of the North Saskatchewan River near Edmonton. M.Sc. Thesis. Dept. of Zoology, University of Alberta, Edmonton, Alberta. 132 pp.

265

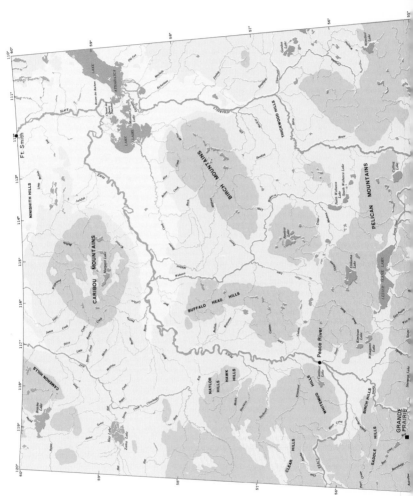

SASKATCHEWAN

COLUMBIA

ALTITUD

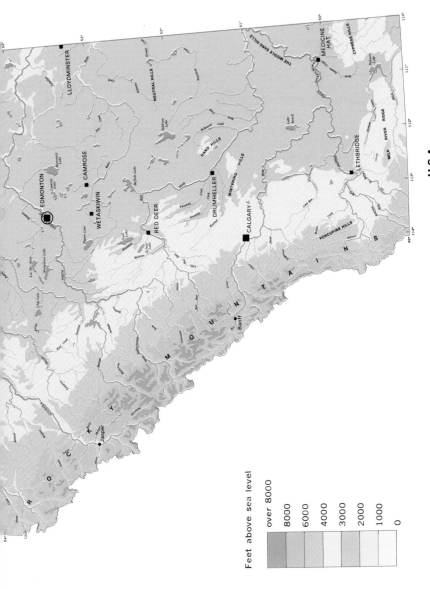

Feet above sea level

over 8000
8000
6000
4000
3000
2000
1000
0

U.S.A.

ALBERTA

267

PATERSON, C. G. 1969. Occurrence of *Coregonus artedii* and *C. zenithicus* in Barrow Lake, Alberta. J. Fish. Res. Bd. Canada, 26(7):1934-1939.

PATERSON, R. J. 1968. The lake trout *(Salvelinus namaycush)* of Swan Lake, Alberta. M.Sc. Thesis. Dept. of Zoology, University of Alberta and Research Dept. 2, Alta. Fish and Wildl. Div., Fish Sect. 149 pp.

PINSENT, M. E. 1967. A comparative limnological study of Lac La Biche and Beaver Lake, Alberta. M.Sc. Thesis. Dept. of Zoology, University of Alberta, Edmonton, Alberta. 149 pp.

PREBLE, E. A. 1908. A biological investigation of the Athabasca-Mackenzie region. U.S. Department of Agri., Bur. Biol. Survey, North American Fauna, No. 27. 574 pp.

PRICE, C. E. and H. P. ARAI. 1967. The monogenean parasites of Canadian freshwater fishes. Canadian J. Zool., 45(6):1235-1245.

RAWSON, D. S. 1937. Biological examination of the Kananaskis lakes, Alberta. Unpubl. Rept. to Alberta Depts. Lands Mines. 12 pp.

RAWSON, D. S. 1939a. A preliminary biological examination of some Alberta provincial waters. Rept. to Alberta Dept. of Agriculture. 47 pp.

RAWSON, D. S. 1939b. A biological survey and recommendations for fisheries management in waters of the Banff National Park. Rept. to National Parks Bureau, Ottawa. 128 pp.

RAWSON, D. S. 1940. The eastern brook trout in the Maligne River system, Jasper National Par. Trans. Amer. Fish. Soc., 70:221-235.

RAWSON, D. S. 1947. Lake Athabasca. Chapt. VI. *In* North West Canadian fisheries surveys in 1944-1945. Fish. Res. Bd. Canada, Bull. 72:69-85.

RAWSON, D. S. 1948. Biological investigations on the Bow and Kananaskis rivers. Unpubl. Rept. to Calgary Power Co. and Calgary Fish Game Assoc. 72 pp.

RAWSON, D. S. 1953. The limnology of Amethyst Lake, a high alpine type near Jasper, Alberta. Canadian J. Zool., 31:193-210.

RAWSON, D. S. and D. A. ELSEY. 1950. Reduction in the longnose sucker population of Pyramid Lake, Alberta in an attempt to improve angling. Trans. Amer. Fish. Soc., 78(1948):13-31.

ROBERSTON, M. R. 1967. Certain limnological characteristics of the La Biche and Wandering Rivers. M.Sc. Thesis. Dept. of Zoology, University of Alberta, Edmonton, Alberta. 74 pp.

SCOTT, W. B. and E. J. CROSSMAN. 1969. Checklist of Canadian freshwater fishes with keys for identification. Life. Sci. Misc. Publ. Royal Ont. Mus., 104 pp.

SMITH, S. B. 1968. Racial characteristics in stocks of anadromous Rainbow trout, *Salmo gairdneri* Richardson. Ph.D. Thesis. Dept. of Zoology, University of Alberta, Edmonton, Alberta. 160 pp.

SOLMAN, V. E. F., J. P. CUERRIER, and W. C. CABLE, 1952. Why have fish hatcheries in Canada's National Parks? Trans. 17th North Amer. Wildl. Conf., Washington, D.C., 226-234.

STENTON, J. E. 1950. Artificial hybridization of eastern brook trout and lake trout. Canadian Fish Cult., 6:1-4.

STENTON, J. E. 1952. Additional information on eastern brook trout and lake trout hybrids. Canadian Fish Cult., 13:1-7.

THOMAS, R. C. 1953. Experiments on mortality in hatchery-reared trout. M.Sc. Thesis. Dept. of Zoology, University of Alberta, Edmonton, Alberta. 56 pp.

THOMAS, R. C. 1957. Effect of the Pocaterra power development on Lower Kananaskis Lake. Unpubl. Rept. to Alberta Dept. Lands and Forests. 12 pp.

THOMAS, R. C. 1958. Alberta lake fisheries. Alberta Resources Conference. Queen's Printer, Edmonton. 18 pp.

TRAUTMAN, M. B. 1957. The fishes of Ohio. Ohio State University Press. 683 pp.

TURNER, W. 1968. Preliminary biological survey of Wabasca lakes area. Alberta Fish and Wildlife Division. Survey report 2.

VICK, S. C. 1913. Classified guide to fish and their habitat in the Rocky Mountain Park. Dominion Parks Branch, Dept. of the Interior, Ottawa. 24 pp.

WARD, J. C. 1951. The biology of the Arctic grayling in the Southern Athabasca drainage. M.Sc. Thesis. Dept. of Zoology, University of Alberta, Edmonton, Alberta. 71 pp.

WHITEHOUSE, F. C. 1919. Notes on some of the fishes of Alberta and adjacent waters. Canadian Field-Nat., 33:50-55.

WHITEHOUSE, F. C. 1946. Sport fishes of western Canada, and some others. McClelland and Stewart Ltd., Toronto, 129 pp.

WILLIAMS, M. B. 1921. Through the heart of the Rockies and Selkirks. Canada Dept. of the Interior, Ottawa. 105 pp.

WILLOCK, T. A. 1968. New Alberta records of the silvery and brassy minnows, stonecat and sauger, with a preliminary list of fishes of the Milk River in Alberta. Canadian Field-Nat. 82(1):18-23.

WILLOCK, T. A. 1969a. Distributional list of fishes in the Missouri drainage of Canada. J. Fish. Res. Bd. Canada, 26(6):1439-1449.

WILLOCK, T. A. 1969b. The ecology and zoogeography of fishes in the Missouri (Milk River) drainage of Alberta. M.Sc. Thesis. Carleton University, Ottawa, Ontario.

ZELT, K. A. 1970. The mayfly (Ephemoptera) and stonefly (Plecoptera) fauna of a foothills stream in Alberta, with special reference to sampling techniques. M.Sc. Thesis. Dept. of Zoology, The University of Alberta. 93 pp.

269

INDEX TO COMMON AND SCIENTIFIC NAMES

271

sport
fish
in
alberta

Northern Pike

An Artist's Conception of the
Sport Fishes Of Alberta

Golden Trout

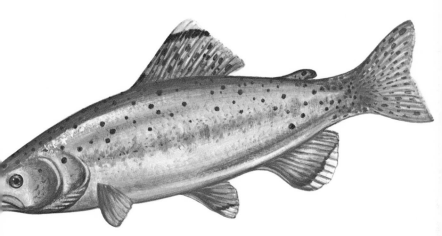

Rainbow Trout

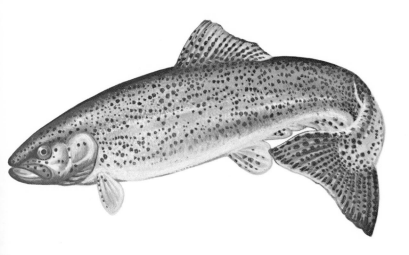

Cutthroat Trout

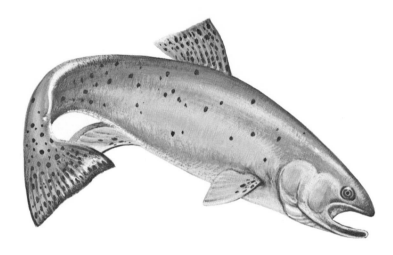

Yellow Perch

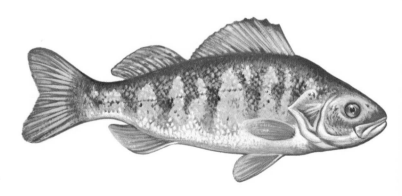

Mountain Whitefish

Goldeye

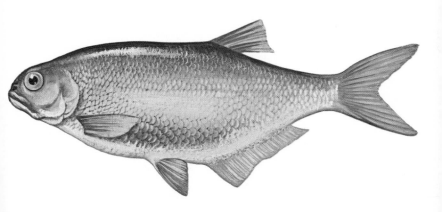

Kokanee

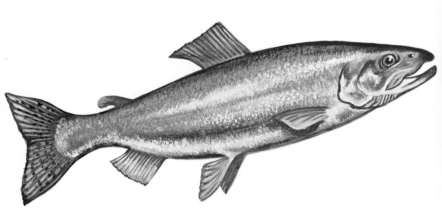

Brook Trout

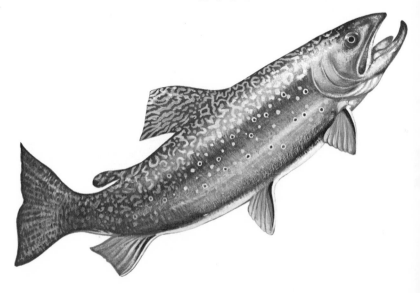

Brown Trout

Dolly Varden

Lake Whitefish

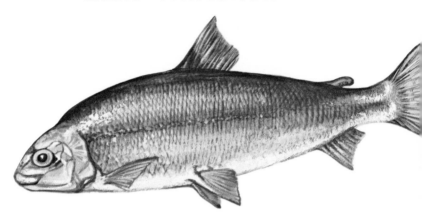

Lake Trout

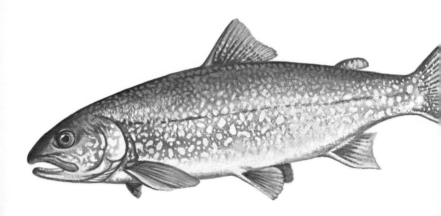

Arctic Grayling

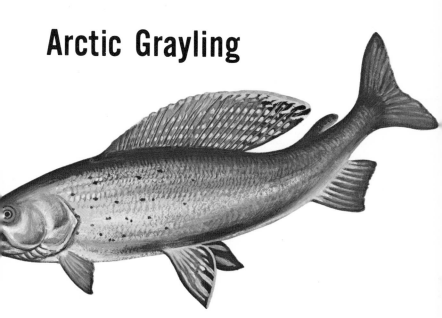

Walleye

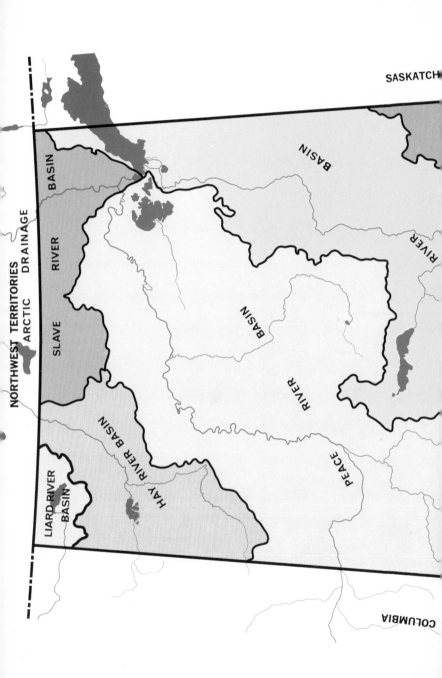

SASKATCH

NORTHWEST TERRITORIES
ARCTIC DRAINAGE

SLAVE RIVER BASIN

BASIN

RIVER

BASIN

RIVER

PEACE

LIARD RIVER BASIN

HAY RIVER BASIN

COLUMBIA

MAP SHOWING MAJOR DRAINAGE B